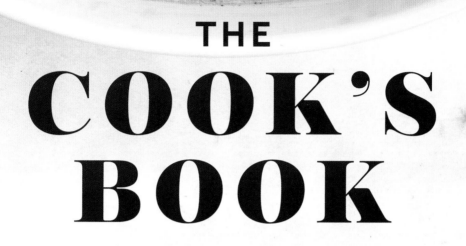

THE
COOK'S
BOOK

Recipes for Keeps & Essential Techniques
to Master Everyday Cooking

Bri McKoy

Revell
a division of Baker Publishing Group

© 2023 by Brianne McKoy

Published by Revell
a division of Baker Publishing Group
Grand Rapids, Michigan
www.revellbooks.com

Printed in China

Library of Congress Cataloging-in-Publication Data
Names: McKoy, Bri, 1984– author.
Title: The cook's book : recipes for keeps & essential techniques to master everyday cooking / Bri McKoy.
Description: Grand Rapids : Revell, a division of Baker Publishing Group, [2023] | Includes bibliographical references and index.
Identifiers: LCCN 2022044701 | ISBN 9780800742942 (cloth) | ISBN 9781493441372 (ebook)
Subjects: LCSH: Cooking. | Cooking—Technique. | Cooking—Equipment and supplies. | LCGFT: Cookbooks.
Classification: LCC TX714 .M38395 2023 | DDC 641.3—dc23/eng/20221122
LC record available at https://lccn.loc.gov/2022044701

The author is represented by Alive Literary Agency, www.aliveliterary.com.

Interior design by Jane Klein.

Principal photography by Laura Klynstra and food styling by Mumtaz Mustafa.

Photos on pages 121, 125, 156, 166, 168, 208, 240, 262: Bri McKoy.

Photo on page 208: Shutterstock

Baker Publishing Group publications use paper produced from sustainable forestry practices and post-consumer waste whenever possible.

23 24 25 26 27 28 29   7 6 5 4 3 2 1

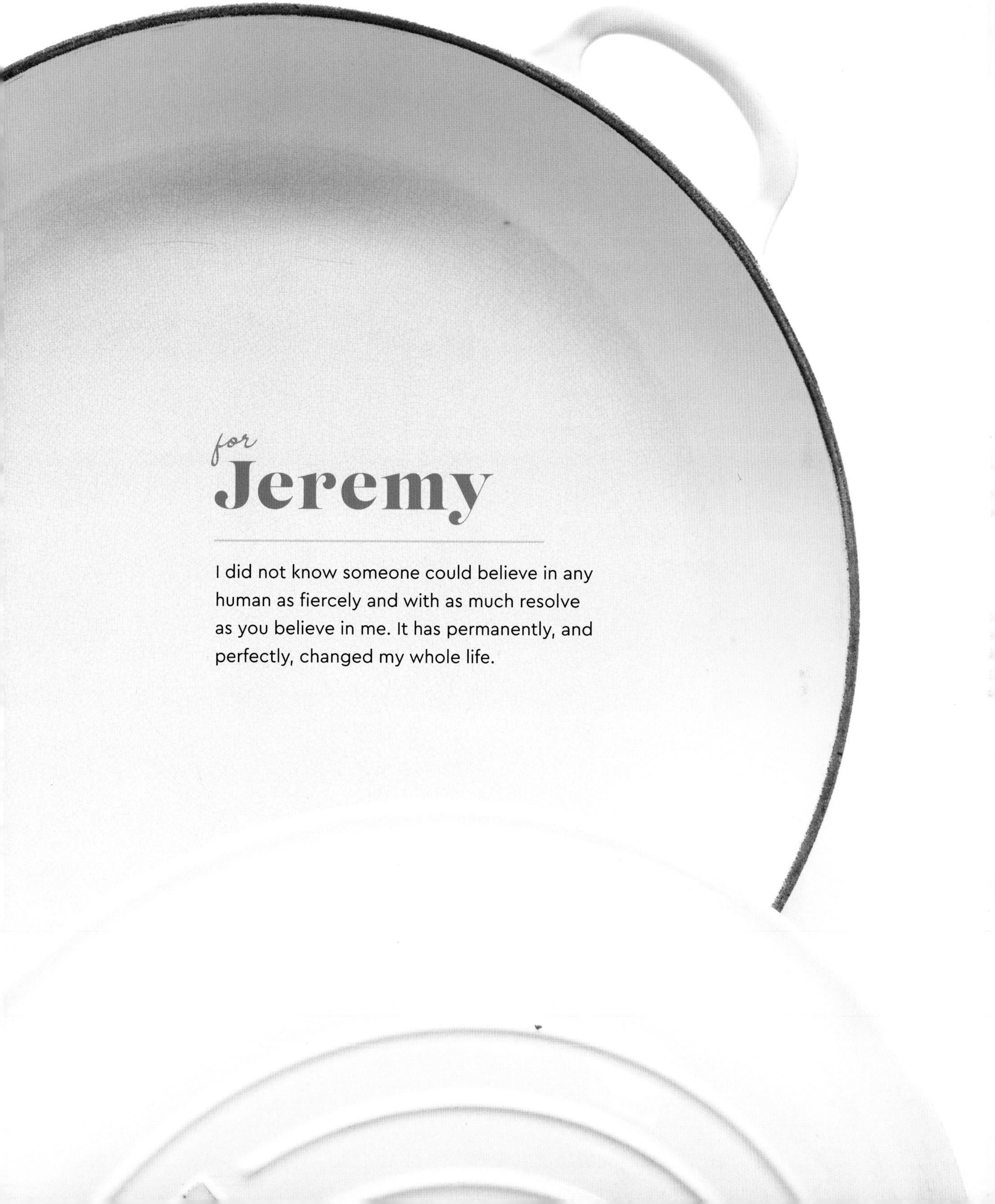

for
Jeremy

I did not know someone could believe in any human as fiercely and with as much resolve as you believe in me. It has permanently, and perfectly, changed my whole life.

CONTENTS

PART 1

A KITCHEN THAT WORKS FOR YOU

PART 2

USING YOUR SENSES

PART 3

THE MOST POWERFUL KITCHEN TECHNIQUES

PART 4

THE MEATS

PART 5

ADDING FLAVOR LIKE A PRO

HOW TO MAKE
THE COOK'S BOOK
YOUR BOOK

This book is created with recipes that teach how to cook. This book is *your* book. You're the cook. Put your name on it. Mark it up with a pen, Sharpie, washi tape, sticky notes, splattered sauce. Think of this more like a craft book, ready for you to add your own delicious mark to it.

I created this book to teach the most essential techniques for everyday cooking through sharing skills and recipes. Each recipe in this book will teach powerful cooking techniques. Every time you make a recipe, you'll learn a skill that you will use over and over again as you bring other recipes to life—even recipes that are not in this book.

The first time you use this book, move through it chronologically. Try not to skip ahead. Each skill being taught builds on the previous ones, and each recipe incorporates skills from previous lessons.

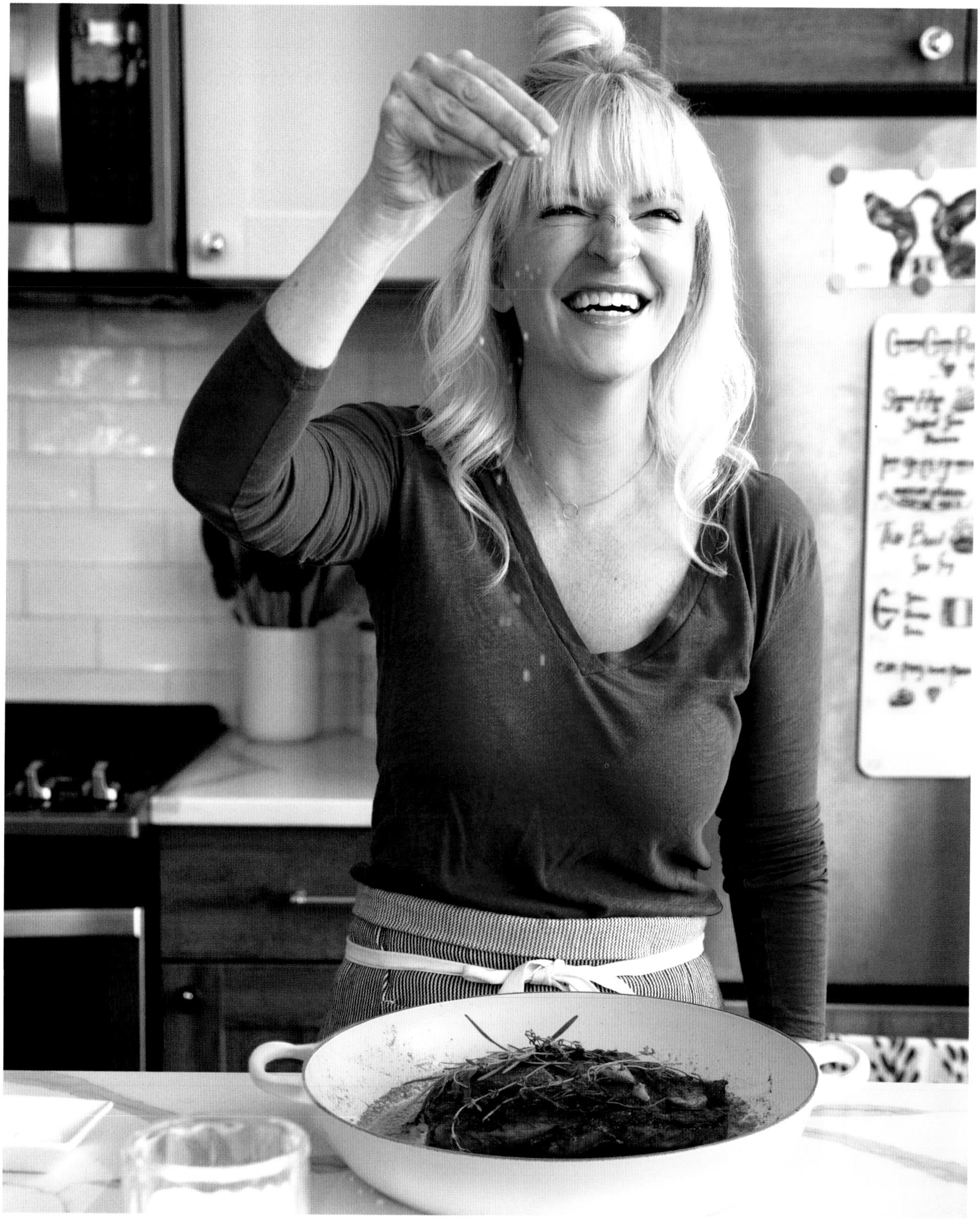

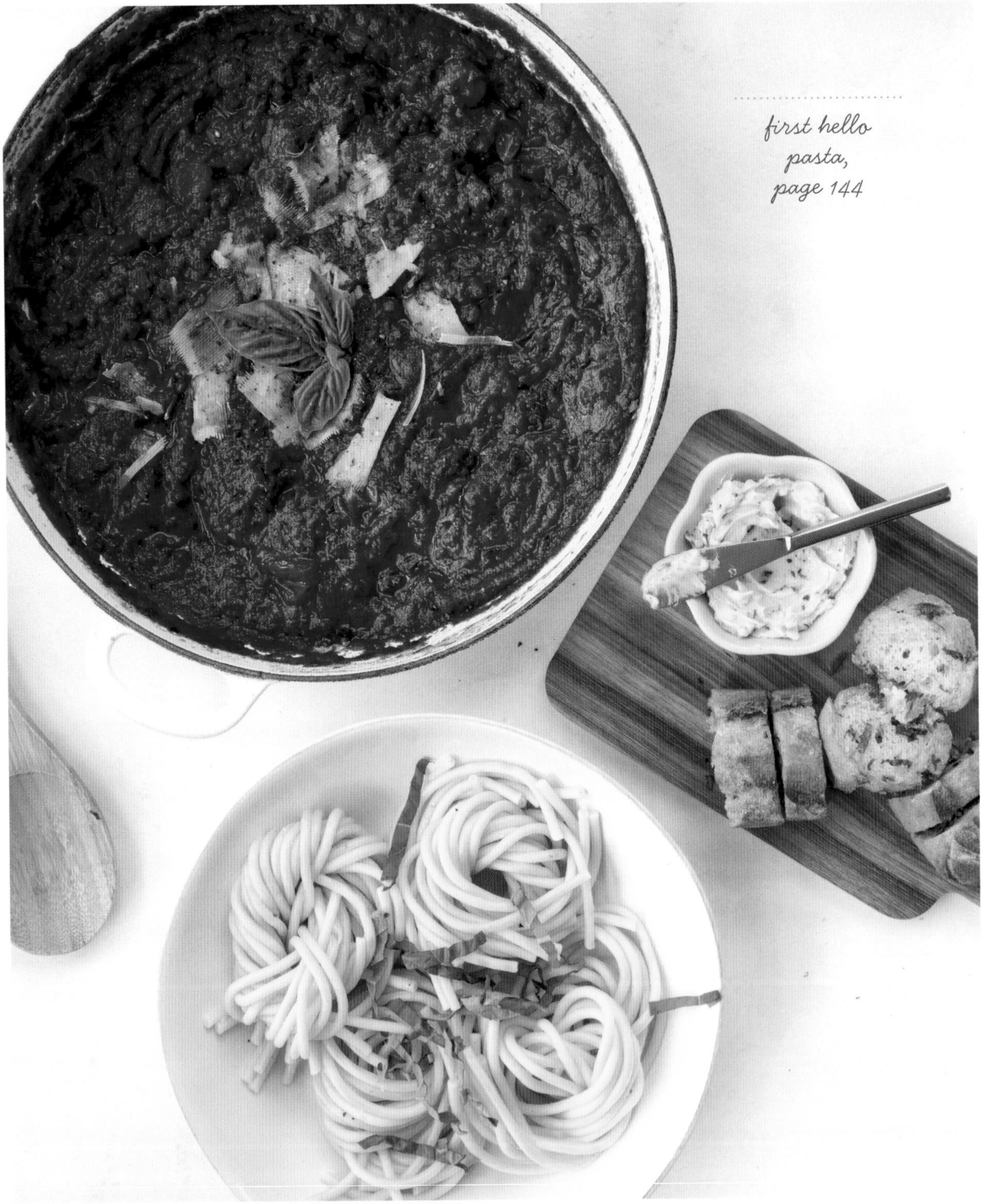

first hello pasta, page 144

aperitif

YOU CAN FIND JOY AND CONFIDENCE
IN EVERYDAY COOKING

Between mouthfuls of salty, lime-laced pad thai, my new husband, Jeremy, looked at me across the table full of takeout containers and said, "We should probably learn how to cook."

The audacity of the suggestion almost had me laughing out loud, and I thought maybe Jeremy should try his hand at stand-up comedy. I thought I was going to choke on my takeout from the eruption of laughter about to come forth, but I looked up to scan his face and saw how utterly serious he was. I then thought he was trying to end our marriage. Which was unfortunate because it was so new, and I really did like him. But I was not interested in learning how to cook. Ever. And I made that explicitly clear by responding with a lot of exasperation and hand-waving and high-pitched speaking that basically was me stating, "No. Next."

Maybe you've had a similar conversation or an experience when you first realized that you probably needed to learn to cook. Hopefully it was less traumatic than the conversation Jeremy and I had. Before that discussion, I had lived twenty-six years without knowing how to cook, and I found this to be an important part of my DNA. My interest was solely in the eating part. I had a lot of other talents and ways I gave back to society. Cooking was not one of them. (To be honest, this was quite remarkable given that my mom is an amazing home cook. She learned to cook from her mom, who had learned from her mom. But I'd broken that line.)

Once I calmed down and agreed that going into debt in our late twenties from ordering pad thai takeout every night could put a damper on things, I realized that maybe cooking was an idea. I mean, it wasn't a great idea, but it was still an idea.

A few weeks later, I found myself looking at cookbooks at Barnes & Noble. I wanted a cookbook for someone who did not want to cook. *You can keep your anchovy salad and your extremely involved roasted Cornish hens,* I thought. *I need something simple. Simple but satisfying! Easy but mouthwatering!*

And I found it: *The Cooking Light Cookbook.* I was delighted in my discovery and promptly purchased it. It would take me a few weeks before I realized that this cookbook was focused on healthy cooking, not a light amount of cooking. I thought *light* meant less cooking—as in light, not heavy, on cooking. But there I was in our postage-stamp size of a newlywed apartment, flipping through a cookbook I'd thought was geared toward less cooking.

Because cookbooks overwhelmed me and I did not want to return to Barnes & Noble only to stare at more cookbooks and mostly consider why every cookbook had a smiling person on the front cover (Why are they so happy in the kitchen? Who smiles like that while holding a very sharp knife?!), I made it my mission to just stick with this one cookbook.

I cooked through practically the full book. At first I followed the recipes exactly, keeping the pages in pristine condition. But as I continued to work my way through the book, I realized I had thoughts. A lot of thoughts. And I needed to record these ideas and thoughts on the recipes themselves. I felt delirious with power when I started marking up the pages: "Too salty . . . I think?" or "Meh." or "Mom loved!"

After going through that cookbook, I bought another. And then another. I was cooking so often I felt like I was really learning to cook. And in some ways I was—but I was actually just learning how to read a recipe. I lost count of the number of times I threw out a meal because I'd burned it or oversalted it or took it out of the oven still raw. There was no trying to save a recipe or figure out what went wrong. It was just bad. Next recipe, please!

Then I started a food blog, because of course I did. I started sharing my own recipes. Lots of recipes. Some people would comment and ask me what to do if something went wrong and I was like, *Um, I don't know. Read the recipe. Obviously.*

I kept cooking, and I did have some wins here and there. But still it seemed as if we were eating more fails than should be natural for a "food blogger." One evening as I was rinsing my overly salted roasted butternut squash in the sink, it came to my attention that maybe I didn't know *how* to cook. Maybe I just knew how to read a recipe. And if anything went wrong, I didn't know how to correct it or save the dish. (And yes, in case you didn't catch that, I had added too much salt to my butternut squash, then roasted it and sampled it only to discover it tasted like a salt cube. So I thought I could just rinse the salt out and serve the soggy but less salty butternut squash.)

I didn't know *why* I was adding salt. I was just adding it.

I didn't know that deglazing a pan could add incredible, restaurant-quality flavor to a dish. I was just annoyed there was stuff sticking to my pan. (Also, what even is deglazing?)

The concept of elevating a dish by adding citrus or fat was not in my vocabulary.

My chicken was served either raw or burnt. And I preferred the burnt version because at least it didn't have salmonella. I liked to call it "Dry but You're Not Going to Die Chicken." A Bri specialty.

Somewhere during this journey in the kitchen, I decided I wanted to learn *how* to cook. I obviously loved recipes; I had a whole blog full of them. But when I stepped into the kitchen there was a lot that the recipe didn't know about me. Things like . . .

- what pan I was using
- where the hot spot on my burner was
- whether I was using a gas or electric stove
- how juicy my lemon was
- what kind of salt I was using

A recipe is an excellent compass, but when we step into the kitchen, *we* become the navigators. The compass is only helpful if we know how to navigate our own kitchen. If I wanted to become a master navigator, I knew I needed to go beyond the recipe on the page. I was going to have to learn *how* to cook by understanding the skills and techniques that turned everyday ingredients into incredible dishes. I had a new mission.

Learning how to cook brought me more confidence in the kitchen. I still enjoy using recipes, but now I'm able to read one through and know exactly what I'm going to change or add. Confidence gives me a sense of control over my meals, but it also helps me take back control when things start to go wrong with a recipe. And thankfully, confidence is not perfection. I will inevitably burn another meal. I will still sometimes oversalt the chicken. I will occasionally forget an ingredient. But now I don't panic when that happens. Instead, I pause to access the "cooking knowledge" file folder in my head and come up with a plan. Ten years ago I was rinsing overly salted squash in the sink. Today if I tasted that salty, roasted squash, I would turn it into a soup by throwing it in the blender and adding stock, fresh garlic, and a little bit of nutmeg and cream.

This is the difference between knowing how to read a recipe and knowing how to cook.

Confidence in the kitchen gives us the ability to pivot, to understand what went wrong and when, and then to adjust. But in addition to gaining confidence, I also found an unexpected joy in noticing and experiencing the act of cooking: washing carrots, slicing onions, hearing the sizzle of oil when the chicken hits the pan at the exact right moment. I began to appreciate my ingredients and tools more. I stopped to smell my ingredients and to taste along the way. I was less frazzled and more able to interact with people in my kitchen while I cooked. I realized that confidence and joy were intertwined.

> *Confidence*
> in the kitchen gives us the
> **ABILITY TO PIVOT,**
> to understand what went
> wrong and when, and
> **THEN TO ADJUST.**

And that is why I wrote this book. I want to give you the recipes and skills you need in the kitchen in order to bring more people to your table—and to do it with confidence and joy.

The key below will help you identify specific kitchen adventures I've included that will sharpen certain techniques, such as chopping an onion or properly salting salsa.

ICONS KEY

how to add extra flavor to the dish

a helpful tip about the dish

sharpening techniques through hands-on experiences

put effort on the front end of this dish

A HOME COOK'S
MANIFESTO
FOR EVERYDAY COOKING

1 YOU ARE THE MOST IMPORTANT ITEM IN YOUR KITCHEN.

2 A RECIPE IS A COMPASS, NOT A GPS.

3 ADDITION IS EASIER THAN SUBTRACTION IN COOKING.

4 BRING ALL YOUR SENSES TO THE PARTY.

5 NOT ALL SALT IS THE SAME.

6 READ THE FULL RECIPE BEFORE COOKING.

7 COOK EARLY.

8 A SHARP CHEF'S KNIFE IS THE BEST SOUS CHEF.

9 MISTAKES ARE THE BEST TEACHERS.

10 IF YOU NEED A KITCHEN WIN, START SIMPLE.

When I first went into the kitchen to learn to cook, my only real guiding light was a recipe and Google. My only objectives were: buy groceries, cook food. But there is so much more that goes into everyday cooking, and this manifesto has become the foundation that continues to give me wins in the kitchen. It has also allowed me a safe place to land when things don't go according to plan.

You are the most important item in your kitchen. There was a time when I thought if I had all the right fancy kitchen tools, I would achieve expert home cook status. But a high-end stand mixer cannot tell me my dough is too dry. Only my hands can. A pricey stainless-steel pan cannot tell me my sauce is too salty. Only my taste buds can. You are the most important thing in your kitchen when it comes to bringing meals together.

A recipe is a compass, not a GPS. I used to cling to a recipe like it was the law. It didn't matter if I thought my sauce already had enough lemon juice in it—the recipe said to add the juice of the whole lemon. I was giving the recipe all the control. But there is so much a recipe does not know about us, our preferences, and our kitchens. It doesn't know how fresh our cilantro is. It doesn't know what brand of salt we're using. Think of a recipe as a compass pointing you in the right direction. You can deviate from it and still end up at your destination.

Addition is easier than subtraction in cooking. We have all oversalted something. If you haven't, you will, and it will be a great learning experience. One that might come with the perk of emergency takeout. It is so much easier to add something more to the dish than to take something away. If I'm reading a recipe and it says to add 1 tablespoon salt and I waver, I might only add ¾ or ½ tablespoon salt. I can always add more salt later. Same with lemon juice or red pepper flakes. Adding just a little more is so much easier than trying to figure out how to make something less salty or less spicy. (It can be done, but the easier route is addition over subtraction.)

Bring all your senses to the party. Using the senses available to you—touch, taste, hearing, smell, sight—will change everything when it comes to cooking. We're often taught to rely most heavily on our sense of taste to bring a dish together, but using all of our other senses is what levels up our game in the kitchen.

Not all salt is the same. We'll cover this more in the next section. Find the salt you love to use for cooking and learn its saltiness!

Read the full recipe before cooking. Reading the full recipe hours before you begin cooking lays a foundation for success. If I am cooking from a

A pricey stainless-steel pan *cannot tell me* my sauce is too salty. ONLY MY TASTE BUDS CAN.

recipe, I like to read the recipe the morning of, preferably while enjoying my coffee. This gives me an idea of how much time the dish will take in case I need to give myself an earlier start. Or if the recipe will come together super fast, I'll want everything ready and chopped before I even turn on the burner. This might mean I can chop all the ingredients on my lunch break or get the chicken marinating in the morning.

Cook early. A few years ago it occurred to me how ridiculous it is that we are required to cook a meal at the end of the day. This is like asking a marathon runner to start running at 5:00 p.m. after they get off work. It's not ideal. So I take a break from work to cook the full meal around 2:00 p.m. This works well with soups and dishes such as casseroles that can easily be reheated, and it's great for people who do not batch cook and who have access to their kitchen earlier in the day. I don't do this every day, but even doing it once a week helps. It especially helps in the winter months when the sun goes down so early. I cook my full meal and then put it in the refrigerator. At around 6:00 p.m., I pull it out, reheat, and serve.

If you do not have access to your kitchen throughout the day, assess if there is anything you can prep earlier before leaving the house or even the night before. In *The Lazy Genius Kitchen*, Kendra Adachi teaches about asking the magic question, "What can you do now to make life in your kitchen easier later?"[1] Even if it's only chopping all the ingredients in the morning and putting them in a container to pull out at dinner time, this small step will have you more motivated to make dinner by the time six o'clock rolls around.

A sharp chef's knife is the best sous chef. Okay, maybe having an actual trained sous chef in your kitchen would be nice. But we are everyday home cooks, not the royal family. (Unless you are the royal family, and then thank you for reading!) In this vein, I need you to listen very carefully: you might hate cooking because your knife is dull and you are spending entirely too much time sawing through your vegetables. I understand. I used to use a dull knife because I thought I was not skilled enough for a high-quality

1. Kendra Adachi, *The Lazy Genius Kitchen: Have What You Need, Use What You Have, and Enjoy It Like Never Before* (Colorado Springs: Waterbrook, 2022), 183.

> *We are allowed* TO GET A LITTLE ANNOYED OR FRUSTRATED WHEN WE MAKE A MISTAKE IN THE KITCHEN, **BUT DON'T FORGET** IT MEANS YOU PROBABLY JUST GRADUATED FROM A COURSE YOU DIDN'T EVEN KNOW YOU WERE ENROLLED IN.

sharp knife. Then one day I was in my friend's kitchen and she asked me to cut up an onion. I took her knife and the first slice through the onion was so effortless I almost started crying. (That could have just been the onion, but we'll never know!) I chopped that onion in record time, and my hand didn't hurt afterward. The next day I went straight to my kitchen store, bought a high-quality knife, and have never looked back.

Mistakes are the best teachers. Some of the most powerful lessons I have learned about cooking have come through my mistakes. I graduated from Salt 101 the day I oversalted that butternut squash. I graduated from Trust Your Sense of Smell the day I burned my chicken because, yes, it *did* smell like it was burning but the recipe said to cook for ten minutes and it had only been six. My favorite course was when I graduated from Turn Down the Burner (Advanced Level) after always keeping my heat on high because *Don't I want this to cook all the way through? Isn't high heat cooking my food? Are medium and low heat even there for a reason?*

We are allowed to get a little annoyed or frustrated when we make a mistake in the kitchen, but don't forget it means you probably just graduated from a course you didn't even know you were enrolled in.

If you need a kitchen win, start simple. When I was learning to cook, I thought winning in the kitchen meant bringing together some kind of elaborate meal. But then I realized a kitchen win means I made a delicious meal that my family loved and I didn't lose my mind while doing it.

Kitchen wins build on each other and can make us feel more and more confident in the kitchen. So start simple. Get a store-bought rotisserie chicken to make the soup or casserole. Or take something premade, such as premarinated kabobs from the butcher shop or meat counter, and pull together a simple but delicious side dish.

A NOTE ON SALT

Personally, I think we all should have been learning about the different types of salt in high school, right after our math lessons. As an adult I've needed to know way more about salt than I've needed to break out my TI-83 graphing calculator and do trigonometry.

As I was learning to cook, I made many mistakes that resulted in TMS (too much salt). This happened because I didn't understand anything about salt. I just added it when it was called for. So I took a new approach— I became salt-shy. Sometimes I'd omit the salt altogether because of flashbacks to my ruined chicken casserole. But then I learned that salt-shy is almost worse than TMS. It turns out that salt can make or break a whole dish.

Let's start here: Food needs salt.

Salt is like the spotlight on a stage. All the characters can be there. They can know their lines and be in costume. They can even be ready to start the show. But if the spotlight isn't on, it's going to be a pretty boring show. Everything will seem very muted and hard to distinguish. But as soon as the spotlight comes on, everything comes to life.

Salt also makes food more of what it already is. It makes potatoes more potatoey, tomatoes more tomatoey, bread more bready. Butter more buttery. Eggs more eggy. Salt does not change an ingredient's makeup; it just makes the ingredient more of what it already is.

WHAT IS SALT?

Salt is a mineral: sodium chloride. In *Salt, Fat, Acid, Heat*, Samin Nosrat notes that it is also one of the several dozen essential nutrients we need to survive.[1] There are so many different varieties of salt in the world, and they each serve a different purpose.

Unless otherwise noted, I used Diamond Crystal kosher salt for all of my recipes. If you are using Morton kosher salt, you will want to cut the salt by one-third (more about this below).

Salt can get a bad reputation because many of us have had the misfortune of eating something that's oversalted. That really sticks with us, especially because sometimes too much salt can ruin a whole meal.

As previously mentioned, I have oversalted butternut squash. The route there was quite simple: I only had half the butternut squash the recipe called for, but I didn't think to cut the other ingredients, particularly the salt, in half. I ended up with what tasted like roasted salt cubes. You all, I WASHED THE ROASTED BUTTERNUT SQUASH IN THE SINK. I thought it would help remove the salt. I did not consider that I would then have soggy roasted butternut squash on my hands.

Which brings me to my next point with salt—and I will say this until my dying day: addition is easier than subtraction in cooking, especially with salt. It's a great deal easier to add more salt to a dish than it is to take salt away.

> The next time you chop a tomato, take a bite of it plain. Then sprinkle a little salt and take another bite. This is an excellent way to understand how salt makes a food become more of what it is.

Reading a recipe that calls for what you think could be too much salt? Try adding only some of the salt and then taste. Not sure about the type of salt you have on hand? Taste the salt first! The raw salt. If your mouth tastes like saltwater after that first taste, you have very salty salt. If the salt tastes salty but pleasant and pure, you have a milder salt.

Whenever you're working with something unfamiliar, *always* taste first and err on the side of less is more.

---

1. Samin Nosrat, *Salt, Fat, Acid, Heat: Mastering the Elements of Good Cooking* (New York: Simon & Schuster, 2017), 20.

Table Salt

Kosher Salt

Coarse Kosher Salt

Fleur de Sel

Pink Himalayan Salt

Sea Salt

POPULAR TYPES OF SALT

Let's talk about all the different varieties of salt and how and when to use them so they shine!

Table Salt

Table salt is for the table! It is 99 percent sodium chloride, so it is intense. When I first started learning to cook, I only had table salt on hand. This salt is very fine and extremely salty. It is best used as just a sprinkle after you have served someone their food and they want a bit more salt. If you find you only have table salt on hand for cooking, you will want to cut the salt in half if the recipe calls for kosher salt. For example, if a recipe calls for 2 tablespoons kosher salt, you will only want to add 1 tablespoon table salt. That's how much saltier it is.

Kosher Salt

Kosher salt is a little chunkier than table salt and does not contain additives, so it has a purer tasting saltiness. This is the salt you want for everyday cooking. Not only is it less salty but because the crystals are larger, it's easier to sprinkle over your pan. Not all kosher salts are the same, so be sure to taste the crystals to assess saltiness. If I could come into your kitchen and give you one ingredient to cook with, it would be Diamond Crystal kosher salt. Diamond Crystal has the most pure taste and is not extremely salty. Its crystals dissolve uniformly and quickly in food as it is being cooked, which means you are less likely to oversalt your dish.

Morton kosher salt is another popular brand to use for cooking but is much saltier and denser than Diamond Crystal. This means it will take more time to dissolve, so the chances are high that you'll think you did not salt your dish enough and then keep adding more. Which means your dish will be very salty.

If you love Morton kosher salt, just know that you will want to add less salt than called for in recipes that use kosher salt (including mine). For example, if a recipe calls for 1 tablespoon (that is, 3 teaspoons) salt, you will only want to use 1¾ teaspoons (slightly more than half the amount) of Morton kosher salt.

Fleur de Sel

This salt, which is known as finishing salt, is more expensive. It is actually harvested by hand using sieves. Think of fleur de sel like your most expensive purse. You don't use it every day. It only comes out on special occasions to really make a statement. My jar of fleur de sel usually lasts for months, if not a whole year.

Fleur de sel crystals are also fairly large and chunky, so a little goes a long way! But a little sprinkle can transform your whole dish. We love to sprinkle it over our salads, roasted veggies, finished steaks, and even over our charcuterie board. Every time I sprinkle something with fleur de sel, I get asked for the recipe.

Flaked Sea Salt

This salt is similar to fleur de sel in that it is also used as a finishing salt. It is a little chunkier, giving it a nice texture and crunch. People love using this salt on top of anything from baked cookies to steaks, and my favorite brand to use is Maldon. Bonus tip: sprinkle a finishing salt like flaked sea salt or fleur de sel from high above the dish for an even distribution!

Pink Himalayan Salt

This salt is mined near the Himalayas in Pakistan. It is unique because it has a pinkish hue. Most people use this salt because it is said to be packed with minerals. You can use this salt just like you would use kosher salt, but it is a bit saltier in nature, so you might want to use less than a recipe calls for.

Sea Salt

Sea salt is known for being unrefined, meaning it still has traces of minerals in it. Because of these minerals, it is also known for its health benefits and flavor. Sea salt is sold in all different sizes, from fine to coarse. If this is your salt of choice, be sure to taste and get familiar with its saltiness!

POPULAR SALT BRANDS

All the recipes in this book were tested using Diamond Crystal kosher salt. As you are getting familiar with different brands of salt and finding which one you prefer for everyday cooking, here is a helpful conversion chart. You may want to make slight adjustments based on your own preferences, but this is a great place to start.

BRAND	CONVERSION
Diamond Crystal Kosher Salt	3 teaspoons*
Morton Kosher Salt	1¾ teaspoon
David's Kosher Salt	1½ teaspoon
Pink Himalayan Sea Salt	1½ teaspoon
Table Salt	1 teaspoon

* 3 teaspoons = 1 tablespoon

While one could go wild with all the different kinds of salts, I recommend having an everyday cooking salt on hand and a finishing salt such as fleur de sel for enhancing dishes.

HOW TO ADD SALT

The type of salt you are using and when you are adding it to a dish also informs *how* to apply the salt to your food. This does not have to be complicated! Here are the top three ways to add salt to your food:

1. *Dump it in.* If you're adding salt to a dish that is in the middle of cooking, you can just plop it right into the dish and mix to continue sautéing with the food.
2. *Sprinkle from up high.* If you're adding salt to a dish that is finished and plated, sprinkle it from up high. This will allow the salt to evenly fall over the food so you don't get some bites with lots of salt and other bites with little to no salt. Use this method for salads, sandwiches, spaghetti, soups, and more.
3. *Rub it in.* If you're using salt to season raw meat, rub it in. This will cause the salt to dissolve into the meat so it's perfectly seasoned.

A KITCHEN

THAT WORKS

for you

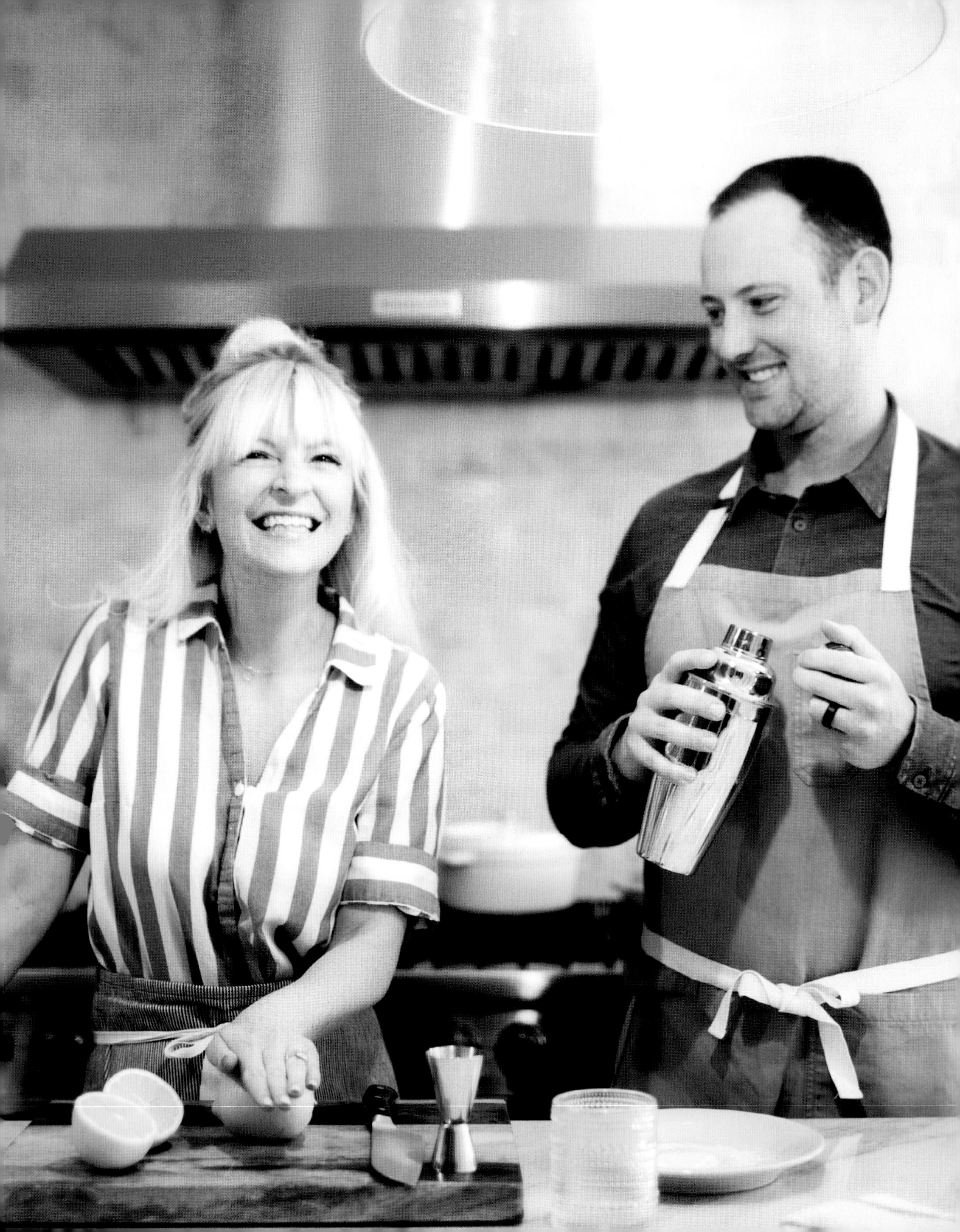

It took me many years to understand that the kitchen in my home was, in fact, *my* kitchen. When it came to the bedroom, the living room, the bathroom, even the outdoor space, I would decorate it all and redesign the space so it was functional for me and my family. Painting, hanging, rearranging . . . we did it all. But I used to approach the kitchen like it was static.

I guess we just don't have enough counter space.

I guess we just won't have a place to put these bowls.

I guess we're just going to have to open the oven a touch in order to open this drawer.

I never felt like the owner in the kitchen because I felt owned by my kitchen.

At the time I'm writing this, my husband and I have lived in six different homes, all with vastly different kitchens. There was even one kitchen that did not have a dishwasher—you know, thrown in for grit and good measure. We've had kitchens with large islands, kitchens with no countertop space, and kitchens with only enough room for one person to stand in. We've had kitchens with cabinets that didn't close and kitchens with paint peeling off the countertops. (Why exactly was there paint on the countertops?) We've had kitchens with state-of-the-art stovetops and kitchens with no vent hood and windows that did not open (that one was really fun because we got to trigger the fire alarm anytime I fried something).

Myquillyn Smith, aka The Nester, was one of the first people who gave me permission to break the conventional rules when it came to making my kitchen my own. Once I realized that I could turn the unused bottom shelf of my linen closet into a wine cellar or that I could shop my own home to make spaces more functional instead of waiting to buy more stuff, everything changed for me.

I got to a place where I made every single kitchen work for me. And to be clear, we did not own any of these homes. These were rentals, and we always got our security deposit back (read: we didn't knock down any walls).

CREATIVE WAYS WE'VE
made our kitchens our own

You might feel like you don't have a lot of options in your kitchen, but if you get a little creative, even small changes can make all the difference.

In one kitchen, we had absolutely no countertop space. Actually we did have a tiny corner, but this was the kitchen with no dishwasher, so that small spot was allotted to holding all of our clean dishes while they dried. Attached to this small kitchen was a place for a small dining room table, which we decided to make into an open-air pantry of sorts. Instead of putting a table there, we put up a few bookshelves and placed all our pots, pans, glassware, and some pantry items on those. It immediately opened up the space for us.

As for the dining table, we put that in the living room. The living room was interestingly large, so we just sectioned it off. One side had the table, and the other side had the couch, chairs, footstools, side tables, and TV. We also put a table on our patio and usually ended up eating our meals outside.

In another kitchen the pantry was so tiny and narrow it quickly became a disaster zone that at any given moment held three to five bags of opened tortilla chips. The first bag I purchased would get lost in the abyss of the deep, narrow pantry. So I would buy another bag, and then that bag would end up finding its way to the dark abyss, and so on and so forth. We did have a narrow nook that the realtor told us was, "A *great* place to put your trash can!" But we decided that nook would be even greater if it had some shelves in it, scaling upward. More space. We searched the kitchen aisles of stores to find something that could fit there but didn't have any luck. So we started thinking outside the box and found what we were looking for in the bathroom aisle. I am happy to report that our tortilla chips stopped being kidnapped by our pantry.

We also used a magnetic strip attached to the wall for hanging knives so a knife block wouldn't take up space. And we stored all our spices on hanging shelves so they wouldn't take up space in cabinets or drawers.

Taking time to make the kitchen your space will give you more joy and even energy to enter it every evening to cook dinner. The best book I know about how to make your kitchen your own is, as previously mentioned, *The Lazy Genius Kitchen* by Kendra Adachi. I think of her book as required reading when it comes to kitchens. If we're going to spend so much time in the kitchen, we don't just need to know how to cook but how to make our kitchens work for us. If *The Cook's Book* is the driving manual for how to navigate the roads and get from point A to B, *The Lazy Genius Kitchen* is the owner's manual for how to operate the vehicle—which is critical, seeing as you will be navigating the roads in . . . the car.

> Identify a pain point in your kitchen.
> You can start with just one. What makes cooking
> dinner more cumbersome than you would like?
> Do you want more counter space? More storage?
> Easier access to appliances? Forget the rules. Get
> creative and make your kitchen work for you.

essential
KITCHEN TOOLS

When I first started learning how to cook, I would devour the first part of a cookbook that told me what tools I needed. I bought several of these special tools only to find that I barely used most of them. For example, a Bundt pan. I have never, not once, used that funky-looking pan. You know why? I don't bake. But maybe you do bake, so maybe you have three Bundt pans in your kitchen!

As I became more comfortable in my kitchen, I realized that just because my neighbor has an emulsifier she swears by does not mean I, too, need an emulsifier. Which is why I am not a fan of telling someone what they should have in their kitchen. I do love sharing things I am absolutely obsessed with in hopes that maybe it will be helpful for someone else. But making it a required item for someone to buy is a bit extreme. Unless I'm able to stand with you in your kitchen and have you tell me what your cooking life is like, you are way more qualified to know what tools you do and don't need.

I also know that when I was a new home cook, I just wanted someone to please, please tell me what to buy and exactly where to get it and the exact measurements, please. So in this section I will share different pots and pans and appliances that are helpful, but *you* get to decide whether you need them. And just because you don't need something right now doesn't mean you can't change your mind down the road. I used to think a toaster oven was the most useless appliance. Why get a toaster oven that takes up so much space when I already have a toaster *and* an oven? Then my season of life changed and I got a toaster oven, and now I will never look back.

Our kitchens get to transform as our seasons of life transform.

UNEXPECTED KITCHEN TOOLS

THAT MAKE COOKING EFFORTLESS

1 **CHEF'S KNIFE OR SANTOKU KNIFE**
(I have the 7-inch)

2 **LARGE WOOD CUTTING BOARD**
(20×15×1.5) or Epicurean cutting board

3 **GARLIC ROLLER**

4 **GARLIC PRESS**

5 **MEAT CRUMBLER**

6 **VEGETABLE PEELER**

7 **BENCH SCRAPER**

8 **OUNCE MEASURER**

9 **SALT CELLAR**

10 **TRASH BOWL**

11 **CITRUS JUICER**

kitchen
APPLIANCES

A kitchen appliance is something that needs to be plugged in or requires power to work. Some kitchen appliances can be inexpensive but mighty. Other kitchen appliances can be an investment but will last for decades. Here are some of the most common appliances for home cooks.

FOOD PROCESSOR

I am obsessed with my food processor, but it's not for everyone. For a long time I used my food processor only for making homemade salsa. But now I also use it for making dips, spreads, and dressings. If you don't make your own homemade salsas and dips, this is not an item you need in your kitchen (at least not now—maybe down the road).

BLENDER

These are probably best known for making smoothies, but a blender can also help you make creamy soups, slushies, and frozen margaritas (you know, the essentials). I have had my Vitamix for nine years, but there are lots of great brands out there that make high-capacity blenders.

INSTANT POT OR PRESSURE COOKER

I waited a few years before getting an Instant Pot (IP) because my slow cooker worked fine for me. I was nervous that the meat would be dry since it was cooking so quickly at such a high temperature. I was also worried the flavor would be lacking since, again, everything cooks so quickly. I finally purchased one with great skepticism, and now I am a believer. My favorite things to cook in it include coconut milk rice (I now cook rice only in the IP), a variety of soups (especially those with frozen chicken), and roasts that only take just over an hour but come out juicy and filled with flavor.

BLUETOOTH SPEAKER

I know this is probably an odd item to add to a kitchen appliance list, but I stand by this. Music in the kitchen not only helps to provide energy or focus but can also be a really pleasant addition when you are entertaining. After we put Bluetooth speakers in the kitchen, we quickly noticed how inviting it was to have music on in the background when we were bringing people to our table.

Part of being a confident home cook is trusting yourself when it comes to making decisions about what you need in your kitchen. And that kitchen can change and grow just like your season of life and family.

Part of being a
CONFIDENT HOME COOK
is trusting yourself
when it comes to making
decisions about what
you need in your kitchen.

POTS *and* PANS

When you are deciding on a pot or pan, you generally have these options: nonstick, cast iron, enameled cast iron, or stainless steel. I have a variety of each, but my go-to pan is enameled cast iron.

You may already have a pan that is your go-to pan, but in case you want to look into other options or are still on the journey to find one, here are some pros and cons of the most widely used varieties.

NONSTICK

Pros: Easy to use. Food will not stick when cooking. Easy to clean (generally dishwasher safe). Lightweight. Can be less expensive than other options.

Cons: Generally, nonstick pans are not as long-lasting as other options. Also, it can be hard to get a good sear on meat or make a delicious, thick sauce because of the nonstick properties.

CAST IRON

Pros: Retains heat beautifully for even cooking. Extremely versatile (I've made chicken kabobs in it one night and pizza the next). Very long-lasting. Can go from oven to stovetop to grill. Gets better over time due to seasoning, and over time can take on nonstick properties. Inexpensive. Can provide a beautiful sear to steaks and meats.

Cons: Not dishwasher safe (but very easy to clean and maintain with kosher salt and oil). Heavier than most pans. Also, some foods can react negatively with cast iron. For example, putting tomatoes in your cast iron can sometimes result in a distinctly metallic taste to your dish.

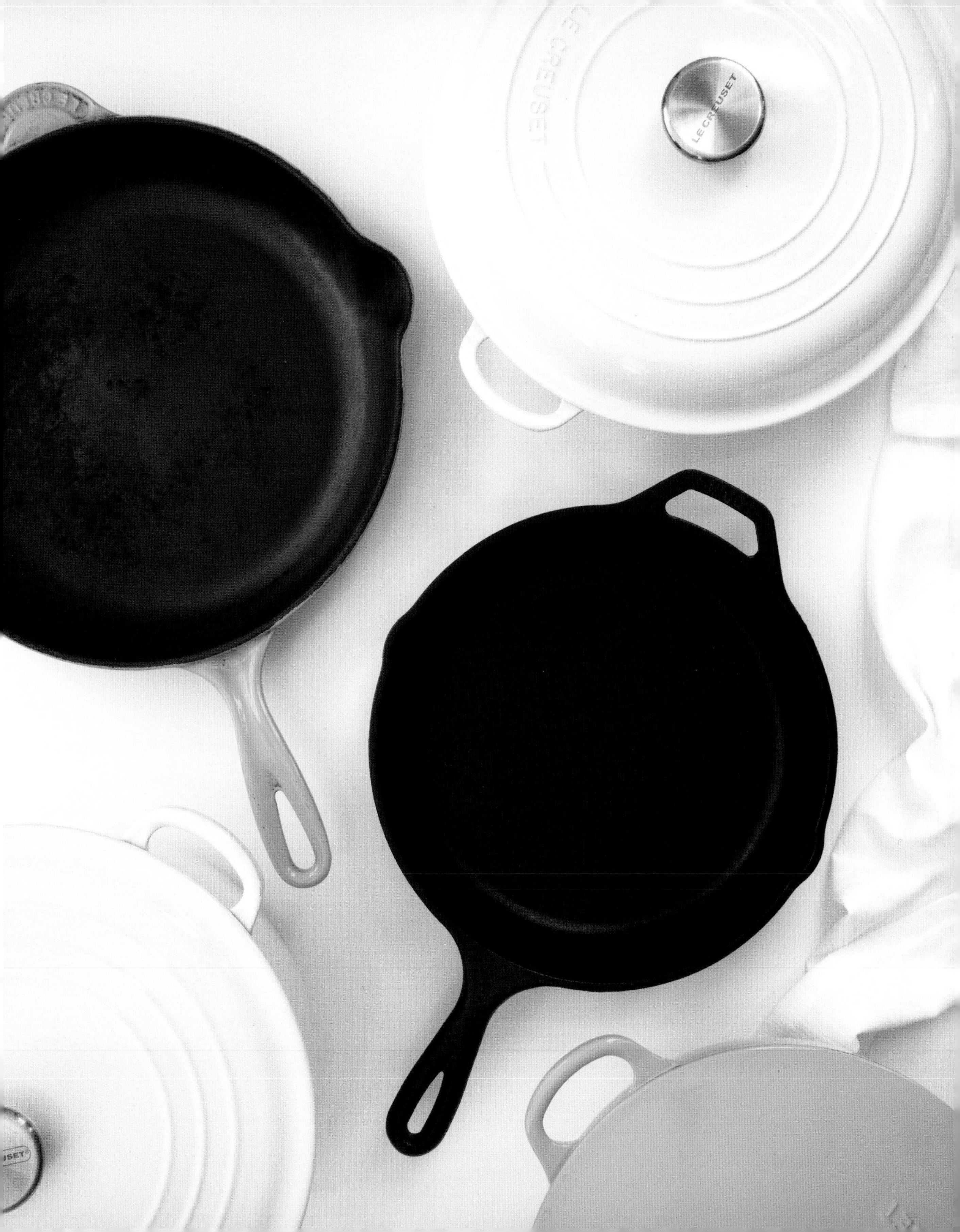
LE CREUSET

Cast iron is different from enameled cast iron in that it does not have an enamel coating. Because it does not have that coating, it requires a different method of cleaning to maintain the iron.

Knowing how to clean cast iron is what will keep it from rusting and make it last a lifetime. To clean your cast iron, while it is still warm, remove any food or stuck on bits by scraping them up with a wooden spoon. You do not want to use any kind of brush with steel wool, as that can strip the cast iron. Add several tablespoons of kosher salt to the pan. Add a little bit of hot water, enough to make a paste. Using paper towels or a cloth, move the salt and hot water paste around the pan to get up any stubborn, stuck-on food. Once everything seems to be up, rinse in hot water. (Do not soak!) Dry the skillet. Add about ½ tablespoon vegetable oil or refined coconut oil to the dry skillet and use a paper towel or dry cloth to coat the whole skillet with the oil. Be sure to rub the oil into the skillet so it is absorbed.

The great news is that lots of cast-iron skillets on the market come pre-seasoned. But if yours is not seasoned, you can easily do this at home! If you buy a cast-iron skillet that is not preseasoned, it will usually come with instructions on how to season it. If not, here is a tried-and-true method.

Preheat the oven to 350°F. Wash the skillet with hot water and dry. Add about 1 tablespoon vegetable oil or coconut oil to the skillet. Using a paper towel or dry cloth, rub the oil all over the skillet. (Not just the inside but the sides, handle, and outside too!) Place the skillet upside down in the middle of your oven (optional: place a sheet pan on the bottom of the oven to catch any oil drippings). Bake for one hour. Turn the oven off and let the skillet cool completely in the oven. Remove when cooled. It's ready to go!

ENAMELED CAST IRON

Pros: This is a cast-iron pan, but it has an enamel coating. My go-to pan for frying, baking, roasting, and sautéing is my enameled cast-iron braiser. Very long-lasting (mine came with a lifetime warranty). Easier to clean than a regular cast-iron skillet due to the enamel. Can go from stovetop to oven to tabletop (it is beautiful to serve from). Maintains heat. Sears meats perfectly. Durable (I've used mine at least four times a week for ten years and it's still going strong). It is the most versatile pan I own. Most brands are dishwasher safe.

Cons: Heavier than a nonstick pan. Can be on the pricier side (an investment). It is not nonstick, so there is a small learning curve for cooking with it (but it gets better with time)!

Some of you might be wondering why you would need both an enameled cast iron and a cast-iron skillet. You don't have to have both! Most commonly, people have a cast-iron skillet and an enameled cast-iron dutch oven (different from a braiser). This is a perfect combination. I love using my cast-iron skillet for browning chicken thighs, making pizza dough, and baking brownies! I've heard baking scones in cast-iron skillets is perfect. And I use my enameled cast-iron dutch oven for roasts, soups, stews, and curry!

Never use something abrasive to clean your enameled cast iron—it will scratch easily! I like to use Scotch-Brite Dobie sponges (I also use these on stainless steel). I also routinely deglaze my pan while cooking (a technique we will cover in part 3), which helps to clean it. Every once in a while (once a month, or even every six to eight weeks), I use Le Creuset enameled cast-iron cleaner on my beloved braiser to keep it a bright white. You simply apply cleaner to the pan and rub it on with a clean cloth!

STAINLESS STEEL

Pros: Beautiful to display. Can be dishwasher safe. Most can go from stovetop to oven. Provides a really nice sear on meats and allows for building beautiful sauces due to the fond (the browned bits of veggies or meat that stick to the pan). Very long-lasting.

Cons: Can be slightly heavier than nonstick pans. Does involve a learning curve for cooking meats and seafood without them sticking to the pan.

Early on when I was learning to cook, I chose to purchase stainless-steel pans. I apparently wanted to start with the steepest of learning curves. But when I did some research, I found that once you learn how to work with your stainless-steel pan, the payoff is massive. You are able to get a really nice, browned crust on your chicken and other meats. You also are able to make really delicious sauces because of the food that inevitably sticks to the pan. I've never looked back.

Every six weeks or so, use Bar Keepers Friend powder cleanser on your stainless-steel sauté pan to keep it beautiful and shiny.

WHICH PAN IS FOR ME?

Most likely, you will have a variety of pots and pans. What's important is that you choose ones you really enjoy cooking in. Delicious food can come from any of them.

You also do not *need* to have a variety of pans all at once. It took me years to acquire the pots and pans in my kitchen. But now I have every pan I could ever need, including my everyday pan that I use to make almost all our meals. Having a dedicated everyday pan is a great move as a home cook, as you become intimately familiar with how to cook everything in it, and most pans get better with time! Here is my lineup:

3½-quart enameled braiser

7¼-quart enameled cast-iron dutch oven (round)

12-inch preseasoned cast-iron skillet

3-quart saucepan (stainless steel or nonstick)

3-quart sauté pan with lid (stainless steel or nonstick)

8-quart stock pot with lid

bringing
YOUR KITCHEN TOGETHER

Now that you know more about the different pots, pans, and appliances available to you, you get to decide what you want in your kitchen. Think of stocking your kitchen as a long-term project. You do not need everything all at once. You can build over time. You can wait for sales or trips to outlets. Here's a checklist to use as a baseline. Feel free to cross out items you know you don't need or want and add items you love that aren't listed.

KITCHEN TOOLS CHECKLIST

BASIC KITCHEN TOOLS

Essential

- ☐ Chef's knife or Santoku knife (7-inch)
- ☐ Large wood cutting board (15×20-inch)
- ☐ Epicurean cutting board (dishwasher safe, perfect for raw meat, doesn't dull knives like plastic or glass cutting boards)
- ☐ Kitchen scissors (also known as kitchen shears)
- ☐ Measuring cups and spoons
- ☐ Ounce measuring cups (measures in ounces and tablespoons)
- ☐ Vegetable peeler
- ☐ Garlic press
- ☐ Garlic roller
- ☐ Cheese grater
- ☐ Bench scraper
- ☐ Trash bowl (any bowl you can set on the counter to collect trash while preparing a meal)
- ☐ Citrus juicer
- ☐ Instant read meat thermometer
- ☐ Silicone meat crumbler
- ☐ Mixing bowls

- ☐ Colander
- ☐ Mesh sieve strainer
- ☐ Funnel
- ☐ Rolling pin
- ☐ Bottle opener
- ☐ Can opener
- ☐ Tongs

- ☐ Silicone spatula
- ☐ Grill spatula
- ☐ Balloon whisk
- ☐ Soup ladle
- ☐ Wooden spoon (or large silicone spoon)
- ☐ Pepper mill

Secondary

- ☐ Paring knife
- ☐ Bread knife
- ☐ Mortar and pestle
- ☐ Microplane grater
- ☐ Airtight containers with labels
- ☐ Wire rack (for baking and cooling)
- ☐ Salt cellar
- ☐ Tea kettle
- ☐ Skewers

- ☐ Bag clips
- ☐ Pizza cutter
- ☐ Pizza stone
- ☐ Silicone jar opener
- ☐ Mason jars with lids (8-ounce and 16-ounce)
- ☐ Wine opener
- ☐ Grilling tongs and spatula
- ☐ Kitchen scale

Bonus

- ☐ Lettuce knife
- ☐ Lettuce keeper
- ☐ Mandoline
- ☐ Salad dressing jar/shaker
- ☐ Large round ice molds

- ☐ Cheese knives
- ☐ Apron
- ☐ Reusable deli food storage containers

KITCHEN APPLIANCES

Essential

- ☐ Stand or hand mixer
- ☐ Slow cooker

- ☐ High-capacity blender
- ☐ Toaster

☐ Instant Pot or pressure cooker
☐ Immersion blender
☐ Coffee/spice grinder

☐ Food processor
☐ Toaster oven

Bonus

☐ Espresso machine
☐ Waffle maker
☐ Soda stream

☐ Electric tea kettle
☐ High-quality Bluetooth speaker(s)
☐ Wine/soda fridge

POTS, PANS, AND SHEET PANS

Essential

☐ Cast-iron skillet (12-inch)
☐ Dutch oven (7¼-quart)
☐ Saucepan (3-quart)
☐ Sauté pan with lid (3-quart)
☐ Skillet (nonstick or stainless steel; 8-inch and 12-inch)

☐ Roasting pan with rack (14×11×5-inch)
☐ Sheet pans (18×13×1-inch and 13×9×1-inch)
☐ Square baking pan (8×8-inch)
☐ Glass baking dishes (7×11-inch and 9×13-inch)

Secondary

☐ Stock pot with lid (8-quart)
☐ Muffin pan

☐ Pie plate

Bonus

☐ Enameled cast-iron braiser (3½-quart)
☐ Tagine (2½-quart)
☐ Butter warmer or small saucepan (1½-quart)

☐ Springform pan (9-inch)
☐ Loaf pan (9×5-inch)
☐ Ramekins (8-ounce)

YOUR PANTRY
and FRIDGE

What is the purpose of a pantry and fridge guide? I'm so glad you asked. A pantry and fridge guide is a list of food items you regularly consume. It can be helpful when you are meal planning every week and when you are grocery shopping. The key here is that it should be helpful. It should not be overwhelming, it should not be burdensome, and—most importantly—it should be yours.

Hot tip: Your pantry and fridge should not look like my pantry and fridge. We are feeding different people who have different tastes, so you get to build the pantry and fridge that best serve you and your family.

To give you a starting point, I have included my own pantry and fridge guide. Feel free to grab a pen and highlighter and make it your own. Once you are able to establish the items that you and your family eat often, it will make grocery shopping a dream.

PANTRY AND FRIDGE GUIDE

PANTRY

- ☐ Baking powder
- ☐ Basmati rice
- ☐ Brown sugar or coconut sugar
- ☐ Canned black beans
- ☐ Canned cannellini beans
- ☐ Canned diced tomatoes (14.5-ounce)
- ☐ Canned crushed tomatoes (28-ounce)
- ☐ Canned tomato sauce
- ☐ Canned whole peeled tomatoes (28-ounce)
- ☐ Chicken stock
- ☐ Coconut milk (canned, full-fat)

- ☐ Cornstarch (or arrow-root powder)
- ☐ Diced green chiles
- ☐ Dried pasta
- ☐ Golden raisins
- ☐ Honey
- ☐ Jar of anchovies in oil
- ☐ Jar of pepperoncini
- ☐ Maple syrup
- ☐ Peanut butter

OILS, VINEGARS, CONDIMENTS, AND SPICES

- ☐ Apple cider vinegar
- ☐ Balsamic vinegar
- ☐ Capers
- ☐ Chili powder
- ☐ Dijon mustard
- ☐ Dried Italian seasoning
- ☐ Dried oregano
- ☐ Dried red pepper flakes
- ☐ Dried yellow curry powder
- ☐ Fish sauce
- ☐ Garlic powder
- ☐ Ground cinnamon
- ☐ Ground coriander
- ☐ Ground cumin
- ☐ Ground nutmeg
- ☐ Hot sauce
- ☐ Hummus
- ☐ Instant yeast
- ☐ Ketchup
- ☐ Kosher salt
- ☐ Olive oil
- ☐ Onion powder
- ☐ Paprika
- ☐ Peppercorns (for freshly cracked black pepper)
- ☐ Red wine vinegar
- ☐ Sour cream
- ☐ Soy sauce or tamari
- ☐ Sriracha
- ☐ Tomato paste
- ☐ Worcestershire sauce

PRODUCE

- ☐ Cherry tomatoes
- ☐ Cucumbers
- ☐ Fresh basil
- ☐ Fresh cilantro
- ☐ Fresh dill
- ☐ Fresh thyme
- ☐ Garlic
- ☐ Ginger
- ☐ Lemons
- ☐ Limes
- ☐ Mini bell peppers
- ☐ Red onions
- ☐ Shiitake mushrooms
- ☐ Sweet onions
- ☐ Sweet potatoes

THE MEATS!

- ☐ Bacon
- ☐ Bone-in pork shoulder
- ☐ Chicken thighs—bone-in, skin-on
- ☐ Chicken thighs—boneless, skinless
- ☐ Chicken wings and drumsticks
- ☐ Chuck roast
- ☐ Ground beef (80/20)
- ☐ Ground pork breakfast sausage
- ☐ Pepperoni

DAIRY

- ☐ Butter
- ☐ Eggs
- ☐ Heavy cream
- ☐ Mascarpone cheese (or cream cheese)
- ☐ Mozzarella cheese
- ☐ Parmesan cheese
- ☐ Sharp cheddar cheese

forever
GROCERY LIST

We shall never reach for an empty jar of Dijon mustard again! This grocery list is for items that are staples in the kitchen but don't need to be purchased every week. Here's how this list works: anytime you get low on an item (say you use tomato paste and realize it's low), check the box on this list so you know you have to get that item next time you go grocery shopping. When you sit down to put your grocery list together, refer to your Forever Grocery List to add any of these items to your weekly list.

FOREVER GROCERY LIST

- ☐ Apple cider vinegar
- ☐ Baking powder
- ☐ Basmati rice
- ☐ Brown sugar or coconut sugar
- ☐ Butter
- ☐ Chicken stock
- ☐ Chili powder
- ☐ Coconut milk (canned, full-fat)
- ☐ Cumin (ground)
- ☐ Dijon mustard

- ☐ Flour
- ☐ Garlic powder
- ☐ Honey
- ☐ Hot sauce
- ☐ Instant yeast
- ☐ Ketchup
- ☐ Kosher salt
- ☐ Maple syrup
- ☐ Olive oil
- ☐ Onion powder
- ☐ Oregano (dried)

- ☐ Paprika
- ☐ Peanut butter
- ☐ Peppercorns (for freshly cracked black pepper)
- ☐ Prepared yellow mustard
- ☐ Red pepper flakes (dried)
- ☐ Sour cream
- ☐ Soy sauce or tamari
- ☐ Sriracha
- ☐ Tomato paste
- ☐ Worcestershire sauce
- ☐ Yellow curry powder

a vision
FOR YOUR KITCHEN

A great way to take ownership of your kitchen is to create a vision for the kind of kitchen you want or the kind of person you want to be in your kitchen. This vision can be a guiding light as you make decisions for how to equip your kitchen and when, how, and what food you cook.

A vision statement is an effective and powerful way to ground yourself as you get in the weeds of being in the kitchen every day, multiple times a day. According to Laurie Beth Jones, author of *The Path*, a good mission or vision statement should be:

1. No more than a single sentence long
2. Easily understood by a twelve-year-old
3. Able to be recited by memory[1]

In chapter 4 of my book *Come & Eat*, I take readers through a step-by-step method of how to create their vision for the table, which can be different from the vision for your kitchen. However, if you have the book, it's a great exercise (and also a great method for creating a vision statement for any area of your life).

Who do you want to be in the kitchen?

For me, I discovered I want to be a confident and joyful home cook. It turns out that the more confident I become in cooking and taking command of my kitchen, the more room there is to be joyful.

---

1. Laurie Beth Jones, *The Path: Creating Your Mission Statement for Work and for Life* (New York: Hachette, 1996), 3.

What tone do you want your kitchen to have?

For me, I want an inviting and safe kitchen. Of course safety is important when it comes to cooking, but I mean in the sense that people feel safe to be in my kitchen and share their life with me while I'm chopping and prepping. I want them to be able to lean over the counter, grab a slice of carrot, and pop it into their mouth knowing I won't get frustrated or annoyed.

As I realized this, I noticed there were lots of ways my kitchen was not inviting and lots of reasons I did not feel confident. My kitchen was not inviting because I often allowed myself to get stressed or frustrated there, which kept people at bay. I noticed that I did not feel confident in the kitchen because, while there were still things I needed to learn, mostly there were lots of ways I put unnecessary pressure on myself.

My vision for the kitchen helped me hone in on what matters. I took a few classes online and in kitchen stores to improve my cooking skills (how to hold a knife, how to make a delicious sauce, how to substitute ingredients, and so on), and as I became more confident I became less stressed. Becoming more confident and comfortable in the kitchen actually helped me to have a more inviting kitchen. I was more at ease with myself, I chose to believe that the people I was feeding were not actively judging my food, and I realized that they would enjoy their meal much more if I was also enjoying myself. I learned to turn on music while I cook. Music always improves my mood and gets me out of my head and more connected to my body (because . . . dancing!).

Your vision in the kitchen is *your* vision. It's all yours, and you get to choose it and own it. Maybe you want to spend less time in the kitchen. Maybe you don't want other people in the kitchen while you're cooking and decide to make it a you-zone during meal prep. Maybe you want your kitchen to be collaborative, which means you actively take steps to invite people into helping you cook meals.

Articulate the truest vision for who you want to be in the kitchen and what you want your kitchen to reflect, and write down three steps you can take to make this a reality. Here is an exercise to help you as you craft your vision for the kitchen.

List three adjectives describing who you want to be in the kitchen.
(Examples: joyful, efficient, calm, consistent, kind, victorious, swift, minimal, present, creative)

1. _____
2. _____
3. _____

List three words describing the kind of space you want your kitchen to be.
(Examples: inviting, safe, loud, clean, structured, private, collaborative, home headquarters)

1. _____
2. _____
3. _____

Using the above, bring together a sentence or two about the kind of person you want to be in the kitchen and the kind of kitchen you want to create. (Example: "I want to be a confident home cook with a joyful and safe kitchen.")

_____

_____

This is the magic of the vision you just created: you can be this person no matter what kind of kitchen you have! I can be a confident home cook in a small kitchen or a kitchen without a dishwasher or a kitchen with a tiny oven. My confidence is based on my knowledge, not the stuff available to me. I can have an inviting kitchen based on my approach to my kitchen, not based on how big my kitchen is. I have filled the smallest of kitchens simply by throwing on some music and pulling out a platter of cheese.

This vision is your guiding light as you take on both the kitchen you have now and future kitchens!

PART 2

USING *your* SENSES

*extra-creamy
chicken piccata
page 91*

FROM RECIPE READER
to home cook

I remember exactly where I was when it occurred to me that I trusted myself in the kitchen more than I ever had before. To start with, I was in my kitchen. I was reading a recipe that called for two small onions. As I was chopping the first onion, I realized how truly pungent it was—very aggressive onion smell. At that moment I decided I did not need to use two small onions. I only needed to use this one very extra onion.

That's the first time I can remember not exactly following a recipe because I trusted my senses more than I trusted the words on a page.

If you've watched any type of food TV show, then you've probably heard celebrity chefs repeat how important it is to taste our food. Taste our food! Taste as we cook. Taste at the end. Taste before we serve. This has been a helpful lesson to me in the kitchen. But I haven't heard as much instruction on listening to my food, looking at my food, touching my food, and truly allowing my senses to guide my decisions as I am cooking a meal.

This lesson may seem like it should be intuitive, but this skill is what took me from being a confident recipe reader to a confident home cook. I truly believe that the most important tool we have in the kitchen is our tongue, closely followed by our additional senses. If you can't use your senses to identify what your dish needs, it doesn't matter how good your knife skills are or if you can cook any kind of meat without burning it. And that's why we'll explore our senses before we dive into cooking techniques.

In this section we will learn the different ways we use all five of our senses to create delicious meals. One of your senses might be stronger than the others, or maybe you don't have all five senses available to you. That's okay! Use and trust what you have.

CALLING ALL
(five) senses

Starting today, we will no longer allow our senses to sit by passively as we cook. We will actively engage them as we step into the kitchen.

TOUCH

It's believed that touch is the first sense humans develop. Touch allows us to experience pain, vibration, temperature, and pressure. Touch is also essential in keeping us safe and informed. Ever get your hand too close to a hot stove? Feeling the heat radiating off the burner alerts you not to touch it.

Touch is for more than safety in the kitchen—it's essential as we cook and prepare our food. There are hundreds of ways touching our food can help inform our cooking decisions, such as how much of an ingredient to use, when a dish is done, or when to omit an ingredient. For example, when you grab a lemon to make a sauce, is it soft instead of firm? If it is softer, this means it is probably very juicy. A juicy lemon means you might not need to use the juice from the whole lemon—maybe just half.

When you pick up a garlic clove, is it less firm and have a little give? This means your clove of garlic is not as pungent as it once was, so you will want to add additional cloves to the recipe.

TASTE

Taste is broken down into the perception of five different tastes: salty, sweet, sour, bitter, and umami (savory). Bonus: spicy is not included as a

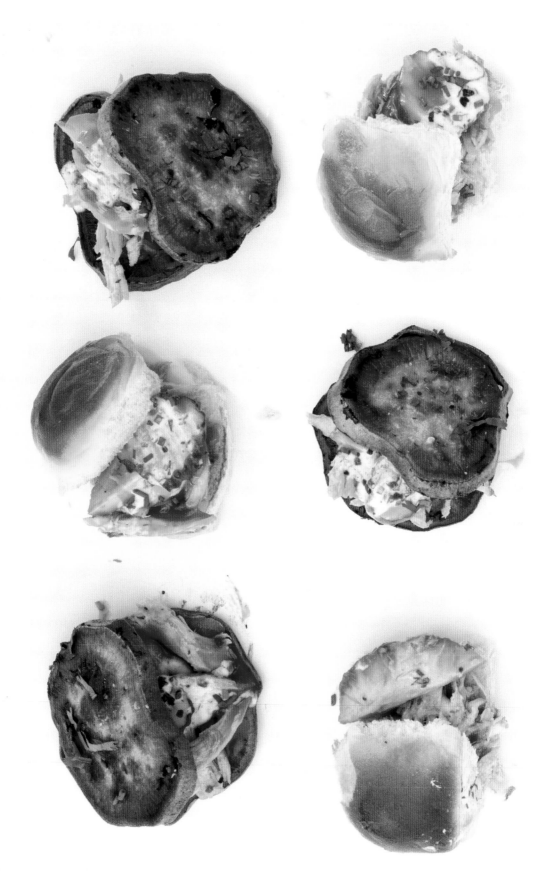

taste—it is actually a pain sensation! The taste buds on the sides of your tongue are much more sensitive than the taste buds in the middle of your tongue, but all areas of your tongue can perceive the different tastes.

The goal with taste is to be able to identify what we are perceiving when we eat our food. A lot of home cooks taste something, and their perception stops at the following:

"Something is off . . ."

"I think it needs something else . . ."

But we're going to become experts with our taste perception. We will taste something and be able to say:

"This is falling flat and needs more salt."

"This is a little bland and needs more citrus."

"The flavors are all there, but I think a little spice will bring everything together."

HEARING

My absolute favorite sound in the kitchen is the sizzle when I put meat in a hot pan. It's beyond satisfying—the loud sizzle signifies that I put the meat in at the right time! Being able to hear your food can be extremely helpful.

Listen to your water come to a rolling boil—you'll know it's ready to go when you hear the gurgling. When you bite into an apple and hear how crisp it is, you know it is perfectly ripe. Your sense of hearing can be powerful as you make decisions while cooking.

SMELL

The smell of food greatly affects how we taste our food. Have you ever plugged your nose to swallow medicine that tastes unpleasant or maybe a green juice you felt you just needed to get down? Plugging your nose drastically reduces your perception of taste. On the flip side, have you ever had a delicious, sizzling plate of fajitas delivered to your table and your mouth started to water before you even tasted the food? That's because your sense of smell is preparing your sense of taste!

If your sense of taste is a queen coming down the red carpet, your sense of smell is the red carpet.

Smell is an important sense because it not only elevates our perception of taste but also informs our decisions as we cook food. Just like in the example above, we want to activate our sense of smell and be able to name what we're working with—an overly pungent onion, a mild-smelling jalapeño, the fragrance of garlic.

SIGHT

Sight might be the first sense we activate when we're cooking. It helps us know if a fruit or vegetable is bad or good. (Hint: brown lettuce is not good!) When we turn a piece of chicken over in a pan, we can visually assess whether it's cooking correctly by looking at the color of the crust forming on the meat.

Actively using our sense of sight in the kitchen enables us to then involve our other senses as we determine our next step in creating everyday meals.

When we purposely activate all the senses available to us as we cook, it will change our cooking game in ways we never imagined. We can rely more on ourselves to make intuitive decisions and less on a recipe. Confidence in ourselves will bloom as we hone our senses.

The following recipe for homemade guacamole is an excellent way to learn how to bring together all five senses in the kitchen.

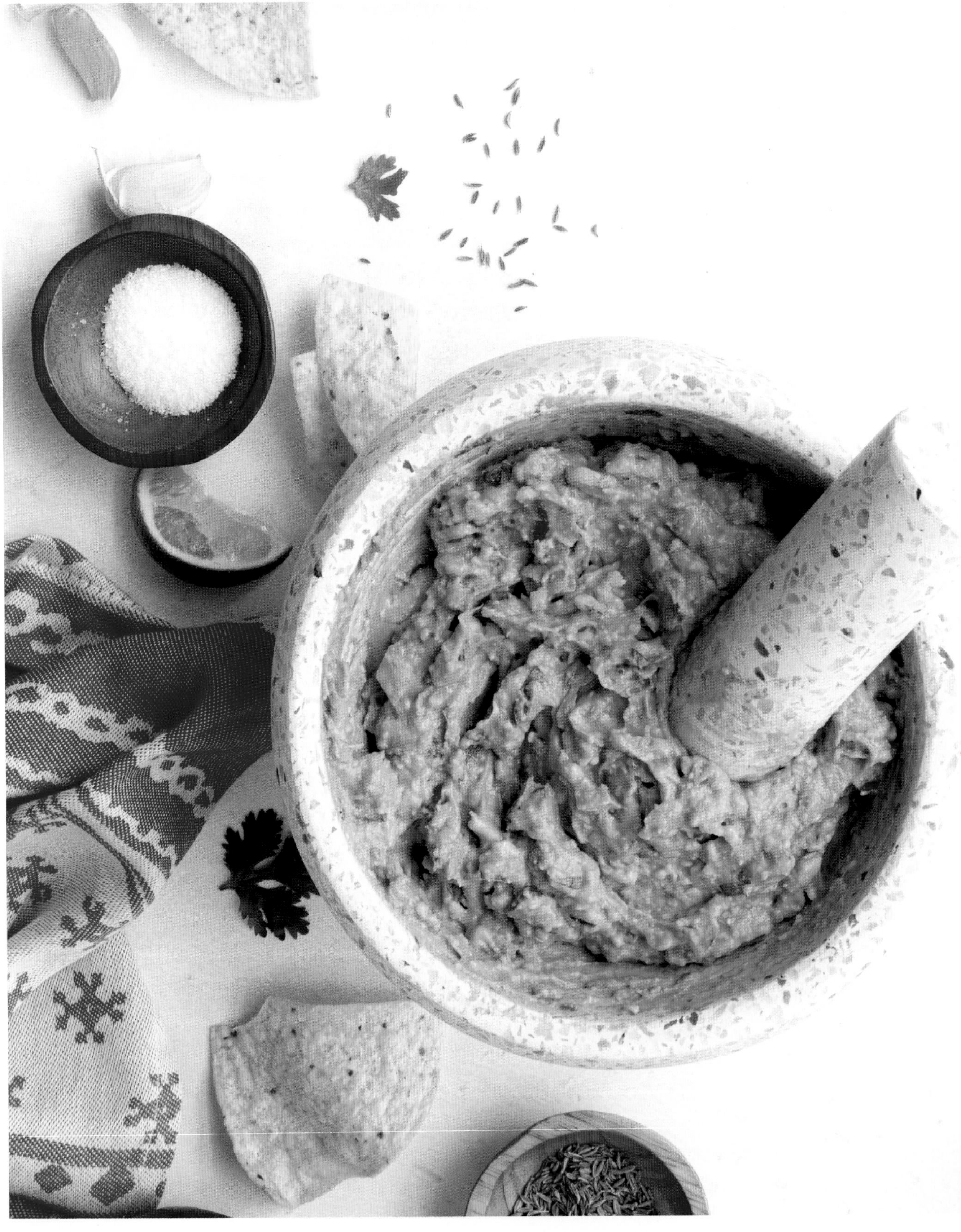

TABLESIDE GUACAMOLE

Bringing together homemade guacamole can teach us so much about our senses! Instead of just following this like a standard recipe, treat it like an experiment following the prompts below. You will learn so much about cooking through these steps.

PREP TIME: 10 MINUTES • COOK TIME: 2–3 MINUTES • SERVES 4

1 garlic clove, minced

2 teaspoons kosher salt

2 ripe avocados

juice from half a lime

juice from an orange wedge

½ teaspoon cumin

2 tablespoons fresh cilantro

¼ cup chopped red onion

¼ cup chopped tomatoes

1 serrano pepper, seeds removed, diced

a few dashes of hot sauce

This list of ingredients is just a guide. If your serrano pepper is very mild, you might want to keep some seeds because they will add heat. If your tomatoes are a little bland, you might need more salt.

A lot of people start with avocados when they're making guacamole, but I start with garlic! The smell of garlic when dipping into fresh guacamole can really activate your sense of taste. Start by making a garlic paste. Just add minced garlic and salt to a bowl or mortar. When you are removing the peel from the garlic, pay attention to how the clove feels. If it's on the softer side, it will be less garlicky and you might want to add another small clove.

Using a pestle or another rounded tool such as a spoon, mash the garlic into the salt to make a paste.

Grab the avocados. Utilize your sense of touch to check if the avocado is ripe. A great way to

VEGETARIAN, GRAIN-FREE, GLUTEN-FREE, DAIRY-FREE

If there is a nice green color under the stem, your avocado is ripe.

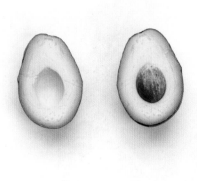

A perfectly ripe avocado will be creamy and easy to mash.

determine whether the avocado is ripe is by gently squeezing it. It should give a little bit. If it's too soft, it may no longer be good. If it's hard, it's not yet ripe. Another way to know if an avocado is ripe is to remove the small stem. If there is a nice green color under the stem, your avocado is ripe!

As you add the avocado to your bowl, make sure it is creamy. You can sense this with your touch as you mash the avocado. Is it creamy? Stringy? Mushy? If your avocado is creamy, there is guacamole in your future! If it is stringy or overly brown, this is where you might need to pivot. If that happens, forgo the guacamole and make a delicious pico de gallo (page 67).

Creamy avocado in hand, turn to your citrus, which comes from the lime and orange.

Firmly rolling a lime under your hand before cutting into it releases its juices, and you definitely want maximum juice from this little sphere. If your lime is soft, this means it is a juicy lime and you'll only need the juice from about half of it. If your lime is hard or quite small, it won't be as juicy and you might need to use the whole lime. The orange is an unexpected citrus for guacamole, but it really adds a little magic to your dip. The juice from the orange will bring a delightful sweetness while complementing the citrus of the lime.

Next, add the cumin. Cumin adds a beautiful note of bitterness to complement the creamy avocado.

Mash everything together and taste before you go any further.

This is where everything changes for you as a home cook. Master home cooks are always assessing their dishes. They're tasting and smelling and feeling every step along the way. If you're just reading the recipe and blindly obeying its orders, you might end up like Michael Scott from *The Office* when he drove into an actual pond because his GPS told him to turn. And so he turned. Into a pond. Obviously, the job of the GPS is to get the driver from point A to point B, but the driver is a very important player. Only the driver can see if there is a roadblock or a large body of water ahead.

You are a very important player in the kitchen, and so are all the senses you have available to you. A recipe cannot tell you if your lime is too juicy or if your avocado is not ripe. You need to use your senses of touch and taste. Think of a recipe as your partner on a seesaw. For a delicious dish to come together, the recipe needs balance and power from you, the cook.

There are still a few ingredients to add to the guacamole, but this is where you first assess the flavor to make sure nothing is off. Are the flavors you've added balanced? The garlic and the citrus should be present in a way that makes you want to go back for more. The delightful bitterness of the cumin should cut through the creaminess of the avocado in a way that complements (but doesn't outshine) the other flavors. If something tastes off, name it.

How is the citrus? Is it muted or not very detectable? Add another squeeze of lime juice.

How is the garlic? Is it overpowering? Make note of that as you add the additional ingredients, knowing you might need to add more avocado to tame the garlic.

Don't worry if you feel like you're fumbling your way through it. You will get better at naming the problem as you continue to hone the skill. And the good news is, guacamole is very easy to fix!

Once you have a good idea of the direction your guacamole is headed, it's time to add the ingredients that won't be mashed. As you prepare each of these items, try to really lean into your sense of smell. If your fresh cilantro has a weak scent, you might want to add a little more. If your serrano smells very spicy, you might want to add less or definitely remove all the seeds.

Now, add all remaining ingredients and stir to combine. Taste again!

umami   *citrus*   *heat*   *freshness*

When I make guacamole, it tastes delicious every time because the basics are there, but I almost always need to tweak something once I get to the finished product. This is because the recipe calls for such fresh ingredients. Your cilantro is not going to taste the same every time, nor will your avocados. This is why tasting, smelling, looking, and touching are so crucial.

Ask yourself the same questions you asked earlier.

Does it need more citrus now? Add more lime juice or even a hit of freshly squeezed orange juice. The orange still brings citrus but adds a beautiful sweetness too.

Is it a little bland? Add a touch more salt.

Do you want more spice? Add more hot sauce or fresh serrano pepper, or perhaps some dried red pepper flakes.

Using your senses from the very beginning of bringing a dish together also allows you to pivot. You might realize your tomatoes went bad or only one of your avocados is ripe. But guacamole is in your future, and here's how.

SIMPLE BUT FLAVORFUL

You can still have a delicious chip dip even if you do not have everything on hand for the Tableside Guacamole. Simple can still be flavorful!

Avocado

Fresh lime juice

Salt

Mash one avocado, add the juice from a wedge of lime, sprinkle in a little kosher salt.

It's delicious and you only need a few ingredients on hand.

ADD A LITTLE FLAIR

Have some additional ingredients on hand to level up your simple guacamole? It's time to add a little flair.

Avocado

Fresh lime juice

Salt

Cilantro

Red onion

Mash one avocado and add juice from half a lime and 1 teaspoon salt. Mix in a handful of chopped cilantro and a handful of diced red onion. Enjoy!

MAKE IT POP

If you are ready to go all out with maximum flavor, make a guacamole that really pops!

Avocado

Fresh lime juice

Fresh juice from an orange

Salt

Cilantro

Garlic clove

Red onion

Pomegranate seeds

Mash two avocados and add the juice from a small lime, the juice from a wedge of orange, and 1½ teaspoons salt. Mix in a handful of chopped cilantro, a minced garlic clove, a handful of diced red onion, and a handful of pomegranate seeds.

Using what you have on hand along with your senses will allow you to create so many variations on a dish you love. Whether making something super simple or more involved, it is a choose-your-own-adventure and *you* are the guide.

As you learn to identify the different taste perceptions, you will be able to more quickly identify what a dish needs. And that's up next.

But first, grab a margarita or cold sparkling water with lime and enjoy your guacamole!

THE FIVE
taste perceptions

Utilizing taste, touch, sight, smell, and sound in the kitchen can be mostly intuitive. But can we identify what things taste like? If something is bitter or too salty? If it's sour or packed with umami?

Making sure tastes are perceived correctly (for example, fresh lemon juice is tart, not sweet) is a game changer. It's a skill that only gets better with time—and lots of tasting.

Remember, there are five taste perceptions: salty, sweet, sour, bitter, and umami.

SALTY

I like to think of salt as a rancher with a lasso wrangling all the flavors together. Have you ever tasted something and it just . . . fell flat? Even if the dish had a variety of spices and ingredients? How can it fall flat with all that flavor? The flavors need to be brought together in harmony, and that's what salt does. In most cases, I think we all know when something is too salty. However, it can be challenging to know when something needs *more* salt.

Here is a rule of thumb when I cook: if I taste something and it's a little flat or off, I always start adjustments with kosher salt—about ½ teaspoon at a time. The missing ingredient is almost always salt.

FIVE GO-TO INGREDIENTS FOR ADDING SALTINESS

1. Kosher salt
2. Fleur de sel
3. Soy sauce
4. Crumbled bacon
5. Parmesan cheese

SWEET

This taste is most often perceived when eating foods rich in sugars. While people mostly think about perceiving the taste of sweet in desserts, it is also important in savory dishes. (Just think of all the recipes for weeknight meals that call for honey or brown sugar or maple syrup.)

FIVE GO-TO INGREDIENTS FOR ADDING SWEETNESS

1. Maple syrup
2. Coconut sugar (or brown sugar)
3. Honey
4. White sugar
5. Liqueur

SOUR

Sour is perceived when eating acidic foods such as lemon. Using something sour in a dish brings brightness, which enhances the dish's flavor. I once steamed broccoli and sprinkled it with fleur de sel and a squeeze of lemon juice. Now, every time I serve this, I get asked for the recipe. The magic is in the squeeze of lemon juice.

FIVE GO-TO INGREDIENTS FOR ADDING ACIDITY

1. Juice from citrus (lemons, limes, grapefruit, etc.)
2. Apple cider vinegar
3. Wine
4. Tomatoes
5. Plain Greek yogurt

(Bonus: condiments such as mustard, ketchup, and mayonnaise can also add a nice acidity to dishes.)

BITTER

The taste perception humans are most sensitive to is bitterness.[1] The most common use of bitterness is to balance sweetness. Think, for example, of using semisweet dark chocolate, which is bitter, in a recipe for rich chocolate cake.

1. Karen Page and Andrew Dornenburg, *The Flavor Bible: The Essential Guide to Culinary Creativity, Based on the Wisdom of America's Most Imaginative Chefs* (New York: Little, Brown and Company, 2008), 3.

Bitterness also shines as a taste that cleanses the palate. For example, think of having a cappuccino after dinner or smelling coffee beans in a department store while testing fragrances.

FIVE GO-TO INGREDIENTS FOR ADDING BITTERNESS

1. Kale or microgreens
2. Capers
3. Dried cranberries
4. Cocoa powder
5. Dried cumin
   (or fresh oregano!)

UMAMI

The best way to describe umami is with the word *savory*. It's the taste perception that has your mouth watering and is generally used to describe rich dishes. Foods that are classified with umami notes include mushrooms, blue cheese, soy sauce, and anchovies.

FIVE GO-TO INGREDIENTS FOR ADDING UMAMI

1. Shiitake mushrooms
2. Garlic (raw or over-cooked garlic can be bitter, but when cooked or roasted, garlic is very rich in umami taste)
3. Soy sauce (Worcester-shire or fish sauce are other options)
4. Molasses
5. Tomato paste

Now that we have covered the five taste perceptions available to us, we will examine each one so we can know what we are tasting in any scenario.

Making homemade salsa is the gateway into maturing taste perceptions. But we're going to make it wrong. And then we're going to fix it. VERY EXCITING!

The skill of using your senses to bring together delicious meals will only mature and advance over time, and you will learn to trust your senses more than you trust a recipe.

And you are worth trusting in the kitchen.

GATHERING SALSA

I call this recipe "Gathering Salsa" because people near and far will find their way to gather in your kitchen. This is perfect for welcoming new neighbors, throwing parties, or enjoying impromptu get-togethers.

 This recipe uses several fresh ingredients, so it might be slightly different every time you make it. Take your time with tasting. This is a great lesson on how to adjust salt and citrus.

PREP TIME: 10 MINUTES • COOK TIME: 3–5 MINUTES • SERVES 10–12

1 (28-ounce) can whole tomatoes, drained

½ cup fresh cilantro, roughly chopped

¼ cup chopped red onion

2 cloves garlic, minced (or 1 teaspoon garlic powder)

1 jalapeño, quartered and sliced thin (remove seeds if you do not want a spicy salsa)

1 teaspoon ground cumin

2 teaspoons kosher salt

1 whole lime, juiced

Before working with your ingredients, taste them individually. Name what you taste.

The tomatoes: canned tomatoes can be a little on the sweet side. I like using canned tomatoes for salsa because they are picked at the height of ripeness and then canned to preserve their ripeness. Sweet and a little acidic.

A leaf from the cilantro: fresh and a little bitter.

A bite of the red onion: pungent and strong.

A tiny bite of the jalapeño: taste this or use your sense of smell to determine if it is mild or spicy.

A granule of cumin: bitter.

A little squeeze of lime juice: citrusy.

Bringing these ingredients together will make a salsa you will return to again and again!

VEGETARIAN, GRAIN-FREE, GLUTEN-FREE, DAIRY-FREE

Method

In a food processor, add tomatoes, cilantro, and red onion. Pulse for 10–15 seconds, or until your desired consistency is reached.

Taste. How does it taste? Say it out loud. One way I really honed my sense of taste was to say what I tasted out loud: "This tastes salty." "This tastes sour." "This tastes garlicky." Do the tomatoes taste a little on the sweet side? Or more on the acidic side?

You're probably realizing what you've created is not that satisfying. It's bland—a little bit "one-note."

What's it missing?

Definitely salt. But it also needs something a little sour (or what I call citrusy) to cut through the strong tomato taste. It would be nice if it also had a bit of garlic, which activates our perception of umami flavor. I know that cumin adds a touch of bitterness, which pairs perfectly with umami flavors.

Add the lime juice, garlic, and cumin. Pulse to bring it together. Taste again.

The sour notes and the umami flavors make it way better! But it still needs something that brings all these flavors together.

Add salt. Pulse. Taste. Now we are getting somewhere. Depending on your preference, you might think this is perfect. I am not a huge fan of too much spice, but I know that a little spice can elevate the other flavors. So now add the jalapeño. Pulse.

Taste!

And now we have used all of our senses, tasting for salty, sweet, sour, bitter, and umami to bring together the most satisfying salsa in all the land.

Just like with the guacamole, since we're using a lot of fresh ingredients in this salsa, we will most likely have to tweak the recipe every time we make it. This does not mean the recipe is wrong or you did something wrong—it just means that sometimes those fresh ingredients will be perfectly ripe and fresh and sometimes they will be a little muted or dull.

Using what you now know about using your senses and taste perceptions, you can pull this dish together in so many different ways, even if you have only a few ingredients on hand. If you start making Gathering Salsa and find that you are out of cumin or don't have a lime, make one of the following variations instead.

SIMPLE BUT FLAVORFUL (PICO DE GALLO)

Fresh tomato	Chop a whole tomato or a handful of cherry tomatoes. Mix in a sprinkle of kosher salt, a handful of chopped white onion, and chopped cilantro. Fresh and delicious!
Kosher salt	
White onion	
Cilantro	

ADD A LITTLE FLAIR

Fresh tomato	Chop a whole tomato or a handful of cherry tomatoes. Mix in a sprinkle of kosher salt, a handful of chopped white onion, and chopped cilantro. Add some fresh chopped pineapple and chopped bell pepper.
Kosher salt	
White onion	
Cilantro	
Fresh pineapple	
Fresh bell peppers	

WHAT THE KALE SALAD

Salad is another great teacher in the kitchen. Listen, if you don't like salads, I'm not here to convince you that you just haven't had a decent one. But I do think most salads are woefully under-seasoned.

 This salad is perfectly satisfying because it has citrus, salt, sweetness, crunch, and creaminess. Anytime you pull a salad together, think of these components that give layers of flavor to your salad.

PREP TIME: 15 MINUTES • SERVES 4–5 AS A SIDE DISH

juice of half a lemon

⅓ cup extra-virgin olive oil

1 tablespoon Dijon mustard

1 tablespoon maple syrup

½ teaspoon kosher salt

1 bunch kale, ribs and stems removed, leaves chopped

3 tablespoons crumbled goat cheese

¼ cup dried cranberries

¼ cup chopped pecans

1 Add lemon juice, olive oil, Dijon mustard, maple syrup, and kosher salt to a small mason jar (or dressing shaker). Secure lid on jar and shake vigorously until combined.

2 Rinse the kale and dry with a cloth or paper towels. To remove the stem, grab onto the stem at the end, then wrap your other hand around the stem and pull up. The kale leaves will come off the stem. Roughly chop leaves and add to a large bowl. Add half the dressing to the kale. Using your hands, massage the dressing into the kale for several minutes. Add goat cheese, dried cranberries, and pecans.

If possible, allow the salad to chill in the refrigerator for about 10–15 minutes. Serve with extra dressing on the side.

VEGETARIAN, GRAIN-FREE, GLUTEN-FREE

TIP: *Kale can be pretty tough, but massaging dressing into the kale allows for better softening and absorption.*

BACK FROM THE CLUB SANDWICH

A basic sandwich gets a glow up with the addition of seasoning it with salt and freshly cracked black pepper, as well as a vinegary bite from candied jalapeños. This is not your basic club sandwich. This is the kind of club you crave when your body is exhausted (say, after clubbing or maybe just running errands) and you want something satisfying but familiar.

 Prepare the candied jalapeños ahead of time and let them chill in the fridge until ready for use. They get better with time and will last in the fridge for weeks!

PREP TIME: 15 MINUTES • SERVES 1

FOR THE CANDIED JALAPEÑOS

1 pounds fresh jalapeños

¾ cup apple cider vinegar

1½ cups white granulated sugar

FOR THE SANDWICH

2 tablespoons butter

3 slices white bread

mayonnaise

2 tomato slices

kosher salt

freshly ground black pepper

3 slices cooked bacon, broken in half

2 slices sharp cheddar cheese

2 slices turkey

2 slices roasted chicken

cilantro microgreens
(optional but so worth it)

FOR THE AVOCADO SMASH

1 avocado

½ teaspoon kosher salt

1 tablespoon candied jalapeños

FOR THE CANDIED JALAPEÑOS

1 Wearing gloves (this is very important when handling this many peppers!), slice off jalapeño stems and discard.

2 Discard most of the seeds by hollowing out the peppers with a small spoon or knife, or just tap the pepper to release most of the seeds. (If you really like heat you can leave the seeds in, but it will be spicy.) Slice the peppers into uniform ¼-inch rounds.

3 In a saucepan over medium-high heat, add apple cider vinegar and sugar. Stir to dissolve sugar and bring to a boil. Reduce heat to medium-low and simmer for 5 minutes to slightly reduce.

4 Raise the heat to medium-high and add the pepper rounds, return to a boil, then reduce the heat again and simmer for 4 minutes.

5 Using a slotted spoon, transfer peppers to a large mason jar.

6 Allow the liquid in the pan to continue to reduce by simmering for another 6–8 minutes.

7 Pour liquid into the jar. Make sure the liquid completely covers the peppers. Allow to sit for 15 minutes to cool down, then secure lid on mason jar. You can flip the jar a few times to ensure the liquid coats all the peppers.

8 Allow to cool and then place in the refrigerator for at least one hour. These get better with time and will last in the refrigerator for up to three weeks.

FOR THE SANDWICH

1 In a large sauté pan, melt butter over medium-high heat. Fry all slices of bread on both sides until golden brown, about 2–3 minutes per side.

2 Make the avocado smash by mashing the flesh of the avocado with ½ teaspoon salt. Mix in 1 tablespoon candied jalapeños.

3 Assemble the sandwich: spread mayonnaise across a slice of bread, followed by some of the avocado smash. Top with turkey, half of the bacon, one slice of cheese, and cilantro microgreens (if using). Sprinkle with kosher salt. Add another slice of bread. Spread on mayonnaise, avocado smash, roasted chicken, the rest of the bacon, tomato slices, and the second slice of cheese. Sprinkle with kosher salt and some freshly cracked black pepper and top with the last piece of bread.

4 Cut the sandwich diagonally in half. Insert toothpicks in each half to keep intact.

Plate sandwich with your favorite potato chips and a pickle spear.

GRANDMA'S SOUR CREAM SALAD

I grew up going to my grandma's house in the summers. Even as a child, after a full day of playing outside with my cousins, I knew I could run into her house at any time and be greeted with the magic of air conditioning and a big help-ing of this fresh, bright, crisp sour cream salad. This dish will always remind me of Grandma's kitchen.

One day I casually shared her recipe on my website, and I was not pre-pared for the cult following. Even people who swore they didn't like sour cream were fans. But the real reason this recipe is in The Cook's Book is be-cause it shows the power of salt.

 To really understand how salt can transform a meal, make this dish without the salt and taste. Then add the salt. It will be a completely different experience.

SERVES 2–3 AS A SIDE DISH

½ cucumber, sliced

1 tomato, chopped (or ½ cup sliced cherry tomatoes)

½ red onion, sliced

¼ cup sour cream (or plain Greek yogurt)

2 teaspoons kosher salt

Add all ingredients to a large bowl and mix. If possible, chill for 20 minutes before serving. Try to share (this will be difficult)!

VEGETARIAN, GRAIN-FREE, GLUTEN-FREE

Starting today, name what you taste. Eating an apple? Sweet and crisp! As you do this, you will become a master at knowing what you are tasting. This skill becomes especially helpful when you are cooking a weeknight meal and, after tasting your food, realize it needs something. For example, maybe your stir-fry tastes a little too salty and maybe even too rich. You will know that something sour can cut through the richness and brighten the dish, so you add a squeeze of lime juice.

the

MOST POWERFUL

KITCHEN

techniques

PICKLED RED ONIONS   83

EXTRA-CREAMY CHICKEN PICCATA   91

SWEET POTATO SHEPHERD'S PIE   93

CREAMY ITALIAN SAUSAGE PASTA   95

HALIBUT WITH CURRY SAUCE   97

When it comes to the art of cooking, there are so many different lessons and techniques you can learn. It can be overwhelming to try to discern which skills are the most worthwhile or important in home cooking. Honestly, there are techniques that just do not matter to me. For example, I am not interested (at least right now) in knowing how to bake a moist and fluffy cake.

But there are three techniques that I believe lay the foundation for every kind of cooking and will allow all other skills to easily build upon this foundation.

1. How to properly hold your knife and use it to make different slices and dices.
2. How to cook food in your pan without sticking.
3. How to properly deglaze your pan to bring extra richness to your dish.

THERE'S A KNIFE
for that

When I was learning to cook, the last thing I wanted in my hand was a sharp knife. I was sure I needed to graduate from some kind of underground knife training course before I could hold one. But what I came to learn is that a dull knife is more dangerous than a sharp knife. A dull knife can easily slip while you are dicing and slicing, which is what can cause injuries. A sharp knife can effortlessly cut through the toughest to most tender veggies and meat.

My least favorite task in the kitchen for a long time was chopping. I later discovered it was because I was using a dull knife. Once I invested in a sharp, high-quality knife, all that changed. Chopping became effortless and even enjoyable.

There are so many amazing brands of knives out there. The best thing you can do is take a trip to your local kitchen store and ask a salesperson to help you make your selection. Hold different knives and see how they feel in your hand. Ask questions about durability, care, and customer favorites. I did this years ago and walked out with a 7-inch Wüsthof Santoku knife. I've never looked back.

Having a chef's knife and then any combination of the other knives mentioned above will level up your game in the kitchen! The best part is that when you invest in a high-quality knife, it can last you a lifetime.

CHEF'S KNIFE

A chef's knife is one of the most versatile knives you can own. If you are just now investing in a knife, start here or with a Santoku knife. These knives can chop, slice, dice, and butcher. I use this knife every day.

PARING KNIFE

A paring knife has a much smaller blade and handle. It is a star at peeling fruits and veggies. It is also often used for more intricate knife work. I use mine for slicing lemons, fruits, and smaller vegetables such as serrano peppers.

SERRATED KNIFE

This knife's blade looks almost tooth-like. Because of this, the blade is perfect for slicing through anything with a harder exterior but soft interior without damaging the item you are cutting. (Have you ever tried to cut through a tomato and ended up flattening it, its juice running everywhere? Not with a serrated knife!) I have a serrated knife on the smaller side, which is perfect for slicing—you guessed it—tomatoes.

BREAD KNIFE

A bread knife also has a serrated blade but is typically much longer to easily slice through large loaves of bread. This allows the bread to keep its shape while you slice through the harder crust and soft interior.

VARIETY OF KNIVES

chef

paring

serrated

bread

STORAGE AND CARE

Storage

Storing your knives correctly is not only important for safety but can help with their longevity. A knife's blade dulls slightly every time it is used, and not storing it properly can dull the blade even faster.

Here are a few options for properly storing your knives to protect yourself and the blades. Depending on the setup of your kitchen and your personal preferences, you can choose any of these methods.

Knife Strip. This is my preferred way to store my knives! First of all, I like having my knives on display. Creepy? Maybe. I also like how easy it is to grab a knife when I need it. The strip is magnetic, so the blade quickly attaches to it. It also takes up wall space instead of counter space.

Knife Block. A knife block is very common. These can sit out on the counter or in a drawer. Generally, if you buy a set of knives, you can also get a knife block with the deal.

Knife Guards. If you prefer to store your knives in a sliding drawer, knife guards are perfect! They not only protect the blade but also protect your hand when you are reaching into the drawer to grab a knife.

Care

How you clean and care for your knives is also an important step to keeping the blades sharp and the knives durable. These steps are important and very easy.

Sharp blades have a very thin edge that can easily be damaged or dulled over time. Here's how to keep your blade sharper longer:

1. Use a wood, bamboo, or Epicurean cutting board. Glass or hard plastic cutting boards are not as gentle for the blade. If you do have a glass cutting board, just be mindful that the blade can dull quicker.

2. Hand-wash. The intense and harsh process of a dishwasher can drastically dull the blades. Take a few minutes to hand-wash your knives and dry with a clean cloth.

3. Store knives in a knife strip, knife block, or inside a knife guard.

4. Sharpen. There are so many ways to sharpen a knife. When you purchase your first good knife, be sure to ask the salesperson for recommended care instructions. If you already own a good knife, you can still visit your local kitchen store and ask how to sharpen it. My preferred method is to take my knives to a local kitchen shop about twice a year and have them professionally sharpened. This can be very inexpensive—just a few dollars a knife! Usually the knives are done the same day or the next day.

Pro tip: It doesn't matter how long your knife has gone without sharpening, most kitchen stores will sharpen your knife. Just call ahead and confirm they offer knife sharpening service. Most of the time knives can be sharpened and ready for pickup the same day. I lovingly refer to this as taking my "kids" (the knives) to "camp" (the kitchen store)! If you would like to learn how to sharpen your own knives, most kitchen stores offer classes you can take to learn how to do this at home.

There is a simple at-home method to test if a knife needs to be sharpened. Have someone hold up a piece of paper—carefully—while you slice through that paper with your knife. If the slice is jagged and the knife snags while moving through the paper, it's time to get it sharpened. If you easily and cleanly slice through the paper, your knife gets an A+.

USING YOUR KNIFE

Holding your knife correctly will enable you to chop and slice with ease.

First, where to grab the knife. You want to grab the knife right where the handle ends and the blade begins. This will give you stability and control over the blade. Your thumb and index finger wrap around the handle and will be the fingers that exert the most pressure when you are gripping the knife. The additional fingers curl around the handle. When you use the knife, your knuckle on your index finger should be pointed.

Second, properly using the knife. A knife should never be used like a saw, going back and forth as if cutting down a tree. The blade should be able to uniformly cut through the item without strain. The best way to use your knife is to think of the blade as a seesaw, rocking it back and forth without lifting the blade up. The tip end of the blade should stay in contact with the cutting board. This allows you to use the length of the blade so the items are cut all the way through, and it means you are not putting too much strain on one area of the blade. When the full blade is being utilized, your blade will not dull as fast.

Practice properly holding and using a knife (remember: grip, tuck, rock). The best way to do this is to practice on something soft—perhaps a large portobello mushroom or even a banana. In this skill you are working more on getting a feel for holding and using the knife than making the perfect slice.

Third, guide food to your knife. You should use your nondominant hand to guide what you are cutting to the blade. Of course, you need to be careful that you don't also guide those fingers into the blade's path, which is why you want to tuck the fingers slightly under into the palm of your hand. When your fingers are slightly tucked, you can safely move, let's say, a piece of celery into the blade as the knife is cutting. Your knuckles will stop the blade from cutting off any part of your hand. Not cutting off your hand is a very important part of being confident in the kitchen!

Mastering this takes lots of practice. At first it will feel weird to hold the knife this way. Take your time. Before you know it, your knife will feel like an extension of your hand. A cue that helped me as I learned to hold my knife was to always repeat the following: grip, tuck, rock. *Grip* the knife correctly, making sure my thumb and index finger are in the correct position. *Tuck* the fingers on my other hand as I guide food to the blade. *Rock* the knife back and forth as I slice and dice.

GRIP. TUCK. ROCK.

SLICING AND CHOPPING

There are a variety of ways to cut fruits and vegetables, and each way is suited for how the ingredient will be prepared or cooked. The different types of preparation are especially important if using heat to cook your vegetables. We want them to cook uniformly, so whether we chop, dice, or slice, we want each piece to be the same size.

Onions are a great example. They are used in so many different dishes and bring excellent flavor, but they can be annoying to cut. Here's how to start working with an onion before proceeding into any kind of chop or dice:

1. Identify the part of the onion that has the brown sprouts coming out. This is the root. (I like to call it "the party" because it looks like confetti is coming out of the onion.) You do not want to cut this part of the onion off. You want to keep the party.
2. Slice the other end of the onion to create a flat surface. Set the onion up on the flat side you created. Slice through the onion vertically, cutting through the party. Remove the outermost skin and discard.
3. Now the onion is halved, and you can work with it to make any kind of dice or slice.

Here are the most common cuts you'll make as a home cook.

Slice. Slicing is when you cut something (like an onion) lengthwise. The end result resembles a long, thin smile. A recipe might call for a thin slice or a thick slice. Generally you want to slice something thicker if it is going to have a longer cooking time, such as caramelized onions. Caramelized onions cook for a long time, so you want more onion to work with. Thin slices can be used if you want a good bite of what you are slicing—for example, on pizza or in a salad.

Chop, dice, and mince cuts all achieve the same look (think of a tiny square) but at varying sizes. Chop is bigger, dice is medium to small size, and mince is the smallest of them all.

Chop. When an ingredient is chopped, it can usually be a rough chop and can be in bigger chunks. In most cases, *no matter what a recipe says*, you can make the call. For example, I love a chunky chili, so when I chop my vegetables they are on the bigger side.

slice

dice

chiffonade

But I know some of my friends have to dice the vegetables because if their kids see vegetables in their bowl of chili, they'll riot.

Again, it is important to consider cooking times if you are using heat to cook what you have chopped. A bigger piece of chopped vegetable will require a longer cooking time than a very small piece.

Dice. A dice is a medium to small cut that works great if you're not cooking the vegetable for long, or if it's raw and you don't want it to overpower your dish.

Mince. Mince is the smallest cut of all. When a recipe calls for, say, minced garlic, that's when I pull out my garlic press or microplane, which will uniformly cut the garlic into the smallest pieces. In most cases you will see that recipes call for minced garlic because garlic is so pungent. It's important that it is cooked and distributed uniformly throughout the dish.

Chiffonade. This cutting technique is only done for leafy green vegetables and herbs, but I'm covering it since it's widely used. Chiffonade is cutting basil leaves, for example, into long, thin strips. This is done by stacking the leaves on top of each other, rolling them, and slicing perpendicularly through the rolled leaves. Long, thin slices of fresh herbs are great when you really want the flavor of the herb to come out.

An important note on slicing and dicing: As home cooks, we are not serving dishes to people at The French Laundry (unless you are, and then please carry on). So while it's helpful to know the proper way to slice and dice food, we don't need to take ourselves too seriously. If some pieces of onion are bigger than others, we'll survive.

PICKLED RED ONIONS

PREP TIME: 10 MINUTES • COOK TIME: 20 MINUTES

1 red onion, thinly sliced

½ cup apple cider vinegar

½ cup purified water

1½ tablespoons honey

1 teaspoon kosher salt

As you practice perfecting a sliced onion, use the slices to make pickled red onions! These are a great condiment and last up to three weeks in the refrigerator. (Put them on burgers, tacos, salads, sandwiches, breakfast burritos . . . possibilities galore!)

1 In a wide-mouth, 1-quart mason jar, add the onion slices.

2 In a small saucepan, add the remaining ingredients and stir to combine. Allow the mixture to come to a simmer over medium-low heat. Stir until honey is fully incorporated.

3 Carefully pour the hot vinegar mixture over the red onions. Allow to sit for 15 minutes to cool down.

4 Secure lid on mason jar. Allow to sit for at least one hour before enjoying. Refrigerate. These will last up to three weeks in the refrigerator.

VEGETARIAN, GRAIN-FREE, GLUTEN-FREE, DAIRY-FREE

COOK WITHOUT FOOD
sticking to your pan

The first time I pulled up a filet of fish from my stainless-steel pan without any of it sticking to the pan, I quickly readied myself to be offered a TV show on the Food Network. The win felt that monumental.

What I didn't know the many times before that when food stubbornly stuck to my pan is that there's a science, a proven technique, for making sure things don't stick. And once you learn the science, you'll never look back. Yay, science!

PROPERLY HEATING A STAINLESS-STEEL PAN

Properly heating your pan before adding your food is the first and critical step. If your food does stick, it could be because your pan is too cold or too hot, or the food is just not ready to be flipped.

The other thing with stainless-steel pans is there are so many different kinds. Big, small, flat, rounded. Also, stainless steel is composed of a variety of different metals, so no two pans are exactly the same. Because of this, there is no cookie-cutter "Heat for three minutes, no more and no less, and you're ready to add your food" instruction.

Essentially, you need to learn your unique pan by taking the temperature of your pan. And here's how.

Turn your burner on medium heat. If you are using stainless steel, you definitely want medium heat, or maybe a little less than medium-high. Stainless steel does an excellent job at maintaining and evenly distributing heat during cooking. It's what it's known for. So if you crank your stove too high, your pan will get really hot really fast and it will be hard to bring it back down to a good cooking temperature.

As your pan is heating, you will be able to check its temperature every 30 seconds with a droplet of water—⅛ teaspoon, to be exact. Do not try doing this test with ¼ teaspoon, because that's too much water and this test won't work.

1 The first time you drop the water in, you might see this:

The water does not react at all, which means the pan is still too cold and you need to let it warm up a little bit.

Wait about 30–45 seconds and try the test again.

2 If you drop the water in and it bubbles and steams, the pan is still too cold. It will look like this:

Wait another 30–45 seconds and try again. You will probably experience this bubble effect one or two more times (like I did). This is no time to give up.

3 Next, you will probably see this:

These round bubbles are what you are looking for . . . well, the shape is what you are looking for. But you need to see one large ball of water glide along the pan to know your pan is ready.

4 Wait another 30 seconds and add another ⅛ teaspoon of water. This is the one perfect ball of water you are looking for:

Now that the pan is at the *exact* right temperature, you have to act quickly, because the pan is still on the heat source and still climbing in temperature. Add the oil to your pan. It's also good to have your food ready to go before you start this experiment.

When you add anything to a pan, it lowers the temperature. Adding the oil will result in a slight decrease in temperature, but only for a few seconds. You will know your oil is properly heated when you see the first wisp of smoke, or if you move the oil around and you see "legs" form (the kind of legs you see when you swirl a glass of wine).

Now you know approximately how long it takes to properly heat your pan (count up all those 30-second intervals). You only have to do this experiment once, but it teaches you so much information about your pan and your stove!

So what exactly is happening here? Stainless-steel pans have pores in them, and during the heating process these pores open and close. If your pan is not heated properly and you put your chicken (or what have you) in the pan, the opening and closing pores will latch on to your food, causing it to stick when you go to flip it.

When the pan is at the right temperature, the pores are no longer opening and closing. This is why the water test is perfect. When water hits a pan and forms one perfect ball that glides across the pan, the pores are stable. Your pan is heated.

If you have properly preheated your pan but your chicken or meat won't easily come up when you go to turn it, leave it alone for another 1–2 minutes. Your chicken or meat will easily release from the pan when it is cooked on that side.

When water hits a pan and
forms one perfect ball
that glides across the pan,

the pores are stable.

YOUR PAN IS HEATED.

PROPERLY HEATING AN ENAMELED CAST-IRON PAN

The water trick does not work on enameled cast iron because it is made of different materials. But there *is* a simple way to learn how to heat your enameled cast iron.

The first rule of thumb is, unlike with stainless steel, we do not want to heat our enameled cast iron without adding liquid first. Always add the oil or fat of choice (I generally use 1 tablespoon olive oil or coconut oil) and then turn the heat to medium-high. Just like with stainless steel, you never need to turn your heat to high because enameled cast iron is an excellent conductor of heat.

You will know your pan is properly heated when the oil becomes almost as thin as water and easily rolls around in your pan. Every 30 seconds, swirl the oil in your pan. You will notice that the oil gets thinner and more liquidy each time. My pan takes about 1½ minutes for the oil to thin out and move throughout the pan easily. At this point, you're ready to add food!

PROPERLY HEATING A CAST-IRON PAN

Cast iron maintains heat very well but typically does not heat as evenly as stainless steel, and it can take a bit longer to heat. Place your dry cast-iron pan on medium-low to low heat for about 5 to 8 minutes. To ensure even heating, I turn my pan once 180 degrees while it is coming to temperature. Usually, I just hover my hand over the pan to see if I can feel the heat coming off it. If I can, I add a small amount of oil and then my food.

DEGLAZING PANS AND
thickening sauces

DEGLAZING

When cooking, especially in a pan that is not nonstick, it's normal to have some of your food stick to the bottom of the pan. The culinary term for these browned bits is *fond*. The fond might seem annoying—tiny bits of food stuck to the bottom of the pan—but it is, in fact, quite magical. The fond has been caramelizing as it sits on the bottom of your pan, giving it a depth of flavor that can add richness to your dish. You want that fond off the pan and in your food!

It might seem frustrating to get stuck-on food off the bottom of the pan, but this is where deglazing comes in. With deglazing, stuck-on bits will easily release from the pan and join the rest of the food.

So what is *deglazing*? Deglazing is "the act of adding liquid to a hot pan, which allows all the caramelized bits stuck to the bottom to release."[1]

What kind of liquid should you add? I typically use liquid that is already part of the recipe. If the dish calls for chicken or beef stock, I use that. If the dish does not call for any liquid, you can use water or wine. I use red wine for dishes with beef and white wine for dishes with chicken.

You do not need much liquid. Generally, ¼ cup is enough to get the fond off the bottom. The key is how you add it. Remove any food that might

> Deglazing your pan isn't just great for your food. It's great for the pan because it essentially helps create less cleanup in the end.

1. Alex Delany, "What Does 'Deglaze' Mean? And Do I Need a Degree to Do It?," *Bon Appétit*, February 23, 2018, https://www.bonappetit.com/story/what-does-deglaze-mean.

DEGLAZING

THICKENING

still be cooking in the pan. Then find a spot in your pan that has a concentration of fond and slowly pour some of the liquid in. As you pour in the liquid, use a wooden spoon to work up the fond. It will come up with little effort. Continue to do this on all the spots in your pan where there is fond.

Not only have you cleaned the bottom of your pan, but you have added a richness to your dish that will take the flavor to the next level!

THICKENING SAUCES

Have you ever brought together a delicious sauce that tastes mouthwatering but just needs a bit more thickness? Allowing the sauce or gravy to thicken can help it adhere better to the noodles or meat. A delicious sauce that is not thickened can sometimes look a little sad.

Thankfully, there is a simple way to thicken anything from soups, stews, and sauces to gravies. It is a mixture of one part water and one part cornstarch (or arrowroot powder, which is a paleo option for those with dietary restrictions).

The great thing about cornstarch/arrowroot powder is that it's tasteless and won't mess with the flavor of your sauce. Also, you can add it at the very end. Here are some important things to know when thickening anything:

1. To make the thickener (usually referred to as *slurry*), be sure to mix together equal parts water and cornstarch/arrowroot powder.
2. Be sure the water and cornstarch/arrowroot powder are thoroughly mixed together and clump-free. (If I am thickening a soup, I tend to do 1 tablespoon arrowroot powder and 1 tablespoon water. If I am thickening a sauce, I start with 1½ teaspoons arrowroot powder with 1½ teaspoons water.)
3. You want to add the slurry to the sauce while it is still on the heat.
4. When adding the slurry, be sure to stir your dish rapidly so the mixture is evenly incorporated, or you will have just a blob floating around in your dish.
5. After you thoroughly incorporate the slurry into your dish, let it simmer on the stove for 2–4 minutes and watch it thicken!

EXTRA-CREAMY CHICKEN PICCATA

This dish is the star of thickening sauces. At the end of cooking this meal you will have a mouthwatering sauce, but it will need to be thickened. Once you learn this skill, you'll never look back.

 This dish comes together very quickly, so make sure you prep everything before sautéing the chicken.

PREP TIME: 15 MINUTES • COOK TIME: 25 MINUTES • SERVES 4

1 pound fettuccine or other pasta of choice (or serve with veggies for gluten-free)

1 tablespoon olive oil

1 tablespoon butter

2 large boneless, skinless chicken breasts (2–3 pounds total), halved horizontally to make 4 cutlets (or instead use 4 boneless, skinless thighs)

2 teaspoons kosher salt, divided

¼ cup white wine or chicken stock, for deglazing

1 shallot, chopped

2 cloves garlic, minced

1 cup chicken stock

½ cup heavy whipping cream or half-and-half

⅓ cup finely grated fresh Parmesan cheese

2 tablespoons capers, drained

juice of 1 lemon

1½ teaspoons cornstarch or arrowroot powder (optional)

1 If using pasta, bring a large pot of salted water to a boil. Follow package instructions to cook until al dente.

2 Place a sauté pan on medium-high heat and add 1 tablespoon oil and 1 tablespoon butter. Allow butter to melt and bubble.

3 Season chicken with 1 teaspoon kosher salt.

4 Add the chicken to the pan and cook about 5–6 minutes on each side, depending on the thickness of your chicken. Once chicken is done, remove to a plate and cover with a piece of foil.

5 Take ¼ cup white wine or chicken stock and deglaze the pan by slowly pouring the liquid in and using a wooden spoon to scrape up the browned bits.

6 Add the chopped shallot and let cook for about 2 minutes until softened. Add the garlic. Sauté until the garlic is fragrant, about 1 minute.

GLUTEN-FREE OPTIONAL, GRAIN-FREE

7 Reduce heat to medium and add the stock and cream. Bring the sauce to a gentle boil. Season with the remaining 1 teaspoon kosher salt. Add in the Parmesan cheese and capers and allow the sauce to simmer for about 2 minutes, until it thickens.

8 Stir in the lemon juice and allow to simmer for 1 minute. (Note: If your family doesn't like lemon, start by adding only half the juice and taste from there. Remember, addition is easier than subtraction!) Taste and add any salt or additional lemon juice to your preferences.

9 If you would like a thicker sauce, in a small dish mix 1½ teaspoons cornstarch (or

Why salt pasta water and when? Salting your pasta water will allow the noodles to soak up some of the salt, giving them excellent flavor. Add half a palmful of salt to your water once it is boiling, right before you add the pasta.

arrowroot powder) with 1½ teaspoons water. Add mixture to sauté pan while it is still on the heat and mix to combine. Allow the sauce to thicken for a few additional minutes.

To serve, place chicken on top of pasta or steamed veggies and spoon sauce over it.

TIP: *Chicken is always fully cooked when it registers at 165°F with a meat thermometer. To check the temperature of your chicken, place the tip of the thermometer into the middle of the thickest part of the chicken.*

SWEET POTATO SHEPHERD'S PIE

This recipe is rich and packed with flavor and is a great meal to work on sharpening your knife skills. (See what I did there?!)

 You can make the Savory Mashed Sweet Potatoes several hours or up to 2 days in advance, which could turn this into a 30-minute meal the day of. Just keep them chilled in the refrigerator until ready to use.

PREP TIME: 10 MINUTES • COOK TIME: 1 HOUR 30 MINUTES • SERVES 5–6

1 tablespoon olive oil

1 small onion, chopped

2 carrots, peeled and diced

4 ounces shiitake mushrooms, chopped (if you cannot find shiitake, try a mushroom medley or baby bella mushrooms)

1 pound 80/20 ground beef or ground lamb

2 cloves garlic, minced

3 teaspoons kosher salt

1 teaspoon ground black pepper

1 tablespoon tomato paste

½ cup dry red wine or beef broth

1 (14.5-ounce) can diced tomatoes

Savory Mashed Sweet Potatoes (page 173)

1 In a cast-iron skillet (or other oven-safe pan) over medium-high heat, add the oil. Sauté the onion, carrots, and mushrooms until the onion is translucent, about 5 minutes.

2 Add the ground meat to the pan. Use a spatula or meat crumbler to break up the meat. Cook until browned, about 5–8 minutes.

3 Add the minced garlic, salt, pepper, and tomato paste. Stir to combine and cook until the garlic is fragrant, about 1 minute.

4 Use the wine or broth to deglaze the pan, slowly pouring it in and scraping up any browned bits stuck to the bottom.

5 Add the diced tomatoes and mix. Allow to simmer on the stove on medium-low heat for 10 minutes.

6 Turn off the stove and remove the pan from heat. Turn the broiler on.

GRAIN-FREE

7 Spread Savory Mashed Sweet Potatoes on top of the meat mixture. Use a spatula to evenly spread, covering the top of the meat mixture.

8 Place under the broiler and cook until the top of the pie begins to brown—about 3 minutes.

9 Sprinkle with fresh thyme, salt, and a few cracks black pepper.

To serve, dish up right from the cast-iron skillet. If desired, top with Parmesan cheese or crushed red pepper flakes.

TIP: *You can make the whole shepherd's pie up to two days in advance. Keep chilled in the refrigerator. When ready to eat, heat the oven to 350° and bake for 25 minutes.*

CREAMY ITALIAN SAUSAGE PASTA

This dish gets its decadence and richness from deglazing! It absolutely transforms this meal.

The mushrooms in this pasta make it extra rustic with an amazing depth of flavor. If you don't like mushrooms, try this dish anyway but dice the mushrooms extra small. Because you get to decide.

PREP TIME: 10 MINUTES • COOK TIME: 25 MINUTES • SERVES 5–6

1 pound orecchiette or other pasta of choice

2 tablespoons butter

1 tablespoon olive oil

5 ounces shiitake or baby bella mushrooms, chopped

1 shallot, chopped

14 ounces Italian sausage, ground or with casing removed

3 cloves garlic, minced

2 teaspoons kosher salt

¼ cup white wine or chicken stock

¼ cup mascarpone or cream cheese

½ cup chicken stock

¼ cup heavy cream

½ cup frozen peas

1 teaspoon freshly cracked black pepper

½ cup Parmesan cheese, grated

FOR THE TOPPING (OPTIONAL)

1 tablespoon butter

½ cup breadcrumbs or panko

1 teaspoon fresh thyme

1 Prepare your pasta according to package instructions.

2 While pasta is cooking, add the butter and oil to a sauté pan over medium-high heat. Once butter is melted, add the mushrooms. Cook until browned, about 2–3 minutes.

3 Add the chopped shallot and cook for another minute. Add the sausage and use a spatula or meat crumbler to break meat apart while it cooks. Sauté for about 8 minutes, until browned. Add garlic and salt and sauté for an additional minute.

4 Deglaze the pan by slowly pouring in the wine or stock and using a wooden spoon to scrape up the browned bits on the bottom of the pan.

5 Add mascarpone cheese. Stir to combine.

6 Add chicken stock, heavy cream, and peas. Allow to simmer on the stovetop for about 4–5 minutes to heat the peas.

7 Remove from heat and add freshly cracked black pepper and Parmesan cheese. Stir.

FOR THE TOPPING (OPTIONAL)

1 In a small sauté pan over medium-high heat, add butter.

2 Once butter is melted and bubbly, add panko or breadcrumbs. Sauté until browned, about 2 minutes. Toss in fresh thyme. Mix to combine and remove from heat.

Serve sauce over pasta and add topping if desired. Enjoy!

HALIBUT WITH CURRY SAUCE

Cooking fish without having it stick to your pan will also have you wondering when your chef celebrity will begin. I'm here to tell you, it begins now.

PREP TIME: 10 MINUTES • COOK TIME: 25 MINUTES • SERVES 4

1 tablespoon olive oil

2 shallots, chopped

½ tablespoon red curry paste

1½ cups low-sodium chicken broth

½ cup canned full-fat, unsweetened coconut milk

2 teaspoons kosher salt

4 (6-ounce) halibut filets, skin removed

½ cup coarsely chopped fresh cilantro leaves

2 green onions, chopped

juice from 1 lime

1¼ cups basmati or jasmine rice, cooked according to package directions (optional)

1 In a large sauté pan over medium-high heat, add oil. When the oil is hot, add the shallots and cook, stirring occasionally, until they begin to brown, about 3 minutes.

2 Add the curry paste and cook, stirring until fragrant, about 30 seconds.

3 Add the chicken broth, coconut milk, and salt. Simmer until mixture slightly thickens, about 6–8 minutes.

4 Season the halibut with an additional sprinkle of salt. Arrange the fish in the pan and gently shake the pan so the fish is coated with the sauce. Turn heat to medium, cover, and cook until the fish flakes easily with a fork, about 7 minutes.

5 Remove halibut to plates.

6 To the sauce, stir in cilantro, green onions, and lime juice.

To serve, place the halibut on top of rice (optional). Ladle the sauce over the fish. Top with additional cilantro.

GRAIN-FREE, GLUTEN-FREE, DAIRY-FREE

97

PART

4

the MEATS

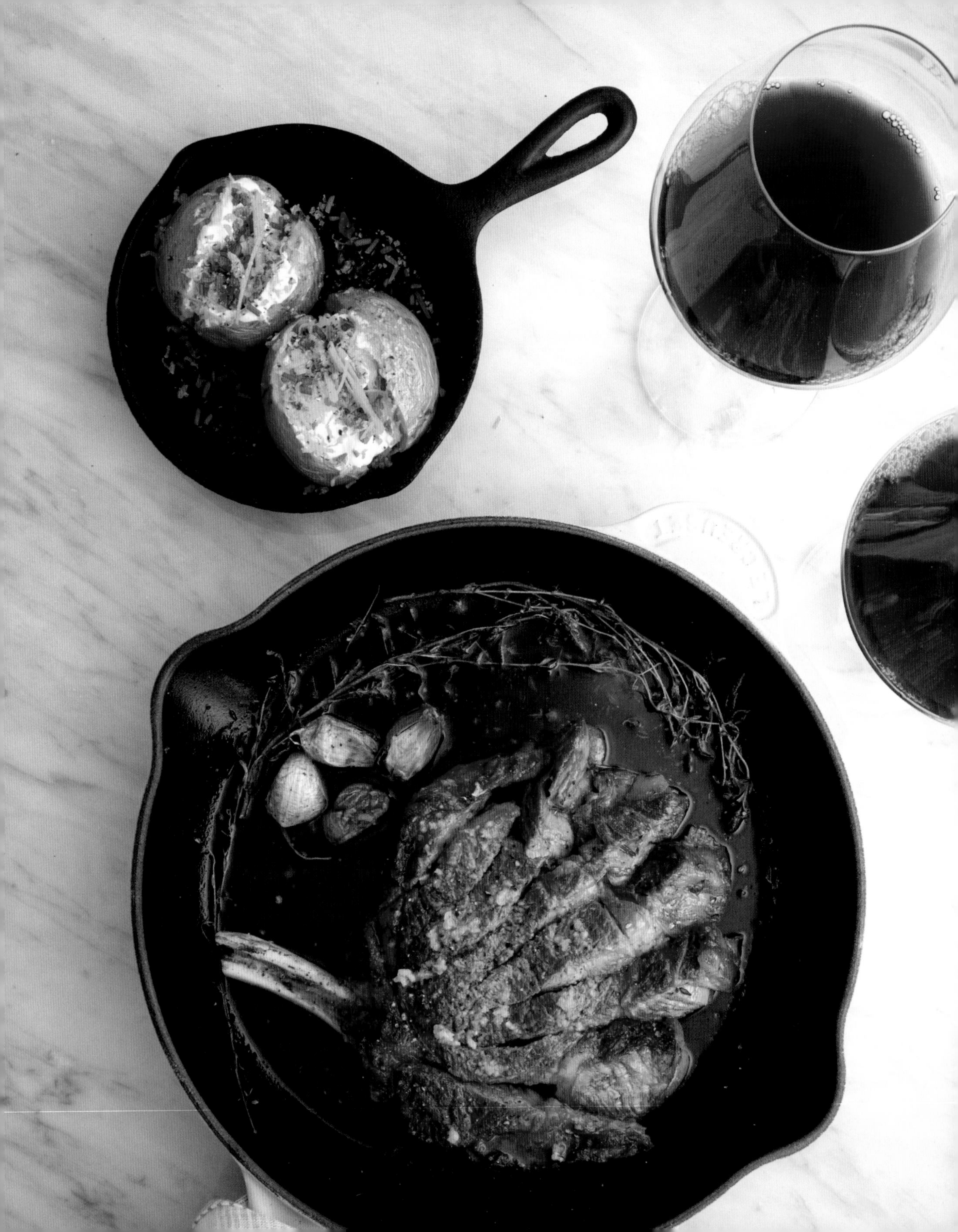

different
CUTS OF MEAT

Here are some universal facts about meat:

- Meat that has bone or skin takes longer to cook than boneless, skinless meat. While it might require longer cooking time, know that bone-in meat is less likely to dry out because the bone insulates the meat, keeping it juicy.
- Most meats have to be cooked to a specific temperature to be considered safe for eating.
- While there are many different cuts of meat out there, you get to decide which cuts of meat are on your regular rotation.

Here is how I approach meat for my everyday kitchen.

MEAT ON REGULAR WEEKLY ROTATION

Boneless, skinless chicken thighs   Boneless, skinless chicken breasts

Bone-in, skin-on chicken thighs   Ground beef (80/20)

MEAT FOR GATHERING (or on Sundays for Slower Meals)

Chuck roast   Chicken drumsticks

Whole chicken   Ribeye steak

Baby back ribs   Bone-in pork butt

Chicken wings

MEAT FOR SPECIAL OCCASIONS

Petite filet mignon

Lamb chops

Bone-in pork chops

Once you identify your go-to meats and which categories the different cuts of meat fit into, it not only simplifies meal planning but also helps you as you try new recipes.

CHICKEN

Quick facts about chicken:

- Chicken is done cooking when it reaches a temperature of 165°F. Unlike red meat, chicken must be cooked fully. It should never be served rare or medium.
- Chicken is made of white and dark meat. White meat comes from the breast and wings. Dark meat comes from the legs, which are generally broken down into thighs and drumsticks.
- I tend to cook with chicken thighs because they are less expensive than chicken breasts and because I prefer the flavor of dark meat. Dark meat chicken is also less likely to dry out as compared to white meat chicken.

Breasts: You can purchase either bone-in, skin-on chicken breasts or boneless, skinless breasts that can be broken down into chicken cutlets or tenders. Because chicken breasts are all white meat, they can dry out quickly during cooking. You generally want to avoid cooking boneless, skinless chicken breasts at high temperatures for long periods of time. I find chicken breasts are ideal for using in soups and stews because they can cook low and slow and therefore don't dry out. They are also great in quick stir-frys!

Wings: Chicken wings are generally sold as wingettes or drumettes and usually have the bone in and skin on. This cut of tender white meat is best known for being served at parties or tailgates. There is not a lot of meat on each wing, but they make the perfect crispy snack.

Thighs: Chicken thighs are readily available as either boneless or bone-in. Because they are dark meat, they tend to have more flavor than white meat chicken and can also withstand higher temperatures and longer cooking times without drying out.

Drumsticks: Chicken drumsticks also come from the leg of a chicken and have dark meat. They are generally cooked and served with the bone in and skin on, which makes them ideal for high-temperature cooking methods such as grilling.

Chicken thighs are a great option for the everyday home cook, as they can be inexpensive and the dark meat is more flavorful.

BEEF

Quick facts about beef:

- Beef comes from a cow and is considered red meat. There are several different cuts of beef, and here we will explore the most widely used ones.

- Beef, unlike chicken, can be cooked to various temperatures. You generally will see this for burgers or steaks. Below is a helpful guide on cooking temperatures for beef.

Chuck: Chuck roasts and steaks come from the neck and shoulders of the cow. The chuck is very flavorful but is best cooked low and slow to render the meat tender. Most people use chuck roasts for the dish best known as pot roast.

Rib and short rib: Beef ribs are perfect for grilling or cooking low and slow in the oven. Short ribs also come from this section and are best when braised.

DONENESS	TEMPERATURE	DESCRIPTION
Rare	120–125°F	Center is bright red, warm throughout, soft to the touch.
Medium-rare	130–135°F	Center is very pink, slightly hot, meat is beginning to firm up.
Medium	140–145°F	Center is light pink, hot throughout, meat becoming more firm.
Medium-well	150–155°F	Mostly brown throughout with just a touch of pink in the center, meat is firm to the touch.
Well-done	160°F	Brown throughout, firm or hard to the touch.

Ribeye steaks, which also come from this area of the cow, are tender and juicy steaks sold either with or without the bone. The bone adds flavor and moisture. This steak is also known for its large ratio of marbling, which refers to the fat in the steak. The fat cooks down, giving the steak robust flavor.

Loin: The beef loin is directly behind the ribs and includes the tenderloin and part of the sirloin. The tenderloin is typically served as filet mignon. This steak can be quite thick but is generally smaller in diameter. The meat is lean and extremely tender; it's perfect for serving with various sauces.

New York strip steak is known for its bold, beefy taste, but it's not the most tender steak. So this cut works perfectly with delicious marinades that can help tenderize the meat and infuse flavor into it.

T-bone and porterhouse steaks both contain a T-shaped bone. These are some of the highest-quality cuts available and can be juicy and tender. Because of that, these steaks can stand on their own without a lot of bells and whistles like marinades and sauces. They are perfect for withstanding high temperature cooking methods, such as grilling.

Round: The round is the rear end of a cow, and this meat is most often used as ground beef. Ground beef is perfect for making burgers, meatballs, and Bolognese or for using in a stir-fry. It cooks fast, especially when cooked over high heat (for example, when grilling).

Hanger and flank: The hanger steak is beloved for its affordability. It can be tough if prepared incorrectly, but when marinated with a strong acid such as fresh citrus juice or vinegar, the meat becomes tender and juicy. It's best cooked to rare or medium-rare. You will generally see this cut of meat in steak tacos. Delicious!

Flank steaks can be inexpensive cuts of meat and are very lean. Similar to hanger steaks, flank steaks should also be marinated with citrus juice or vinegar for a long period of time, cooked for a short period of time, and cut against the grain. This type of meat is great for a stir-fry or fajitas.

Brisket: Brisket comes from the breast or lower chest of a cow. There are two components of this large cut of meat: the point and the flat. The point is denser than the flat and contains hunks of fat. The flat is mostly connective tissue.

The average brisket can be 3–8 pounds and is sometimes sold as only the flat. Brisket needs a much longer cooking time—up to 12 hours at low temperature—to really break down the connective tissue. The flat is usually used to make corned beef, while the point and the flat together (referred to as a "full packer") is used for barbecued or smoked brisket.

Many people think "pot roast" is the actual cut of meat, but this refers to the preparation of the meat. A pot roast is a method where one takes a big, tough cut of meat and cooks it low and slow to render it tender. Ask for a chuck roast when buying meat for pot roasts.

PORK

Quick facts about pork:

- Pork is meat that comes from a pig. Most cuts of pork can be so lean that it needs to be cooked very specifically so it comes out juicy and tender. Pork that has a lot of fat (bacon, for example) can be juicy and full of flavor and more forgiving during cooking.
- Pork, just like chicken, must be cooked through for safe eating. Typically, you want your cut of pork to be at 145°F.

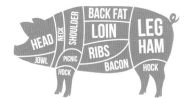

Belly: Bacon and ribs both come from the belly of a pig. Bacon is salt-cured meat that is best prepared alone. It can withstand high-temperature cooking and produces a crispy, flavorful piece of meat.

There are several different ribs you can get from a pig, including spareribs, baby back ribs (explained below under "Loin"), and St. Louis style ribs. Spareribs come from the belly of the pig, are bigger than the other types of ribs, and are more fatty. These ribs can withstand cooking for a long time at a low temperature.

St. Louis style ribs are spareribs that have had the hard breastbone and cartilage removed, making them easier to work with. The meat is fattier than baby back ribs, adding more flavor, and they cook more evenly because of their shape.

Boston butt: Also called simply "pork butt," this comes from the upper shoulder of the pig (not the rear end like its name implies). Pork butt usually has a lot of fat, which results in juiciness and great flavor. Because of this it is also a very forgiving piece of meat to work with. It is best for braising and stewing (think carnitas or BBQ pulled pork).

Picnic shoulder: The meat from the bottom shoulder can be very tough and is generally used for ground pork and sausage.

Loin: From the loin of the pig we get tenderloin and baby back ribs. Pork tenderloin is a very tender cut of meat, but it contains almost no fat. This means it is highly susceptible to drying out and becoming tough. When cooked properly, it can be tender and juicy. Baby back ribs come from the upper ribcage of the loin. These ribs are curvier and shorter than spareribs and are also leaner, which means they have a shorter cooking time.

Ham (or leg): The back legs of the pig are known as ham. Typically when you buy ham it has already been cured or smoked and is ready to eat (think of serrano ham or prosciutto). Ham hocks are also very popular, as they can be braised with dishes such as collard greens to infuse flavor.

This guide has given you a foundational knowledge of meats everyday home cooks can work with. Understanding the different cuts from each animal is one of the best ways to know how to prepare your meat.

cooking methods
FOR MEAT

Most home cooks today have many different options for cooking food. We've come a long way from the days of only being able to cook food over an open fire. Now we have the stovetop, oven, grill, slow cooker, and possibly even pressure cooker. Each of these methods can be well-suited for many different dishes. You might find yourself using one method more than others because it's the one you are most comfortable with. But using multiple methods for cooking can result in quicker cooking and more variety.

Here is a guide to the most common cooking methods.

STOVETOP

The stovetop is probably the most widely used method for cooking meals. On the stove you can sauté, deep-fry, boil, and brown all kinds of food. While it's used most often, it's not always the right method for the job, which is why we sometimes encounter dry or burnt chicken—or even chicken that looks golden brown on the outside but is raw on the inside.

Most stovetops come with an oven. The two are a pair and should be used as a pair. Think of your stovetop and oven as a heroic duo like Batman and Robin. They each can get the job done on their own, but they're much more efficient and effective together.

A great example of using the stove and oven together is when we make steakhouse-style steak. The stovetop helps us get that really nice brown crust on the outside of the steak, and then the oven finishes cooking the steak without the outside becoming burnt.

Each stovetop is different, and each one has hot spots. Knowing your stove's hot spots will level up your cooking game. Ever cook chicken and wonder why one chicken breast is perfectly cooked, a second is still sticking to the pan, and a third is on its way to being burnt? That's due to hot spots.

You can't really fix this. It's just how your stove works. But knowing where your hot spots are helps you know where to place your food in the pan when cooking. For example, if I am cooking chicken thighs, I generally add the thickest thigh to the hot spot area because it will need to cook longer. If I have a smaller, thinner chicken thigh, I place it on a cooler spot in the pan.

If all my cuts of meat are the same in thickness and size (always a good rule of thumb to achieve even cooking), then I know to turn the pieces over the hot spot sooner than the other pieces.

OVEN

Baking is a method of cooking food using dry heat. This is most commonly done in an oven. There are a number of pros for using the baking method. Even heat distribution can easily break down fats, allowing the meat to be infused with flavor. Baking also causes skin on chicken to get crispy, and cleanup is generally easier.

One of the biggest cons of baking is that all ovens are different! When I lived in California, I found that my oven ran hot. I would bake a dish for the time and at the temperature the recipe called for, but my food would burn or be dried out. In another home I found my oven ran a little cooler and took slightly longer than the prescribed time to bake my food.

A great way to learn where your stove's hot spots are is a simple test. Place a sauté pan on the burner you use most often. Add ½ cup water to the pan (enough to cover the surface with a thin layer). Turn the burner to medium-high heat. Watch the water to see where the first bubbles appear. This can take 1–2 minutes. Wherever you see the bubbles appear, that's the spot that gets the hottest fastest.

Knowing your oven will take your cooking to the next level! Does it run hot or cool? Cooking bacon is one great way to figure this out.

Line a rimmed baking sheet with foil or parchment. Add slices of bacon. Do not overlap them and make sure there is some space between each slice. Put the bacon in the cold oven and set the temperature to 400°F. (Note: adding the bacon to the oven while it is preheating allows for evenly crisped bacon.) After 10 minutes, turn each slice of bacon over and cook for an additional 10 minutes.

If your bacon comes out perfectly cooked and crisped, you have a great oven! It runs average. If your bacon is too crispy or you had to pull it out of the oven early because it was overcooking, your oven runs hot. This means you should subtract several minutes from the recipe's prescribed baking time.

If after 20 minutes your bacon needs more time to get perfectly crisp, your oven runs cool. This means you should add to the recipe's baking time.

You can also do this test with a medium-size russet potato! Preheat the oven to 425°F. Scrub the potato, pierce it all over with a fork, and place it on a baking sheet. Once the oven is preheated, place the baking sheet in the oven.

After 45 minutes, pierce the potato with a butter knife. If the knife easily punctures the potato all the way to the middle, your oven runs hot! If the butter knife does not easily move through to the middle of the potato, continue baking for an additional 15 minutes.

After 60 minutes, again pierce the potato with a butter knife. If the knife easily punctures the potato all the way to the middle, your oven runs average! However, if the butter knife still does not easily pierce to the middle of the potato, your oven runs cold. Continue baking for an additional 15–20 minutes.

Because everyone's oven is different (including the people creating the recipes), knowing your oven will help you be in control when preparing a recipe. For example, because I know my oven runs cool, when a recipe says to bake a roast for 2½ hours, I almost always tack on an extra 30 minutes.

Here's the truth about reading a recipe: Yes, someone else created and tested the recipe, but now that it's in your hands—you're in control.

SLOW COOKER

A slow cooker is a countertop appliance used for cooking food over several hours at low temperature. It's great for even cooking. A slow cooker can be used to make tough meat tender and to create amazing flavor in any dish.

A slow cooker is unlike an oven in that it uses liquid to cook food. (You don't want to put a chuck roast in the slow cooker without liquid or it will just dry out.) It's easy to use since you will generally cook the food on high for a few hours or on low for many hours. A slow cooker also enables easy cleanup. I typically try to plan at least one meal a week in the slow cooker or pressure cooker so I know I have a night when cooking dinner won't take much time.

PRESSURE COOKER

The pressure cooker has made quite the comeback over the last decade thanks to the Instant Pot. A pressure cooker is a pot with a locking lid that enables it to build up extremely hot steam and intense pressure. The steam is what cooks the food.

A pressure cooker allows you to cook much faster and hotter than on the stovetop or in the oven. For example, baking sweet potatoes in a 400° oven takes 45–60 minutes. Cooking sweet potatoes at high pressure in the Instant Pot takes only about 20 minutes once it comes to pressure.

The pressure cooker can be intimidating because it can seem unstable. But today's pressure cookers have many safeguards, so the average home cook can feel comfortable using this powerhouse appliance.

GRILL

Flavor! Flavor! Flavor! The star of grilling is the flavor it can impart to food. Few appliances or cooking methods can replicate the flavor food acquires when grilled over an open flame. Grilling uses a significant amount of direct heat (usually through flame) to quickly cook meat and vegetables. In other words, it's a very fast (in most cases) dry-heat cooking method.

Grilling is one of the more unstable ways to cook food. It's important to always pay attention to the heat of the grill and the flame height, and you need to consistently check to see if the food is getting too crisp. But once you master grilling, it might become one of your favorite ways to cook food.

You don't have to know how to cook all the things on the grill. I have just a few recipes I love to make this way—especially for summertime.

Now that we've become much more acquainted with our stove, oven, and other appliances, let's make seven different dishes that use the various cooking methods.

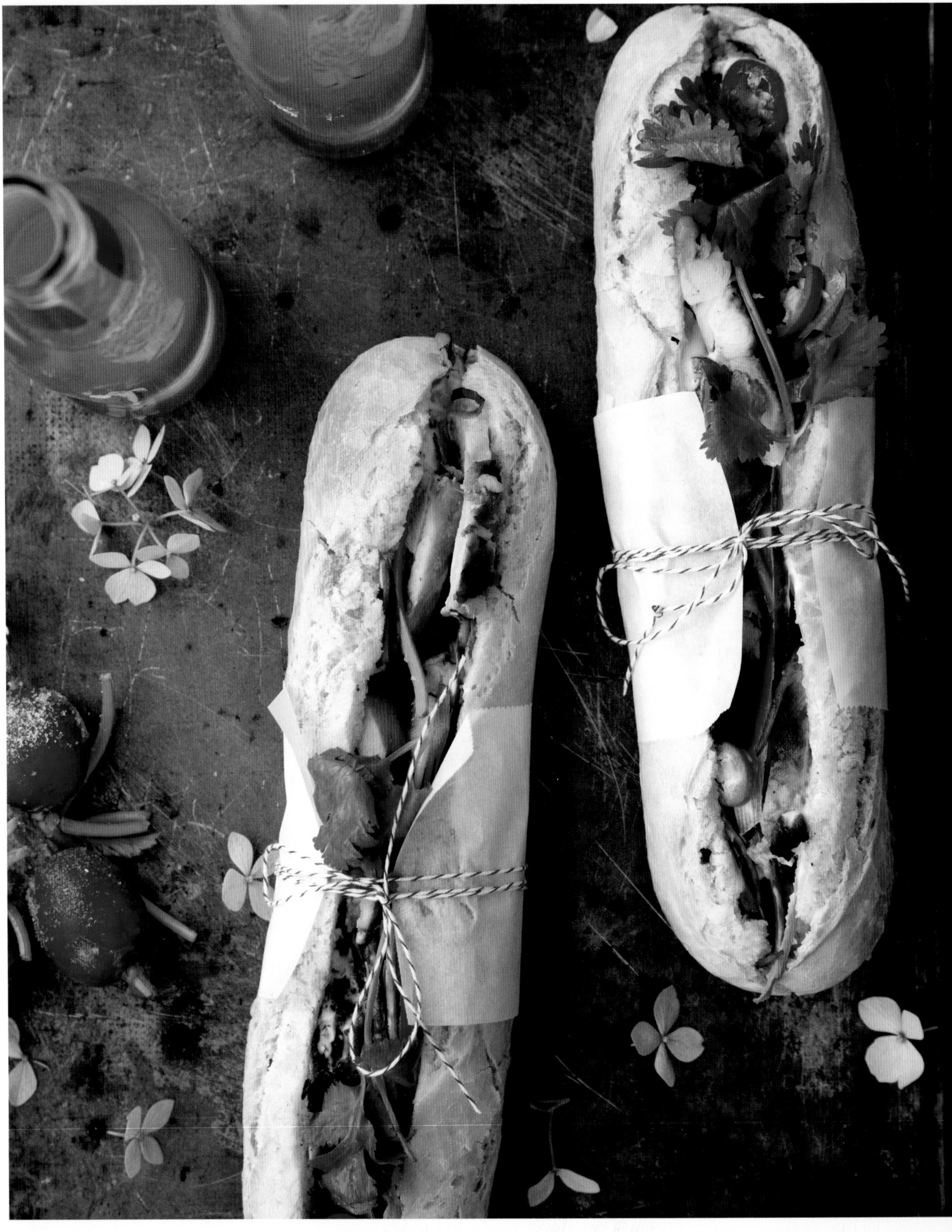

HOMEMADE COCONUT CHICKEN BANH MI

This popular Vietnamese dish is one of my favorites. Our local Vietnamese restaurant shut down during the pandemic, and my cravings got a little out of hand, so here we are. It's the finishing touches that make this sandwich unforgettable and teach the art of adding flavor at the end.

 The baguette is part of what makes a banh mi so delicious. It's crusty on the outside and soft on the inside with a touch of sweetness. Look in your grocery store for take-and-bake demi baguettes (they are usually sold in a package of two).

PREP TIME: 15 MINUTES (2+ HOURS MARINATING) • COOK TIME: 20 MINUTES • SERVES 4

FOR THE CHICKEN AND MARINADE

1 cup (8 ounces) canned coconut milk

2 tablespoons soy sauce

1 teaspoon fish sauce

2 teaspoons kosher salt

1 tablespoon coconut sugar

juice from 2 small limes

2 pounds boneless, skinless chicken thighs

FOR THE DRESSING

1 cup mayonnaise

juice from half a lime

1 tablespoon rice wine vinegar

1 teaspoon kosher salt

FOR THE QUICK-PICKLED VEGGIES

1 carrot, julienned

1 cucumber, julienned

1 tablespoon rice wine vinegar

FOR SERVING

slices of jalapeño (optional)

fresh mint

fresh cilantro

sliced green onions

crusty baguette or lettuce wrap

FOR THE MARINADE

1 Combine all ingredients for the marinade and add to a large dish or resealable plastic bag. Add the chicken thighs and cover or seal. Place in the refrigerator and marinate overnight or for at least 2–4 hours.

FOR THE DRESSING

1 Combine all ingredients in a small bowl and mix to combine. Place in the refrigerator. Can be made several hours or days in advance. Will last in the refrigerator for up to 7 days.

FOR THE QUICK-PICKLED VEGGIES

1 Using a vegetable peeler, julienne (long thin slices) the carrot and cucumber (you can do this by using the julienne blade side of the peeler and just running it down the length of the carrot and cucumber).

2 Add cucumber and carrot to a small jar with a lid. Add the rice wine vinegar. Secure lid and shake to combine, then refrigerate. Can be done several hours or days in advance. Will last in the refrigerator for up to 7 days.

FOR THE CHICKEN: GRILL METHOD

1 Preheat grill to medium-high heat. Rub the grill grates with oil. Remove any excess marinade and place chicken thighs on the grill. Close the lid.

2 Grill for 4–5 minutes. Flip and grill for another 4–5 minutes with the lid closed. Chicken is done when it reaches an internal temperature of 165°F.

3 Remove chicken to plate and cover with foil to rest for about 5 minutes, then slice.

FOR THE CHICKEN: STOVETOP METHOD

The marinade on this chicken really does best when grilled, but if grilling is not an option, please follow these tips and instructions.

1 In a large nonstick sauté pan, add 1 tablespoon olive oil and heat over medium-high heat.

2 While the pan is heating, line a large plate with paper towels. Remove chicken from the marinade and place on the paper towel. Cover with another sheet of paper towel to remove excess marinade from the chicken. (This step is important as the marinade has sugar in it and is quite heavy—the chicken will not cook properly without this step.)

3 Once the sauté pan is heated, add the chicken. Cook for 5 minutes. Flip the chicken and cook for an additional 4–5 minutes. Chicken is done when it reaches an internal temperature of 165°F.

4 Place the chicken on a plate and cover with foil. Let rest for 5 minutes before slicing.

To serve, spread a good dollop of the dressing over the inside of bread. Add the sliced chicken followed by the fresh jalapeños (optional), pickled vegetables, and fresh herbs (mint, cilantro, and green onions). Close sandwich and slice into quarters.

> **TIP:** *Follow the package instructions to heat the baguette. Cut the baguette lengthwise down the middle, making sure not to slice all the way through the loaf.*

MELT-IN-YOUR-MOUTH OVEN RIBS

You can double this recipe by baking more racks of ribs. A good rule of thumb is 4–6 individual ribs per person (this is assuming there will be additional sides such as baked potatoes and salad or vegetables). For each additional rack of ribs, you will need to add 20 minutes to the cooking time.

 These ribs take a few hours in the oven. You can prep them the morning of and keep them in the fridge until you are ready to bake them.

PREP TIME: 15 MINUTES • COOK TIME: 2½ TO 3 HOURS • SERVES 4

FOR THE RIBS

4 pounds or two racks pork baby back ribs (about 22–26 individual ribs)

½ tablespoon garlic powder

2 tablespoons coconut sugar (or brown sugar)

2 teaspoons kosher salt

½ teaspoon freshly ground black pepper

1 teaspoon paprika

1 teaspoon cumin or mushroom powder (optional)

¼ teaspoon cayenne pepper

FOR THE BBQ SAUCE

1 tablespoon olive oil

¼ cup onion, diced

2 cloves garlic, minced

1 tablespoon Dijon mustard

2 teaspoons kosher salt

1 cup tomato sauce (or ketchup)

½ cup maple syrup

¼ cup apple cider vinegar

1 tablespoon Worcestershire sauce

If you like a smooth sauce, you can blend it when it's finished, or use ½ tablespoon onion powder and 1 teaspoon garlic powder in place of the onion and garlic (if you do this, omit step 1 for the sauce method).

I like to use maple syrup and tomato sauce because I prefer a sticky, sweet sauce that is not overly sweet, but you can use ketchup and brown sugar if that's what you have on hand!

GRAIN-FREE, DAIRY-FREE

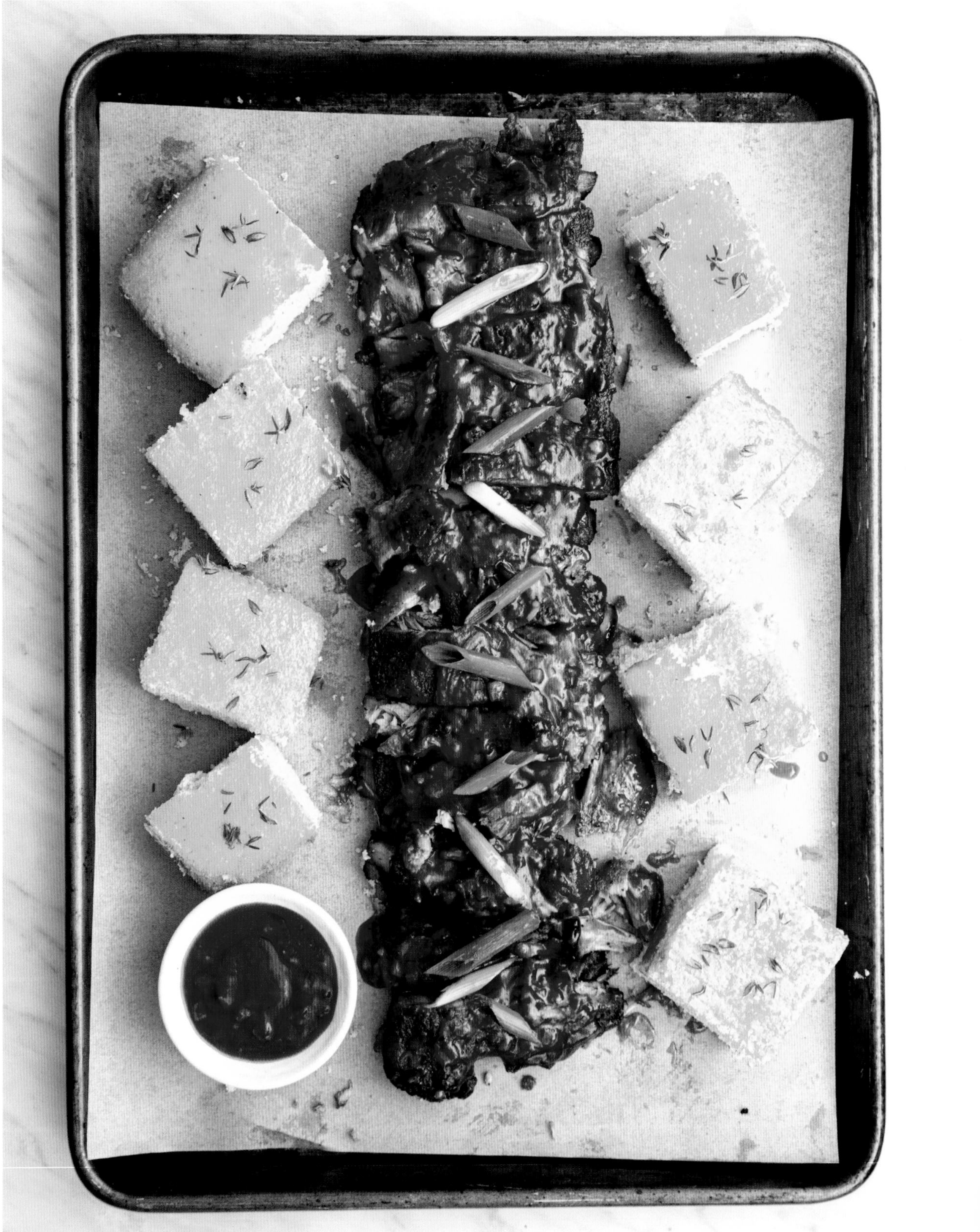

FOR THE RIBS

1 Preheat oven to 275°F.

2 In a bowl, mix together all spices for the ribs and set aside.

3 Line a baking sheet with aluminum foil (this will help with any liquid that oozes from the foil-wrapped ribs). Add another piece of foil onto the baking sheet, big enough to cover one rack of ribs. Place one rack of ribs upside down on foil (the side with less meat and more bone should be facing up). With a sharp knife, score the back of the ribs to cut through the membrane (the membrane is the white piece of tissue on the back side of the ribs). I like to make tiny X's all along the back of the ribs.

4 Rub half the spice mixture over both sides of the ribs. Wrap tightly in foil.

5 Place foil-wrapped ribs right side up on the foil-lined baking sheet. Repeat this process with the other rack of ribs.

6 Place in the oven for 2½–3 hours. If your oven runs hot, check your ribs after 2½ hours. If the meat easily pulls away from the bone when pierced with a fork, your ribs are done! If you prefer to check for doneness with a meat thermometer, ribs are done when they reach 190° to 200°F.

FOR THE BBQ SAUCE

While the ribs cook, make the sauce!

1 In a saucepan over medium-high heat, add oil. Once oil is heated, add onion and sauté for about 3 minutes. Add garlic and sauté for an additional minute.

2 Add all remaining ingredients. Mix to combine. Allow to come to a boil and then turn heat to low.

3 Let simmer for 25–30 minutes, or until the sauce thickens.

To serve, pull ribs out of the oven and move to a platter or individual plates. Cover ribs in sauce. Enjoy!

Optional: Wrap russet potatoes in foil and add them to the oven at the same time you add the ribs. When the ribs are done, you will also have baked potatoes!

This sauce makes the perfect amount for 3 pounds of ribs or 4 pounds of chicken. This means you will have leftover sauce for dipping or using on other meals throughout the week. Want more sauce? If you are making more ribs, you can easily double the sauce!

Now that you are acquainted with whether your oven runs hot or cold, you can guess how long you should cook these. Because my oven runs a little cooler, I bake these ribs for about 3 hours. If you are still unsure about your oven, you can always check for doneness near the end (around 2 or 2½ hours into the baking time).

SMASH BURGER WITH BACON-FAT SWEET POTATO FRIES

Crumbled ground beef is a great candidate for the stovetop! It is hard to burn and also hard to dry out, so it can be on direct heat for a longer period of time when it has sufficient liquid. These burgers get smashed down to within an inch of their lives, so be sure to have a sauté pan or skillet large enough to cook at least two at a time.

 Before cooking, have the sweet potato fries cut and the onions sliced, ready to go.

PREP TIME: 15 MINUTES • COOK TIME: 40 MINUTES • SERVES 6-8

FOR THE BURGERS

2 pounds 80/20 ground beef or 90/10 ground sirloin

2 teaspoons kosher salt

1 teaspoon ground black pepper

1 tablespoon Worcestershire sauce

3 tablespoons butter, melted

FOR THE CARAMELIZED ONIONS AND MUSHROOMS

1 tablespoon olive oil

2 tablespoons butter, divided

1 teaspoon kosher salt

2 sweet onions, halved and thinly sliced

8 ounces shiitake or baby bella mushrooms, sliced (optional)

FOR SERVING

potato buns

American cheese slices

iceberg lettuce

mustard

pickles

tomatoes

Bacon-Fat Sweet Potato Fries (page 180)

FOR THE BURGERS

1 Mix all the burger ingredients together.

2 Form into 6–8 balls slightly smaller than tennis balls. Place on a plate and cover. Place into the freezer to get cold while your pan heats.

3 Heat a large cast-iron skillet over medium-high heat for 3–5 minutes. A hot pan will create the best crust. While the pan is heating, get the caramelized onions and mushrooms going and place the fries in the oven if you haven't yet.

4 Place 2 balls of meat at a time into the pan (you do not need to add oil to the pan because of the butter in the meat). Allow to sear for 1 minute. Using a wide spatula or smaller skillet, smash the balls of meat down until paper thin (you might need to spray oil on the spatula or flat surface you are using to smash the meat to prevent sticking). Allow to cook for an additional 3 minutes.

5 Flip the burgers and cook for an additional 2 minutes. Remove burgers from heat and immediately add sliced cheese. Keep warm.

6 Repeat with remaining burger patties. (The pan may smoke, so be sure to have your vent on and/or windows open.)

FOR THE CARAMELIZED ONIONS AND MUSHROOMS

You can make these up to 2 days ahead of time and refrigerate. Reheat when ready to use.

1 In a large sauté pan over medium-high heat, add olive oil and 1 tablespoon butter. Once butter is melted, add onions (and mushrooms if using). Lower heat to medium and allow to cook for 5 minutes.

2 Decrease the temperature to low. Add salt and the remaining tablespoon of butter and stir to combine. These will cook low and slow for about 25–30 minutes to perfectly caramelize. Stir every 5–8 minutes. The end result will be melt-in-your-mouth, buttery, golden-brown onions and mushrooms.

3 Place burger on bun, add iceberg lettuce, pickles, mustard, bacon, and caramelized onions and mushrooms. Serve with warm sweet potato fries.

The most common varieties of ground beef are 80/20 or 90/10. I typically cook with 80/20. The numbers represent what percentage of the beef is lean and what percentage is fat. So 80/20 refers to beef that is 80 percent lean and 20 percent fat. I like 20 percent fat in my beef because it adds good flavor and keeps the meat from drying out.

SUN-DRIED TOMATO SOUP WITH CHICKEN BREASTS

My all-time favorite way to prepare chicken breasts is in the slow cooker or Instant Pot. This ensures that they do not dry out. Chicken breasts are a great candidate for soups and come out juicy when cooked.

*If this is your first time cooking with sun-dried tomatoes, lean into it! They impart the most incredible flavor. **Bonus:** I know kids who call this "Pizza Soup" because of the richness from the sun-dried tomatoes and Italian seasoning.*

PREP TIME: 10 MINUTES • COOK TIME: 30 MINUTES TO 8 HOURS • SERVES 5–6

1 tablespoon olive oil

½ yellow onion, diced

1 sweet potato or russet potato, peeled and cubed into bite-size pieces

2 cloves garlic, minced

⅓ cup chopped sun-dried tomatoes (in oil)

½ tablespoon dried oregano or Italian seasoning

2 teaspoons kosher salt

1 teaspoon paprika

½ teaspoon ground black pepper

2 pounds boneless, skinless chicken breasts or thighs (fresh or frozen), or 2–3 cups cooked, shredded chicken

4 cups chicken stock

½ cup heavy cream

¾ cup Parmesan cheese, shredded

1 tablespoon cornstarch or arrowroot powder (optional)

FOR SLOW COOKER (8 HOURS)

1 If your slow cooker has a sauté function, turn it on now. Once heated, add oil, onion, and potato. Sauté for 3 minutes. Add garlic and sauté until garlic is fragrant, about 1 minute. (Or sauté these ingredients in a small sauté pan over medium-high heat for 3–5 minutes, then add to slow cooker.)

2 Add sun-dried tomatoes and spices. Mix to combine. Place chicken in the slow cooker. Add chicken stock.

3 Place the lid on the slow cooker. For fresh chicken, cook on high for 2 hours or low for 4 hours. For frozen chicken, cook on high for 4–5 hours or low for 7–8 hours.

4 Once finished, remove chicken and shred. You can do this with two forks or with a stand mixer using the paddle attachment.

GLUTEN-FREE, GRAIN-FREE

5 Add chicken back to the slow cooker. Add cream and Parmesan cheese. Stir to combine.

6 If you want your soup a little thicker, in a separate small bowl mix together equal parts cornstarch (or arrowroot powder) and water. Once combined, stir into the soup. Be sure to stir the soup so the thickening mixture is incorporated throughout the whole soup and does not clump. Allow to cook until thickened, about 5 minutes.

> **TIP:** *Use what's left from the jar of sundried tomatoes for the Eat, Pray, Love Pasta (page 215).*

FOR INSTANT POT (3 HOURS)

1 Follow steps 1–2 for slow cooker.

2 Secure lid and move valve to "Sealing." For fresh chicken, cook on high pressure for 10 minutes. For frozen chicken, cook on high pressure for 15 minutes. Allow the pressure to release naturally for 5 minutes.

3 Move valve to "Venting." Remove the lid. Set IP to "Sauté" function to keep the soup cooking.

4 Follow steps 4–6 for slow cooker.

Serve with additional fresh shredded Parmesan cheese, fresh parsley, and red pepper flakes!

WELCOME HOME POT ROAST

Whenever I walk into a house and smell pot roast, I just feel like I'm home. This is all thanks to my mom, who mastered pot roast and has it in the oven anytime I visit.

 This roast cooks in the slow cooker or oven and takes several hours. You can prep all the veggies the morning of or several hours before cooking the roast.

PREP TIME: 20 MINUTES • COOK TIME: 3–5 HOURS • SERVES 5–6

1 (3–4 pounds) chuck roast

4 teaspoons kosher salt (or about 1 teaspoon per pound of meat + 1 extra teaspoon), divided

3 teaspoons ground black pepper, divided

3 teaspoons garlic powder

2 tablespoons olive oil

1 (10¾-ounce) can cream of mushroom soup

¼ cup dry red wine, such as pinot noir

2 tablespoons Worcestershire sauce

1 small yellow onion, quartered

8 ounces shiitake mushrooms, sliced

4–5 Yukon Gold potatoes, halved or quartered depending on size

3 cloves garlic, crushed

4 carrots, peeled and quartered

2 dried bay leaves

¾ cup beef broth or water

FOR DUTCH OVEN

1 Preheat oven to 325°F.

2 In a small dish combine 3 teaspoons salt, 2 teaspoons black pepper, and garlic powder.

3 Rub the spice mix all over the roast.

4 On the stovetop, heat the oil in a dutch oven over medium-high heat and sear the roast on all sides (about 2 minutes per side).

5 While the roast is searing, prepare the gravy by combining cream of mushroom soup, red wine, and Worcestershire sauce. Set aside.

6 Once meat is seared, remove from dutch oven and add onion, mushrooms, potatoes, garlic, and carrots. Sprinkle with remaining 1 teaspoon salt and 1 teaspoon pepper and cook for 2 minutes while stirring.

GRAIN-FREE

7 Make room for the roast in the middle of the dutch oven and add the meat and its juices back in.

8 Add dried bay leaves.

9 Pour the gravy on top of the roast.

10 Pour the broth (or water) around the roast.

11 Cover with lid and place in the oven for 3½ to 4 hours. The meat should fall apart easily when pierced with a fork.

FOR SLOW COOKER

1 Follow steps 1–3 for dutch oven.

2 Sear roast in a skillet over medium-high heat (2–3 minutes per side), or if your slow cooker has a sauté function, use that for this step.

3 While the roast is searing, prepare the gravy by combining cream of mushroom soup, red wine, and Worcestershire sauce. Set aside.

4 Add onion, mushrooms, potatoes, garlic, and carrots to the slow cooker and sprinkle with remaining 1 teaspoon salt and 1 teaspoon pepper. Mix to combine. Make room for roast in the middle and place roast in the slow cooker.

5 Follow steps 8–10 above, then cook on low for 5 hours or on high for 3 hours. The meat should easily come apart when pierced with a fork.

Shred the pot roast and serve alongside the vegetables. Drizzle gravy over meat.

When it comes to seasoning meat, a good rule of thumb is to add 1 teaspoon kosher salt per pound of meat.

CRISPY CHICKEN WINGS WITH SWEET HEAT SAUCE

You can make the most crispy, finger-licking wings at home! The oven method for cooking really shines with these wings.

 Be sure to use baking powder and not *baking soda* in this recipe. **They are not interchangeable.**

PREP TIME: 5 MINUTES • COOK TIME: 70 MINUTES • SERVES 6 AS AN APPETIZER

3 pounds thawed chicken wings, drumette and flat separated (about 30 wings)

1 tablespoon baking powder

Sweet Heat Wing Sauce (page 164)

FOR SERVING (OPTIONAL)

Fresh Herb Dressing (page 167)

carrots

celery

TIP: *A full wing consists of three connected parts: the drumette, the wingette (or the flat), and the tip. Be sure to purchase wings that have the drumette and the flat already separated (the tip is usually discarded).*

1 Preheat oven to 250°F.

2 Line a large, rimmed baking sheet with foil or parchment paper. Place a baking rack on the baking sheet and liberally coat with oil.

3 Thoroughly dry chicken wings with a paper towel—this helps get them crispy! Place chicken wings in a large bowl and sprinkle with baking powder. Toss well to coat. You want a very fine coating of baking powder on the wings. If you added more than 30 wings, add more baking powder if needed until each wing is lightly coated.

4 Arrange chicken wings on the baking rack in a single layer. Do not overlap the wings or they will not get crispy. Do these in batches if you are making a lot of wings. (If you do not have a baking rack, you can place them directly on the baking sheet, but you will have to flip them over halfway through.)

GRAIN-FREE, GLUTEN- FREE

5 Place the pan in the oven and cook for 30 minutes.

6 After 30 minutes, crank the oven temperature up to 425°F and continue cooking for another 20 minutes.

7 Rotate the pan (and if you are not using a baking rack, flip the wings) and cook for an additional 20 minutes or until wings are crispy and lightly browned. (If you are baking additional wings, they will need more cooking time. As soon as they are golden brown, they are done.)

8 Remove the wings from the oven. In batches, add a few chicken wings to a bowl and toss with some of the sauce. Remove sauced wings from the bowl and continue until all wings have been tossed in sauce.

Serve wings with remaining sauce, herb dressing, celery, and carrots!

Note: If serving as an appetizer, plan about 5 wings per person. If serving as a meal, plan about 8–10 wings per person.

If you have leftover wing sauce, use it to make Sweet & Spicy Chicken Stuffed Sweet Potatoes (page 220).

PART

5

adding flavor

LIKE A PRO

even on sundays
chicken sandwich,
page 131

flavor LAYERING

Simple does not have to equal bland. Quick does not have to mean flavor-less. You can add flavor to your dish at so many different points during the preparation. Welcome to the flavor section!

There are four pivotal points in cooking where you can elevate the flavor of your dish: before, beginning, during, and after. Sometimes a recipe will include these steps, but if not, you can use the methods below to make a dish your own and add the specific kind of flavor you enjoy.

BEFORE

The best way to ensure your dish will be flavorful before you start cooking is through seasoning, marinating, or brining.

Seasoning is the act of adding any kind of herbs, spices, or condiments to your food before you start the cooking process. Seasonings and salt can better penetrate meat before cooking when it is still cold. Salting food before you cook it lays the foundation for a really flavorful meal.

Marinating can provide two wins. First, it can add incredible flavor to your dish on the front end so you don't have to fuss with it too much after you start cooking. Second, it can tenderize your meat. For example, marinating a flank steak for several hours will ensure the meat is tender and juicy.

Brining is different from marinating in that it usually involves submerging the meat in water. This water is usually heavily salted. Brining helps keep meat juicy and is generally used with large meats such as a whole turkey or chicken.

BEGINNING

A great way to add flavor in the beginning of a dish is to sear your food (usually meat). Searing is the act of browning the food on each side. You aren't trying to cook the food all the way through, you just want a nice sear to appear on all sides of the food. This browning amplifies the savory flavor of a dish and also gives nice coloring to the food. As we know, we eat with our eyes first!

DURING

The best way to add flavor during cooking is by deglazing the pan and thickening sauces, which we covered in part 3. I do this all the time, even if the recipe doesn't call for it. If there are browned bits forming on the bottom of my pan, I know I want that flavor in my dish and will be deglazing!

AFTER

The number of times I followed a recipe and it resulted in a dish that was just *meh* is alarming. But I know that even if a recipe doesn't turn out as I hoped, I can rescue it at the end by adding fresh herbs, a sauce, citrus, or finishing salt.

Simple
DOES NOT HAVE TO
EQUAL BLAND.

EVEN ON SUNDAYS CHICKEN SANDWICH

This recipe really allows the technique of marinating meat to shine! The sandwich is crispy on the outside but juicy on the inside. Bonus: you can enjoy it—even on Sundays!

 This chicken needs time to marinate!

PREP TIME: 10 MINUTES (PLUS TIME MARINATING) • COOK TIME: 20 MINUTES • SERVES 6

FOR CHICKEN

3 boneless, skinless chicken breasts, filleted to make 6 cutlets

1 cup pickle juice (from a 32-ounce jar of dill pickles)

1 egg

¼ cup heavy cream

½ cup flour (or tapioca starch for gluten-free)

2 tablespoons paprika

2 teaspoons kosher salt

1 teaspoon garlic powder

¼ teaspoon cayenne pepper (optional)

3 tablespoons high-heat oil such as avocado or vegetable oil

FOR BUNS (OPTIONAL—BUT DO IT!)

6 brioche buns

4 tablespoons butter

1 teaspoon garlic powder

TOPPINGS

mayonnaise

pickle slices

lettuce

tomato

avocado

FOR CHICKEN

1 Place chicken cutlets in a resealable plastic bag and add the pickle juice; marinate in the fridge for 1–3 hours.

2 After marinating, open the bag and discard the juice.

3 In a shallow dish, mix together the egg and heavy cream.

4 In a separate shallow dish, mix together all the dry ingredients.

5 Working with one cutlet at a time, coat the chicken in the egg mixture and then fully coat in the flour mixture. Pat as much of the flour mixture into the chicken as you can. Set aside.

6 Add oil to a braiser or large sauté pan on medium-high heat.

7 Fry your chicken cutlets in batches until golden brown, about 4–5 minutes on each side. Add extra oil as needed for subsequent batches.

8 Remove each batch to a paper towel to remove excess oil, then set cutlets on a baking sheet and place in oven set at warm or 170°F to keep the chicken warm and crisp until serving.

FOR BUNS

1 Turn on broiler.

2 Melt butter and mix in the garlic powder.

3 Place brioche buns on a baking sheet cut side up and brush halves with the garlic butter.

4 Broil in oven until golden brown, about 2–3 minutes.

To serve, spread mayonnaise on each bun, then add chicken. Follow with any remaining toppings you like such as pickles, lettuce, avocado, and tomato. Enjoy!

how to fillet chicken breasts

TIPSY BRAISED SHORT RIBS
WITH MASCARPONE MASHED POTATOES

We are searing these beef short ribs, and I promise you, the effort in the beginning is going to have a major payoff. This is a perfect way to learn how you can add flavor right at the beginning of cooking!

PREP TIME: 20 MINUTES • COOK TIME: 4½ TO 5 HOURS • SERVES 5–6

FOR THE SHORT RIBS

- 2 tablespoons high-heat oil such as avocado oil or vegetable oil
- 4–5 pounds bone-in short ribs, at least 1½ inches thick
- 5 teaspoons kosher salt, divided
- 2½ teaspoons freshly cracked black pepper, divided
- 2 yellow onions, quartered
- 4 stalks celery, halved crosswise
- 3 carrots, halved crosswise
- 10 cloves garlic, smashed
- 3 tablespoons tomato paste
- 1 (750 ml) bottle dry red wine such as a cabernet sauvignon
- 2 cups beef stock
- 8 sprigs fresh thyme
- 10 sprigs fresh parsley
- zest from one lemon, grated
- 1½ tablespoons cornstarch or arrowroot powder (optional)

FOR THE MASHED POTATOES

- 7 medium (about 5 pounds) russet or Yukon Gold potatoes, peeled and chopped
- ½ cup heavy cream
- 11 tablespoons butter, softened
- 8 ounces mascarpone cheese or cream cheese
- 1 tablespoon + 1 teaspoon kosher salt
- 1 teaspoon ground black pepper

Not all grocery stores carry bone-in short ribs. Be sure to ask the butcher at the meat counter or make a trip to your local meat market.

FOR THE SHORT RIBS

1 Preheat oven to 275°F.

2 Pat the short ribs dry. Mix 4 teaspoons salt and 2 teaspoons pepper together and sprinkle evenly over the meat.

3 In a large dutch oven over medium-high heat, add oil. Working in batches, brown short ribs on all sides, about 2 minutes per side. Move ribs to a platter.

4 Pour out excess oil/fat from dutch oven, reserving about 2 tablespoons in the pot.

5 While still over medium-high heat, add onions, celery, carrots, and garlic to the pot and cook, stirring often, until onions are browned, about 5 minutes.

6 Add the tomato paste, stirring to coat the veggies. Allow the paste to cook for about 1–2 minutes so it caramelizes (it will get darker in color).

7 Deglaze the pan by slowly pouring in ¼ cup of the red wine, scraping up all the browned bits.

8 Add the short ribs back to the dutch oven with any accumulated juices on the platter. Stir in the remaining wine and bring to a boil.

9 Lower the heat to medium and simmer until wine is reduced by half, about 20 minutes.

10 Stir in stock. Be sure the meat on the short ribs is covered in liquid. Add thyme and parsley. Bring to a boil, cover, and transfer to the oven.

11 Cook until short ribs are tender, about 3½ to 4 hours.

12 Transfer short ribs to a platter. Discard the veggies and fresh herbs (they have imparted all their flavor and are now just sad). Spoon fat from the surface of sauce and discard.

13 Place the dutch oven over medium-high heat and season the sauce with remaining 1 teaspoon salt and ½ teaspoon pepper. To thicken, if desired, make a slurry with equal parts cornstarch (or arrowroot powder) and water. Mix thoroughly. Slowly add to the simmering sauce while stirring vigorously. Allow the sauce to thicken for about 3–5 minutes. Remove from heat. Stir in the lemon zest and then taste for any seasoning adjustments.

FOR THE MASHED POTATOES: STOVETOP

1 Add the potatoes to a large pot. Cover with water and bring to a boil over high heat. Once the water is boiling, add a generous pinch of salt, reduce heat to medium-high, and allow the potatoes to cook for 20 to 25 minutes or until fork tender.

2 Drain the potatoes in a large colander. Place them back into the dry pot and put the pot on the stove over low heat.

3 Pour in the heavy cream. Mash the potatoes over low heat until desired consistency. (For truly creamy potatoes, use a ricer or mash in a stand mixer with the cream.)

4 Add the butter, mascarpone cheese, salt, and pepper. Mash to combine.

5 Taste and add any additional salt to your liking. Top with a few pats of butter and freshly cracked black pepper. Cover until ready to serve.

FOR THE MASHED POTATOES: INSTANT POT

1 Place 4 cups of water into the IP. Add peeled potatoes. Secure lid and set valve to "Sealing." Cook on high pressure for 12 minutes.

2 Allow to naturally release for about 5 minutes, then move valve to "Venting" to release the steam. Drain water from potatoes and place them back in the IP.

3 Follow steps 3–5 of stovetop method.

In a bowl or plate with curved edges, add a scoop of mashed potatoes. Place 1 short rib on top. Drizzle with sauce. Enjoy!

These are most delicious when the short ribs are made the day before. Cook as instructed above but hold off on removing the short ribs from the sauce. As soon as the short ribs come out of the oven, allow the pot to cool and then cover and place in the refrigerator overnight. When ready to enjoy, remove the lid and scrape off the fat that has settled on the top. Warm in the oven at 350° for 30 minutes and then finish making the sauce.

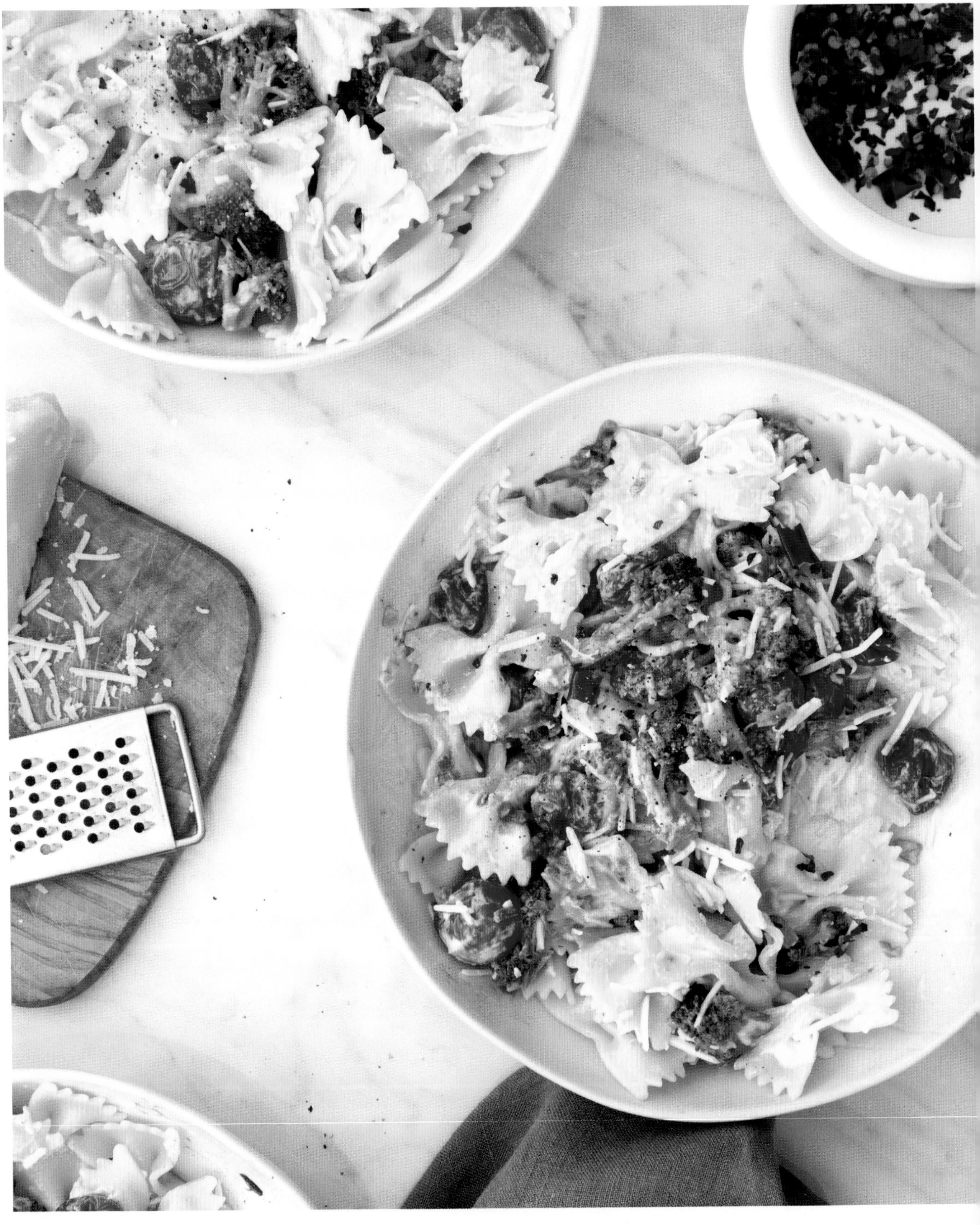

SPRING IS HERE PASTA

This is a dish that is absolutely transformed by adding flavor at the end of cooking.

This dish uses crème fraîche, which is French for "fresh cream." It is a thick, cultured cream that has a tangy taste like sour cream. It is usually found in the specialty cheese section at the grocery store.

PREP TIME: 5 MINUTES • COOK TIME: 20 MINUTES • SERVES 5-6

1 pound bowtie pasta (or pasta of choice)

1 tablespoon butter

1 tablespoon olive oil

2 shallots, chopped

1 cup broccoli florets, roughly chopped

1 cup cherry tomatoes

2 teaspoons kosher salt

2 cloves garlic, minced

¼ cup white wine or chicken stock

juice from 1 lemon

1 cup (8 ounces) crème fraîche or sour cream

1 cup shredded fresh Parmesan cheese

1 Cook pasta according to package directions.

2 In a sauté pan over medium-high heat, add butter and olive oil.

3 Once the butter is melted, add shallots and sauté for 2 minutes.

4 Add broccoli, tomatoes, and salt, and sauté for an additional 3–4 minutes until broccoli is cooked. Add minced garlic and sauté until fragrant, about 1 minute.

5 Deglaze the pan by carefully pouring in ¼ cup white wine or stock and scraping up the browned bits with a wooden spoon or spatula.

6 Drain the pasta and add it to the pan with the broccoli.

7 Add the juice from one lemon, crème fraîche, and Parmesan cheese. Mix until thoroughly combined.

Dish out pasta and sprinkle with more Parmesan cheese. For a little heat, sprinkle with red pepper flakes. Enjoy!

STICKY HONEY CHICKEN

PREP TIME: 5 MINUTES • COOK TIME: 30 MINUTES • SERVES 4–5

2 pounds boneless skinless chicken thighs

1 teaspoon kosher salt

½ teaspoon ground black pepper

1 tablespoon olive oil

2 tablespoons butter

3 tablespoons soy sauce or coconut aminos

⅓ cup honey

3 tablespoons tomato sauce

3 cloves garlic, minced

1 teaspoon sriracha (optional)

juice from half a lime

1 cup fresh sugar snap peas (optional)

FOR SERVING

2 cups cooked basmati or jasmine rice (optional)

sesame seeds (optional)

avocado

lime

1 Make rice according to package instructions, if desired.

2 Trim excess fat from chicken thighs and sprinkle evenly with salt and pepper.

3 In a large sauté pan over medium-high heat, add oil and butter.

4 Once butter is melted, add chicken thighs. Brown chicken in batches until cooked, about 4–5 minutes per side.

5 Remove chicken from pan to a bowl or plate and cover with foil.

6 In the same pan, over medium heat, add the soy sauce, honey, tomato sauce, garlic, and sriracha. Mix and let simmer for 2 minutes while it thickens.

7 Add lime juice and sugar snap peas, if desired. Simmer for an additional minute.

8 Meanwhile, shred chicken with two forks or in a stand mixer using the paddle attachment. Add shredded chicken to the sauce in the sauté pan. Mix to combine.

Serve over basmati rice, cauliflower rice, or steamed veggies. Serve with a sprinkle of sesame seeds, slices of avocado, and a wedge of lime.

fresh and dried
HERBS AND SPICES

Using fresh and dried herbs as well as spices are key ways to add flavor. If I'm reading a recipe and it's lacking in spices, herbs, or seasoning, I skip right past it.

FRESH HERBS

Fresh herbs can be delicate and make so many dishes pop with freshness. Here are the most commonly used fresh herbs for the everyday home cook.

Parsley

This is a bright green, leafy herb. Most grocers carry flat-leaf parsley and curly-leaf parsley. It has a very bright, leafy taste with a small hint of bitterness. Parsley is most widely used for adding freshness or a pop of color to dishes at the end.

Cilantro

Cilantro comes from the coriander plant. To some people it tastes bright with a little hint of bitterness, and it can have some peppery notes. But for others, cilantro tastes like soap. If cilantro tastes like soap to you, I recommend you not use it even if a dish calls for it. The best substitute for cilantro is parsley since it's in the same plant family, but know that it will not bring exactly the same effect to your dish.

To freeze most leafy green herbs like parsley and cilantro, thoroughly wash and dry the leaves. Chop them up and add them to an ice cube tray with just about 1 tablespoon of water or oil. Once they are frozen, you can add the cubes to a baggie and keep them in your freezer until you are ready to use them.

The best way to store bunches of fresh cilantro or fresh parsley is to trim the ends and gently wash and dry it as soon as you bring it home. Place the cilantro or parsley in a jar filled with about an inch of water, then place a plastic baggie over top of the leaves and put in the refrigerator. This can keep your herbs fresh for weeks (assuming they were at peak freshness when you purchased them).

Chives

Chives have a very delicate onion flavor. They are like a small whisper of an onion. Because of this they can be used fresh and do not need to be cooked like other onions or shallots.

Mint

Mint has a delightful, sweet taste on the palate and can also deliver a cooling sensation. I love using mint in honey simple syrup or even in beverages because of these tasting notes. Mint is also a very fun surprise in salads. If you ever have leftover mint, chop a few leaves up and add it to your salad.

Fresh mint can be stored the same way as fresh parsley and cilantro.

Dill

I am a dill fanatic! I don't use it too often in my cooking, but when I do, I lose my mind. It has a slight lemony flavor with some grassy notes. It's a favorite of mine to use in sauces, as it brings a freshness I cannot get with any other herb.

To store fresh dill, spray the dill with a little bit of water. Wrap loosely in paper towels and store in your refrigerator's vegetable drawer. It will last a little over one week.

Thyme

Thyme pairs really well with eggs, cheese, beans, tomatoes, and potatoes. Fresh thyme is probably the herb I use most often. The tiny leaves can easily be removed by running two pinched fingers down the stick of the thyme, or fresh thyme can also be used by tying whole sprigs into a small bunch and throwing it into a soup or stew to flavor the dish while it cooks.

Fresh thyme can last up to two weeks in the refrigerator just by keeping it in the container or bag it came in.

Thyme and rosemary are fresh herbs that can stand up to heat, unlike other delicate fresh herbs.

Rosemary

This herb is a shrub that is known for its pine-like flavor. It is perfect for throwing a few sprigs into a cast-iron skillet while searing a steak or adding to oven-roasted potatoes. I love rosemary, but a little goes a long way (and I have actually found that when a dish calls for rosemary, I almost always reach for the thyme I already have on hand). Just like thyme, rosemary can last up to several weeks in your refrigerator in the container or bag it came in.

Basil

This is another popular herb for home cooks. It is most often used fresh and has a bit of a peppery flavor with some sweetness and just a little hint of mint or anise. It is commonly used in caprese (tomatoes, mozzarella cheese, basil, olive oil, and balsamic vinegar) and pesto. It is also delicious on pizza, in salads, and on sandwiches.

THAI BASIL STIR-FRY

This dish absolutely transforms with the addition of fresh Thai basil and lime juice!

 This dish comes together so fast. Be sure all veggies are prepped before cooking.

PREP TIME: 10 MINUTES • COOK TIME: 30 MINUTES • SERVES 4

1 tablespoon olive oil

1 pound 80/20 ground beef

1 red bell pepper, sliced

½ red onion, diced

2 cloves garlic, minced

¼ cup chiffonaded fresh Thai basil leaves (or regular basil)

1 inch of fresh ginger, grated

3 tablespoons soy sauce or coconut aminos

1 tablespoon coconut sugar or brown sugar

1 teaspoon fish sauce

1 teaspoon kosher salt

juice from half a lime

TOPPINGS

1 carrot, shredded

2 green onions, sliced

fresh basil

fresh jalapeño, sliced

lime wedges

1 Heat oil in a large skillet over medium-high heat.

2 Add ground beef, crumbling with a meat crumbler or wooden spoon. Allow to cook for 5 minutes.

3 Add bell pepper and red onion. Sauté for 3 minutes.

4 Add garlic, basil, and ginger, stirring until fragrant, about 2 minutes.

5 Add soy sauce, coconut sugar, fish sauce, and salt. Stir to combine.

6 Sauté for an additional 2–3 minutes to allow the sauce to caramelize the beef.

7 Turn off heat. Squeeze the juice of half a lime over the meat and mix to incorporate.

Serve over Creamy Coconut Rice (page 179) or lettuce greens. Top as desired with shredded carrots, green onions, fresh basil, sliced fresh jalapeño, and a lime wedge.

GRAIN-FREE, GLUTEN-FREE, DAIRY-FREE

DRIED HERBS

Dried herbs are great for home cooking and can be helpful when fresh herbs are not available. For example, you can easily use dried thyme or parsley or oregano.

Dried herbs are just that—herbs that have been cleaned, chopped, and dried. They are great because they have a longer shelf life than fresh herbs, but they do lose their potency over time.

Something to note about dried herbs is they are much more potent than fresh herbs. Because they are dried, their leaves have shrunk. Therefore, a good rule of thumb is that 1 tablespoon of fresh herbs is the equivalent of 1 teaspoon of dried herbs.

I don't have a lot of dried herbs on hand because I prefer to use fresh. However, there are a few dried herbs that I believe shine better, so I always keep the following on hand:

oregano
Italian seasoning (which usually includes dried oregano, thyme, sage, and rosemary)
sage

That's it. That's all I have on hand because, like I said, I prefer fresh herbs. But a few other common dried herbs you might want include:

rosemary
thyme
dill
parsley

FIRST HELLO PASTA

This dish highlights how you can combine dried herbs with fresh herbs to create a dish that tastes like it has been simmering all day. I call it First Hello Pasta because I always make it the first time we have new people over. Several years ago, I got a DM from an Instagram follower. She was having a first date over for dinner but didn't know what to make. I directed her to this dish. He fell in love with it and then with her and then they got married. (Yes, for real.)

PREP TIME: 5 MINUTES • COOK TIME: 30 MINUTES • SERVES 5–6

1 pound pasta of choice (we like using spaghetti noodles)

2 tablespoons olive oil

½ red onion, diced

1 pound ground beef (preferably 80/20)

3 cloves garlic, minced

1 tablespoon dried oregano

¼ teaspoon red pepper flakes (optional)

1 cup dry red wine, such as a cabernet sauvignon or merlot

1 (28-ounce) can crushed tomatoes

2 tablespoons tomato paste

1 tablespoon kosher salt

½ teaspoon ground black pepper

¼ cup chiffonaded fresh basil leaves

¼ cup heavy cream or half-and-half

½ cup freshly grated Parmesan cheese

1 Cook pasta according to package instructions.

2 Heat 2 tablespoons olive oil in a large skillet over medium-high heat. Add the onion and sauté for 3 minutes.

3 Add the ground beef and cook for 5–7 minutes until the meat has lost its pink color and starts to brown, breaking apart the meat with a meat crumbler or wooden spoon.

4 Stir in the garlic, oregano, and red pepper flakes and cook for 1 more minute.

5 Carefully pour 1 cup of the wine into the skillet, stirring to scrape up any browned bits.

6 Add the tomatoes, tomato paste, salt, and pepper, stirring until combined. Bring to a boil, lower the heat, and simmer uncovered for 10 minutes.

7 After 10 minutes, add basil and cream and simmer for 8–10 more minutes, stirring occasionally until thickened. Once thickened, remove from heat and add the Parmesan.

Serve over noodles or with a side of steamed veggies!

GRAIN-FREE, GLUTEN-FREE OPTIONAL

DRIED SPICES

Dried herbs and dried spices both come from plants, but dried herbs come from the leaves of the plant and dried spices come from the root, stalk, or seeds of the plant. I have more dried spices on hand than I do dried herbs.

Here is a list of the most commonly used dried spices for the everyday home cook.

Dried Spices for Heat

Cayenne pepper

Red pepper flakes

Essential Everyday Spices

Garlic powder

Ground cumin

Paprika

Onion powder

Chili powder

Spices for Curries and Asian Dishes

Curry powder

Ground cardamom

Ground ginger

Turmeric

Spices for Baking or Sweets

Ground cinnamon

Ground nutmeg

Favorite Blends

Trader Joe's Everything but the Bagel Sesame Seasoning Blend

Trader Joe's Chili Lime Garlic

Nom Nom Paleo Magic Mushroom Powder

I highly recommend going through your jars of dried herbs and spices! Some of them are probably years old, and that means they must go. After one year, most dried spices really start to lose their flavor. As you empty your spice and herb jars, take note of which ones you use the most and which ones you only used one teaspoon of. For example, I had a whole jar of dried fennel sitting in my cabinet for years. I don't love fresh fennel, but I tried a recipe that called for dried fennel, so I thought I needed it. Well, I didn't! I will never buy a jar of dried fennel again.

TAMALE CASSEROLE

This dish uses popular dried seasonings to achieve the most delicious flavor in every bite!

PREP TIME: 5 MINUTES • COOK TIME: 35 MINUTES • SERVES 6–8

FOR THE CORNBREAD

1 package (8.5 ounces) cornbread mix (such as a small box of Jiffy)

¼ cup frozen corn

¼ cup sour cream

¼ cup heavy cream

1 (4-ounce) can diced green chiles

1 egg

1 tablespoon olive oil

FOR THE CHICKEN

1 tablespoon olive oil

½ yellow onion, chopped

3 cloves garlic, minced

2 cups cooked, shredded chicken (I like to buy rotisserie chicken!)

1 teaspoon chili powder

2 teaspoons kosher salt

1 teaspoon cumin

juice of 1 lime

1 (4-ounce) can diced green chiles

1 (28-ounce) can crushed tomatoes

1 (15-ounce) can black beans, drained and rinsed

1 cup shredded sharp cheddar cheese or Mexican cheese blend

FOR GARNISH

sliced avocado

shredded cheese

lime

cilantro

hot sauce

If you have leftover chicken mixture, you can put it in a freezer bag or container and freeze it for up to one month. Simply thaw overnight in the refrigerator and place on top of a new batch of cornbread!

FOR THE CORNBREAD

1 Preheat oven to 400°F.

2 In a large bowl, mix all cornbread ingredients together except the oil.

3 Evenly coat the bottom of a braiser or oven-safe 8×8 baking dish with 1 tablespoon oil. Pour the cornbread batter into the dish. Place in the oven and bake for 20 minutes.

FOR THE CHICKEN

1 In a soup pot or large sauté pan, heat oil over medium heat. Sauté onion until soft, about 3–4 minutes. Add garlic and stir until fragrant (about 1 minute). Add shredded chicken and stir in chili powder, salt, cumin, lime juice, and green chiles. Sauté for a few minutes, allowing the aromatics to coat the chicken.

2 Add tomatoes and beans. Bring to a boil, then turn the heat to low and simmer for 10 minutes.

3 Spread chicken mixture on top of cornbread. Add shredded cheese and place under broiler until cheese gets bubbly, about 3–5 minutes. Remove from the oven and serve.

Dish up and garnish as desired with sliced avocado, more shredded cheese, lime, cilantro, and hot sauce.

PINEAPPLE CARNITAS WITH CITRUS SLAW

Pork absorbs flavors really well and is a great candidate for using dried herbs and spices to reach peak flavor.

 While the carnitas cooks in your slow cooker, prep the slaw and pickled pineapple so they have time to sit in the refrigerator before serving.

PREP TIME: 20 MINUTES • COOK TIME: 6–8 HOURS • SERVES 6–8

FOR THE CARNITAS

3 pounds bone-in pork shoulder or butt, fat trimmed

1 tablespoon olive oil

2 teaspoons ground cumin

2 teaspoons chili powder

2 teaspoons dried oregano

1 tablespoon kosher salt

½ teaspoon ground cinnamon

1 yellow onion, quartered

4 cloves garlic, smashed

1 cup pineapple juice

juice from 2 oranges (about ¾ cup)

1 tablespoon honey

FOR THE CABBAGE SLAW

1 bag (14 ounces) coleslaw mix

½ cup chopped fresh cilantro

¼ cup lime juice

2 tablespoons mayonnaise

½ teaspoon kosher salt

3 green onions, green and white parts, sliced

FOR THE PICKLED PINEAPPLE

1 cup fresh pineapple, cubed

1 tablespoon apple cider vinegar

1 teaspoon maple syrup

1 tablespoon fresh cilantro, chopped

½ jalapeño, diced (remove seeds for less heat)

FOR SERVING

small corn tortillas or basmati rice

sour cream

hot sauce

avocado

GRAIN-FREE, DAIRY-FREE

FOR THE CARNITAS

1 In a large dutch oven over medium-high heat (or in your slow cooker if it has a sauté function) add 1 tablespoon oil. In a small bowl combine the cumin, chili powder, oregano, salt, and cinnamon. Rub the spice mixture all over the pork. Add the pork to the heated oil and sear on each side for about 2 to 3 minutes.

2 Add the seared meat to the slow cooker. Add remaining ingredients.

3 Cook on high for 6 hours or on low for 8 hours (the meat should shred easily with a fork).

4 Remove the pork and shred, discarding the bone, then add back to the slow cooker to let it soak up all that delicious juice (it's citrusy and sweet!).

5 If you would like your carnitas crispy, spread the shredded pork on a sheet pan lined with parchment paper or foil and place under the broiler for 5–8 minutes.

FOR THE CABBAGE SLAW

1 Add all the ingredients to a large bowl and mix to combine.

2 Refrigerate for at least 1 hour before serving.

FOR THE PICKLED PINEAPPLE

1 Add all the ingredients to a bowl and mix to combine. Refrigerate for at least 20 minutes before serving.

Serve carnitas in small corn tortillas or over a bed of rice. (Be sure to warm your tortillas in a microwave or using a dry sauté pan. I like to put a clean dish towel on a large plate and wrap the tortillas in the towel to keep them warm.) Top with slaw and pickled pineapple. Garnish with favorite toppings like avocado, hot sauce, and sour cream.

PART

6

let's get SAUCY!

SAUCES
can make a dish
fancy
without
making it fussy.

the

MINDSET

Sauces, dips, and dressings are my love language.

My deep love for sauces goes back to childhood. Some of my fondest memories with my dad come from selecting a variety of sauces that were available whenever our family ordered takeout. Pizza and chicken nuggets were highly prized because we would make sure to get enough sauces to fill up one plate.

This is not an exaggeration.

It was not unusual for my dad and me to each grab two plates for dinner. Plate 1: pizza slices. Plate 2: a smattering of the best sauces the pizza parlor had to offer (buffalo sauce, garlic butter, ranch, zesty ranch). With each bite we got to change the flavor profile of our meal. It was low-key magical, and I am happy to report I never grew out of this "plate of sauces" delight.

Sauces have the power to level up any meal. They can make a dish fancy without making it fussy. They are generally easy to whip up, get better with time, and are extremely versatile.

All the sauce recipes in this book can be used with many different cooking methods (marinating, braising, sautéing, baking, pressure cooking). These sauces can also be used to accompany the meal (dipping, drizzling, coating). Most wonderfully, they can be used on all different types of meat or veggies.

A great way to choose a sauce for your dish is to think about what the dish offers you. Following is a helpful guide that has never led me astray when I have created sauces and then paired them with my dishes.

THERE'S A SAUCE
for that!

The magic of a sauce is that it can take a simple or routine dish to the next level. Is BBQ chicken always on rotation? Make my Fresh Herb Dressing to elevate the dish! Taco night always on Tuesdays? Refresh the dish by making my Avocado Crema! Yellow curry is delicious, but when you add a cooling sauce like my Cilantro Lime Yogurt Sauce, it transforms the whole dish into something with layers of flavor.

   The next two recipes showcase how sauces and dressings can elevate a dish.

flavor profile	*needs something*	*sauce*
Spicy with strong flavors	Cooling and fresh	Cilantro Lime Yogurt Sauce
Fresh and salty	Smoky and sweet	Chipotle Honey Vinaigrette
Herbal and charred	Bright and creamy	Tzatziki
Bland or one-note	Citrusy and savory	Peanut Lime Soy Sauce
Savory and sweet	Vinegary and sour	Zesty Lime Garlic Sauce
Hot and crispy	Spicy and sticky	Sweet Heat Wing Sauce
Cold and crunchy	Citrusy and creamy	Fresh Herb Dressing

SWEET & STICKY GLAZED SALMON

This one is for the salmon haters. Or, I should say, this one is for the people who hate salmon but want to love it! I've made this for so many people, my husband included, who were sure they didn't like salmon. And now they're believers. Not only is this cooked perfectly, but the sauce takes it to the next level.

PREP TIME: 5 MINUTES • COOK TIME: 15 MINUTES • SERVES 4

FOR THE SALMON

3 tablespoon dark brown sugar

1 tablespoon low-sodium soy sauce

4 teaspoons Dijon mustard

1 teaspoon rice vinegar

4 (6-ounce) salmon fillets, about 1-inch thick (frozen salmon is fine, just make sure you thaw it in the refrigerator the night before)

cooking spray or olive oil

1 teaspoon kosher salt

FOR THE BUTTERY RICE

2 cups cooked basmati rice

2 tablespoons butter

1 tablespoon olive oil

¼ cup chopped shiitake mushrooms

¼ cup frozen peas

FOR THE SALMON

1 Preheat oven to 425°F.

2 Combine the brown sugar, soy sauce, Dijon mustard, and rice vinegar in a saucepan; bring to a boil. Remove from heat.

3 Place fish on a foil-lined jelly roll pan coated with cooking spray. Sprinkle salmon fillets with salt (about ¼ teaspoon each).

4 Bake salmon for 12 minutes. Remove from the oven.

5 Preheat broiler.

6 Brush some of the glaze mixture evenly over salmon, then broil 3 inches from heat for 3 minutes, or until fish flakes easily when tested with a fork.

GRAIN-FREE OPTIONAL, DAIRY-FREE

1 Combine the brown sugar, soy sauce, Dijon mustard, and rice vinegar in a saucepan; bring to a boil. Remove from heat.

2 Spray the skin of the fish with oil. Place fish, skin side down, on the air fryer basket coated with cooking spray; sprinkle fish with salt.

3 Place in the air fryer and set it to 400 degrees. (If your toaster oven doubles as an air fryer, be sure you're using the air fryer function.) Cook for 8–10 minutes. Remove from the air fryer.

4 Turn on broiler. Brush some of the glaze mixture evenly over salmon, then broil 3 inches from heat for 3 minutes, or until fish flakes easily when tested with a fork.

FOR THE BUTTERY RICE

1 Add butter and olive oil to a sauté pan over medium-high heat. Once melted, add mushrooms and allow to brown for about 3 minutes. Add the cooked basmati rice and frozen peas. Sauté until the peas are cooked through, about 4–5 minutes. Remove from heat.

Plate up rice and place salmon on top. Serve with reserved sauce!

TACOS IN A BLANKET WITH TEX-MEX QUESO

The queso takes this dish to the next level. But be careful, you might eat all the queso before you get to add it to the Tacos in a Blanket!

The first Taco in a Blanket you make in your pan will take more time to cook than all the others. If the pan is getting too hot, just move it off the burner and let it cool slightly, then proceed with the additional Tacos in a Blanket.

PREP TIME: 10 MINUTES • COOK TIME: 20 MINUTES • SERVES 4

FOR TACO MEAT

1 tablespoon olive oil

¼ cup chopped red onion

1 pound ground beef

1 tablespoon chili powder

2 teaspoons salt

2 teaspoons ground cumin

½ teaspoon paprika

1 teaspoon garlic powder

1 tablespoon tomato paste

FOR TEX-MEX QUESO

1 cup heavy cream or half-and-half

10–15 slices (8–12 ounces) white American cheese (cheese from the deli melts the best)

2 tablespoons salsa verde or 3 tablespoons canned green chiles

FOR TACOS IN A BLANKET

4 large soft tortillas (Get the burrito size! Smaller sizes will not work for this, unless you want to make a mini version.)

1 (15.4-ounce) can refried beans

4 tostadas or favorite tortilla chips (even cool ranch or nacho flavor!)

1 cup sliced cherry tomatoes

sour cream

shredded iceberg lettuce (optional)

1 tablespoon olive oil

shredded cheddar cheese (optional)

hot sauce (optional)

FOR TACO MEAT

1 In a sauté pan, add the oil and turn heat to medium-high. Once the pan comes to temperature, add the onion and sauté for 2 minutes.

2 Add ground beef. With a meat crumbler, break apart the meat. Brown for 6 minutes.

3 Add all the seasonings and the tomato paste. Mix to incorporate all ingredients.

4 Turn heat to medium and cook for an additional 3–5 minutes.

5 Turn off heat and set aside.

FOR TEX-MEX QUESO

1 Add 1 cup cream to a saucepan over medium-high heat and allow to come to a simmer.

2 Add cheese slices a few at a time. Allow the cheese to melt and get bubbly (this will take about 2-3 minutes; be sure to stir to incorporate everything). Do not walk away from your pan or your stove will be wearing a new queso cape. Stir until the sauce is thick and creamy.

3 Add salsa verde or green chiles. Stir to combine. Remove from heat.

FOR TACOS IN A BLANKET ASSEMBLY

1 Lay your large, soft tortilla flat and spread about 2 tablespoons of refried beans over the middle. Make sure there is at least 2 inches of tortilla around the edges without anything on it. We will need to fold the tortilla, so do not overfill!

2 Add the tostada or tortilla chips on top of the refried beans.

3 Add 2 tablespoons meat. Top with a few sliced cherry tomatoes, some of the Tex-Mex Queso, a few shreds of iceberg lettuce if desired, and sour cream.

4 Place a small sauté pan on medium heat. Add 1 tablespoon oil.

5 Once the pan is heated, fold your Taco in a Blanket (pull the edges of the soft tortilla over the tostada). If it does not fold completely, add some shredded cheddar cheese as a "cover" or another tortilla to keep everything from spilling out. Carefully add to the pan with the folded part down. Gently press down and hold to keep it all secure.

6 Allow to sauté for about 2 minutes. Once golden brown, flip. Sauté for an additional minute.

7 Place finished Tacos in a Blanket on a baking sheet in the oven to keep warm. Repeat assembling and cooking remaining Tacos in a Blanket.

Cut in half and serve with your favorite hot sauce and extra queso!

THE SCIENCE
of a sauce

With just a few ingredients, you can create a simple but flavor-packed sauce that will give your dish a glow up. Below are some essentials for making a delicious sauce. Just using two or three of these ingredients is where you find the magic.

SALT

Nearly all sauces have some salt! Think of salt as the wrangler of all the flavors in the sauce. It brings them together in perfect harmony. Most fresh sauces only need a little salt, but it is a game changer. A great rule of thumb is to start with just ½ teaspoon of salt and add from there. Remember that it's always easier to add salt than to subtract it.

SWEET

When creating a sauce that is spicy or smoky, a little sweetness is always a good idea. On the obvious side, it can tame the spiciness, but more practically, sweetness complements the spice. My favorite sauce sweeteners are honey and maple syrup.

FRESH HERBS

The power of fresh herbs is in their freshness! Cooking any kind of fresh herbs with heat generally tames their flavor. In a sauce or dressing, a fresh herb gets to sing. Dill is great when you need a bit of a grassy note. Cilantro has a little bite and instantly adds freshness. Basil has a beautifully mild sweetness. Chives are pungent and can make a dull sauce come alive.

CITRUS

Citrus, such as fresh lemon or lime juice, is the quickest way to add a little tartness to your sauce while brightening the flavor.

UMAMI

When you want to create a rich sauce that is truly mouthwatering, adding ingredients with umami flavors is always a big win. These ingredients include soy sauce, garlic, fish sauce, and Worcestershire sauce.

SPICE

Adding a little bit of spiciness to a sauce can make it a great accompaniment to a meal that is very fresh or bland in nature. I love using red pepper flakes, sriracha, or hot sauce. I also love using adobo sauce, which is smoky and has delicious heat.

EXTRA-VIRGIN OLIVE OIL

I do not use expensive, high-quality olive oil when I am cooking with heat. But using cold-pressed extra-virgin olive oil in a dressing is a game changer. High-quality olive oil has subtle grassy notes and can be a touch herbal in flavor.

The best way to find good quality extra-virgin olive oil is to go to an olive oil store where you can sample the various oils. It will be a little more pricey, but if you stick to using the good olive oil only in dressings, it will go a long way.

everyday SAUCES

AVOCADO CREMA

1 garlic clove, minced

¼ cup chopped cilantro

juice from 1 lime

½ teaspoon kosher salt

1 avocado, skin and pit removed

1 cup plain Greek yogurt

¼ cup heavy cream

1 Add first 4 ingredients to a food processor.* Pulse 10–15 times.

2 Add avocado, Greek yogurt, and heavy cream to the food processor. Pulse until smooth and creamy (about 15 pulses). Store in the fridge for up to 5 days.

If you do not have a food processor, fully mash avocado in a bowl until creamy. Add the rest of the ingredients and stir vigorously to combine.

pair with TACOS, TAMALE CASSEROLE (PAGE 146), BEAN DIP, FANCY NOT FUSSY SHEET PAN NACHOS (PAGE 212)

CILANTRO LIME YOGURT SAUCE

¾ cup plain Greek yogurt

¼ cup finely chopped fresh cilantro

1 garlic clove, minced

juice from 1 lime

½ teaspoon kosher salt

3 tablespoons cold, filtered water

Add all ingredients to a bowl. Mix to combine.

Note: I like to use cold, filtered water instead of a heavy cream to thin out this sauce, but you can add as little or as much water (up to 4 tablespoons) as you like for your desired consistency. Store in the fridge for up to 5 days.

pair with CHICKEN BURGERS, MAKE ME SMILE YELLOW CURRY (PAGE 257), SWEET & SPICY CHICKEN STUFFED SWEET POTATOES (PAGE 220), TAMALE CASSEROLE (PAGE 146)

ZESTY LIME GARLIC SAUCE

⅓ cup mayonnaise or plain Greek yogurt

2 teaspoons Dijon mustard

zest of 1 small lime

juice from half a lime

1 garlic clove, minced

¼ teaspoon kosher salt

Add all ingredients to a bowl. Mix to combine. Store in the fridge for up to 5 days.

pair with BACON-FAT SWEET POTATO FRIES (PAGE 180), EVEN ON SUNDAYS CHICKEN SANDWICH (PAGE 131), SMASH BURGER (PAGE 118)

BBQ SAUCES
and marinades

STICKY & SWEET BBQ SAUCE

1 tablespoon olive oil

¼ cup diced onion

2 cloves garlic, minced

1 cup tomato sauce (or ketchup)

1 tablespoon Dijon mustard

2 teaspoons kosher salt

½ cup maple syrup (or brown sugar)

¼ cup apple cider vinegar

1 tablespoon Worcestershire sauce

1 In a saucepan over medium-high heat, add oil. Once oil is heated, add onion and sauté for about 3 minutes. Add garlic and sauté for another minute.

2 Add remaining ingredients. Mix to combine.

3 Allow to come to a boil and then turn heat to low. Let simmer for 25–30 minutes, or until the sauce thickens.

Note: For a smooth sauce, either use an immersion blender at the end or substitute ½ tablespoon onion powder and 1 teaspoon garlic powder for the fresh ingredients. Will keep in the refrigerator for up to 2 weeks.

pair with ANY AND ALL BBQ!

SWEET HEAT WING SAUCE

8 tablespoons butter (1 stick)

½ cup Frank's RedHot (or your favorite hot sauce)

½ cup honey

2 cloves garlic, minced

1 Combine all ingredients in a small saucepan over medium heat.

2 Once butter is melted, whisk to combine and remove from heat.

Notes: If you would like a thicker sauce, whisk together 1 teaspoon cornstarch (or arrowroot powder) with 1 teaspoon water. Pour mixture into sauce while whisking. Whisk to combine until the sauce is thickened!

For a sweeter sauce, add more honey. For a spicier sauce, add more hot sauce.

pair with CRISPY CHICKEN WINGS (PAGE 124), SWEET & SPICY CHICKEN STUFFED SWEET POTATOES (PAGE 220)

HONEY MUSTARD SAUCE

4 tablespoons honey

2 tablespoons warm water

3 tablespoons Dijon mustard

1 tablespoon apple cider vinegar

1 In a small mason jar, add the honey and warm water. Whisk to thin out the honey.

2 Add the Dijon mustard and apple cider vinegar. Secure lid and shake until mixed together. Store in the fridge for up to 7 days.

pair with EVEN ON SUNDAYS CHICKEN SANDWICH (PAGE 131), SMASH BURGER (PAGE 118), SALADS

DRESSINGS
and dips

TZATZIKI

¾ cup plain Greek yogurt

½ English cucumber, chopped
(or one small regular cucumber,
seeds removed, chopped)

juice from half a lemon

3 cloves garlic, minced

1 tablespoon fresh dill

1 teaspoon kosher salt

In a bowl, mix all ingredients together. Refrigerate ahead of time, if you can, to allow all flavors to come together.

pair with SPICED CHICKPEAS (PAGE 219),
GREEK PLATTER (PAGE 252), AS A DIP FOR VEGGIES

CHAMPAGNE VINAIGRETTE

2 tablespoons champagne vinegar

½ teaspoon Dijon mustard

1 garlic clove, minced

½ teaspoon kosher salt

½ cup olive oil

Add first four ingredients to a bowl and whisk together. Slowly drizzle in the olive oil while continuously mixing until incorporated. (If you have an immersion blender, use for about 30 seconds until combined.) Store in the refrigerator for up to 5 days.

pair with ANY SALAD—ESPECIALLY ONE WITH
GOAT CHEESE AND DRIED FRUIT!

CHIPOTLE HONEY VINAIGRETTE

½ cup olive oil

¼ cup apple cider vinegar

3 tablespoons honey

1 small chili in adobo

2 teaspoons adobo sauce (start here and add more adobo sauce if you want more heat)

2 cloves garlic

½ teaspoon cumin

½ teaspoon kosher salt

juice from 1 lime

2 tablespoons cold water

1 Add all ingredients into a blender. Blend until smooth.

2 After blending, taste. If you want a little more heat, add more adobo sauce (by the teaspoon). If you want a lot more heat, add another chili. If the dressing is too spicy, add another tablespoon of honey. Store in the fridge for up to 7 days.

pair with BURRITO BOWLS, SALAD, TACOS IN A BLANKET (PAGE 157)

FRESH HERB DRESSING

3 green onions, white and green parts, sliced

½ cup chopped fresh basil leaves, lightly packed

1 tablespoon chopped fresh dill

2 tablespoons freshly squeezed lemon juice

1½ tablespoons Dijon mustard

1 tablespoon olive oil

2 cloves garlic, chopped

½ teaspoon kosher salt

½ cup plain Greek yogurt

½ cup heavy whipping cream

1 Place green onions, basil, dill, lemon juice, mustard, olive oil, garlic, and salt in the bowl of a food processor.* Blend for 15 to 20 seconds to make a smooth mixture.

2 Add the yogurt and heavy whipping cream and blend until smooth. Transfer the dressing to a container, cover, and refrigerate for 1 hour to allow the flavors to develop. This can be stored in the refrigerator for up to one week.

If you do not have a food processor, finely chop green onions, basil, dill, and garlic. Mix with the lemon juice, Dijon mustard, olive oil, salt, Greek yogurt, and heavy whipping cream.

pair with CRISPY CHICKEN WINGS WITH SWEET HEAT SAUCE (PAGE 124), CHICKEN SLIDER, WEDGE SALAD

GREEK VINAIGRETTE

½ cup olive oil

¼ cup red wine vinegar

2 cloves garlic, minced

juice from half a lemon

1 teaspoon dried oregano or Italian seasoning

¼ teaspoon kosher salt

Add all ingredients to a mason jar. Shake well to combine. Store on your counter for up to 3 days.

pair with GREEK KABOBS, COUSCOUS, SALAD

umami-packed
SAUCES

HONEY GARLIC SAUCE

3 tablespoons soy sauce or coconut aminos

⅓ cup honey

3 tablespoons tomato sauce

3 cloves garlic, minced

1 teaspoon sriracha (optional)

juice from half a lime

1 In a saucepan over medium heat, add the soy sauce, honey, tomato sauce, garlic, and sriracha. Mix and let simmer for 2 minutes while it thickens.

2 Add lime juice. Simmer for an additional minute. Remove from heat. Can be stored in the refrigerator for up to 7 days.

pair with STICKY HONEY CHICKEN (PAGE 138), POURED OVER STIR-FRIED VEGGIES, DIPPING SAUCE FOR EGG ROLLS

PEANUT LIME SOY SAUCE

2 tablespoons creamy peanut butter

2 tablespoons soy sauce

1 tablespoon maple syrup

2 tablespoons rice wine vinegar

juice from half a lime

1 teaspoon sriracha (optional)

1 In a small saucepan, mix all ingredients together.

2 Heat over medium heat for about 3–5 minutes or until the peanut butter melts and all ingredients are incorporated. Remove from heat. Can be stored up to 7 days in the refrigerator.

pair with CHICKEN SKEWERS, DIPPING SAUCE FOR VEGGIES SUCH AS SUGAR SNAP PEAS, LETTUCE WRAPS

HONEY SOY GLAZE

⅓ cup low-sodium soy sauce

⅓ cup honey

3 tablespoons rice vinegar

1 teaspoon cornstarch (or arrowroot powder)

1 teaspoon water

1 In a small saucepan over medium heat, add soy sauce, honey, and rice vinegar. Stir and allow to simmer until all ingredients are incorporated, about 2 minutes. Turn heat to low.

2 In a small bowl, mix together cornstarch or arrowroot powder and water until combined. Pour mixture into saucepan. Mix vigorously to incorporate the slurry with the soy glaze. Allow to simmer until thickened, about 2 minutes. Remove from heat. Allow to cool for a few minutes before pouring into an airtight jar. Lasts in the refrigerator up to 7 days.

pair with TOSS WITH BLISTERED SHISHITO PEPPERS, DRIZZLE OVER EDAMAME, DIP FOR POTSTICKERS

PART

side

HUSTLES

Never wonder what side dish to pair with a meal again!
(I mean, "never" is kind of dramatic, but stick with me here.) These tried-and-true side dishes are quick but delicious and so versatile. I love them so much I call them my "side hustles."

SAVORY MASHED SWEET POTATOES

2 large sweet potatoes
(about ½ pound each)

2 cloves garlic, minced

1 tablespoon olive oil

3 tablespoons butter

1 teaspoon kosher salt

1 tablespoon fresh thyme

1 Preheat oven to 400°F.

2 Place sweet potatoes on a foil-lined baking sheet.

3 Bake for 45 minutes (or until juice from the potatoes is oozing).

4 Remove from the oven and allow to cool.

5 Meanwhile, sauté garlic in the olive oil and butter over medium heat until garlic is fragrant and turning light brown and butter is melted, about 3–4 minutes.

6 Remove skin from the sweet potatoes and mash (using a stand mixer, masher, or food mill) to desired consistency.

7 Add salt, thyme, and garlic mixture to the sweet potatoes. Mix until well combined.

8 Serve warm.

INSTANT POT VARIATION

1 Add steamer basket to IP and pour in 1 cup water.

2 Place sweet potatoes into the IP and close and lock the lid.

3 Move the valve to the "Sealing" position. Set on high pressure for 25 minutes.

4 When complete, allow pressure to naturally release for about 10 minutes before moving the valve to "Venting."

5 Remove the lid and follow steps 5–8 above.

VEGETARIAN, GRAIN-FREE, GLUTEN-FREE

"WHAT'S THE RECIPE?" ROASTED BROCCOLI WITH LEMON

This roasted broccoli will have people asking you for the recipe. I'm serious. Every time I've made my broccoli exactly like this, I get asked for the recipe. The magic is in the freshly squeezed lemon juice and a sprinkle of fleur de sel added at the end.

PREP TIME: 5 MINUTES • COOK TIME: 35 MINUTES • SERVES 4–5 AS A SIDE DISH

2 heads broccoli, florets removed (I use kitchen shears to cut the florets off the stem), or 4 cups broccoli florets

2 tablespoons olive oil

1 teaspoon kosher salt

2 tablespoons butter, cut into little pats

juice from half a lemon

1 teaspoon fleur de sel (or other finishing salt)

1 Preheat oven to 450°F.

2 Oil a baking dish or rimmed baking sheet covered in foil. Add broccoli florets. (Make sure you have a baking dish or sheet pan large enough that the broccoli is not overlapping. Vegetables will steam if they are placed on top of each other. We want them to get crisp and roasted.)

3 Add olive oil and kosher salt and toss to coat broccoli.

4 Roast for 15 minutes, then remove broccoli and top evenly with the pats of butter. Return to the oven and roast for an additional 15–20 minutes, or until the broccoli is nice and crisp.

5 Remove from the oven. Squeeze some of the lemon juice over the broccoli (just a little squeeze and then taste—add another squeeze if desired). Sprinkle fleur de sel over the broccoli. Toss and taste. Add more lemon juice or fleur de sel to your liking.

VEGETARIAN, GRAIN-FREE, GLUTEN-FREE

EAT THEM STRAIGHT OUT OF THE PAN GREEN BEANS

PREP TIME: 5 MINUTES • COOK TIME: 15 MINUTES • SERVES 4–5 AS A SIDE DISH

1 tablespoon olive oil

2 tablespoons butter

1 (10-ounce) bag haricot verts (these French green beans are skinnier and sauté very nicely)

¼ cup sliced shiitake mushrooms (optional; if I have leftover shiitake mushrooms for the week, I throw them in the pan)

2 cloves garlic, smashed

2 teaspoons kosher salt

half of a lemon, thinly sliced

1 In a large sauté pan over medium-high heat, add the oil and butter. Once melted, add the green beans and shiitake mushrooms if using. Allow to sauté for 4 minutes.

2 Add smashed garlic and salt. Continue to sauté for about 8 minutes. We want the beans nice and crisp, so try not to move them around too much—just toss them every 2–3 minutes.

3 Once the green beans are tender and slightly charred, add the slices of lemon. Toss with the green beans and allow to sauté for an additional 2 minutes.

4 Remove from heat, discard lemon slices, and serve immediately!

VEGETARIAN, GRAIN-FREE, GLUTEN-FREE

BRIGHT MEDITERRANEAN COUSCOUS

PREP TIME: 20 MINUTES • COOK TIME: 5 MINUTES • SERVES 4–5 AS A SIDE DISH

1 cup prepared couscous

8 whole pitted dates, chopped

¼ cup chopped red onion

¼ cup chopped fresh parsley

2 tablespoons chopped fresh mint

juice from 1 lemon

2 tablespoons olive oil

1 tablespoon red wine vinegar

½ cup feta cheese

½ cup halved cherry tomatoes

1 teaspoon kosher salt

1 In a big bowl, add the prepared couscous. Mix in all remaining ingredients.

2 Taste and add any additional salt or freshly cracked black pepper to your preference. (Remember that feta can be pretty salty, so you might not need salt.)

VEGETARIAN

"DO I HAVE TO SHARE?" BALSAMIC GLAZED CARROTS

PREP TIME: 10 MINUTES • COOK TIME: 30 MINUTES • SERVES 4–5 AS A SIDE DISH

FOR THE CARROTS

1 pound carrots

2 tablespoons olive oil

½ teaspoon kosher salt

FOR THE BALSAMIC GLAZE

1 cup balsamic vinegar

1 tablespoon honey

FOR THE CARROTS

1 Preheat oven to 425°F.

2 Peel carrots and cut in half lengthwise and then into thirds. On a large baking sheet, add carrots, olive oil, and salt. Toss to coat.

3 Roast in the oven for 30 minutes.

FOR THE BALSAMIC GLAZE

1 While carrots are roasting, add the balsamic vinegar and the honey to a small saucepan, stirring to combine.

2 Bring to a boil, then lower the heat to simmer for about 15 minutes. Remove from heat. As the glaze cools, it will thicken. Can be stored in the refrigerator for 2 weeks in an airtight jar.

Plate roasted carrots and drizzle with balsamic glaze.

VEGETARIAN, GRAIN-FREE, GLUTEN-FREE, DAIRY-FREE

A REASONABLE AMOUNT OF MASHED POTATOES

Are creamy, buttery mashed potatoes the secret MVP of every meal? Obviously. But I tend to reserve them for big gatherings or holidays. Then one day it occurred to me—I can make a small pot of mashed potatoes for just a few people. I've never looked back.

PREP TIME: 10 MINUTES • COOK TIME: 30 MINUTES • SERVES 2–3 AS A SIDE DISH

2–3 russet potatoes, scrubbed, peeled, and cubed

3 teaspoons kosher salt, divided

1 tablespoon olive oil

3 tablespoons butter

2 cloves garlic, minced

3 tablespoons mascarpone cheese or cream cheese

¼ cup heavy whipping cream

1 teaspoon ground black pepper

1 In a small pot, add potatoes. Cover potatoes with water and add 1 teaspoon salt. Place the pot on high heat and allow the water to come to a boil. Once water comes to a boil, lower heat to medium and allow to cook for 10 minutes or until potatoes are tender and easily pierced with a fork.

2 Meanwhile, in a small sauté pan, add butter and oil over medium heat. Allow butter to gradually melt until it turns golden brown. It will begin to bubble and have a nutty aroma. Add minced garlic and sauté for 1–2 minutes or until garlic is fragrant. Remove from heat and set aside.

3 Once the potatoes are cooked, drain and then return the potatoes to the pot. Pour garlic and butter mixture over the potatoes. Add mascarpone cheese, heavy cream, remaining 2 teaspoons salt, and pepper, and mash. Taste! Add extra salt or butter if needed.

VEGETARIAN, GRAIN-FREE, GLUTEN-FREE

CREAMY COCONUT RICE

1¼ cups basmati rice (other rice options do not work as well, and some burn)

1 (13.5-ounce) can full-fat, unsweetened coconut milk

½ cup water

1 teaspoon kosher salt

INSTANT POT

1 Mix together the canned coconut milk, water, and salt. Be sure the coconut cream is incorporated. Add rice and coconut milk mixture to IP. Stir to fully combine.

2 Lock lid and move valve to "Sealing." Cook on high pressure for 4 minutes. (If doubling the recipe, add 2 minutes to cooking time.) Allow for a natural pressure release for 7 minutes. Move valve to "Venting."

3 Uncover and give the rice a good stir. Serve immediately!

STOVETOP

1 Add the coconut milk and water to a pot. Add the rice and salt. Stir to incorporate.

2 Bring to a boil over medium-high heat. Turn the heat to low and cover. Cook for 10 minutes. Stir. Cover and cook for an additional 10 minutes.

3 Uncover and give the rice a good stir. Serve immediately!

VEGETARIAN, DAIRY-FREE

BACON-FAT SWEET POTATO FRIES

PREP TIME: 20 MINUTES • COOK TIME: 30 MINUTES • SERVES 4 AS A SIDE DISH

4–8 slices bacon (generally 1–2 slices for each person you're serving)

1 (15-ounce) bag frozen sweet potato fries or 2 pounds sweet potatoes

FROM FROZEN

1 Line a rimmed sheet pan with foil and add slices of bacon.

2 Place sheet pan in cold oven. Set temperature to 400°F.

3 After 10 minutes, flip each slice of bacon and place back in the oven for another 10 minutes. Check to see if the bacon is done to your preference. For crispier bacon, bake for another 2–3 minutes.

4 Remove sheet pan from oven. Place bacon on a plate lined with paper towel and set aside. Keep the parchment paper or foil with the bacon fat on the pan.

5 Place sweet potato fries on the pan. Use tongs to toss in the bacon fat. (If there is not much grease on the pan, add ½ tablespoon olive oil.)

6 Place sweet potato fries in the oven and bake according to package instructions.

7 Sprinkle with kosher salt or fleur de sel and serve warm!

FROM FRESH

1 Follow steps 1–4 above to make the bacon.

2 Scrub sweet potatoes and cut in half. Cut each half into strips. You should have around 20–25 strips total. Add to the sheet pan with the bacon fat.

3 Mix together 1 teaspoon kosher salt, ½ teaspoon freshly cracked black pepper, and 1 teaspoon garlic powder. Sprinkle over fries on the sheet pan and use tongs to toss the fries in the seasoning and bacon fat.

4 Bake in the 400° oven for 15 minutes. After 15 minutes, flip potatoes and cook for an additional 15 minutes or until fries are crispy.

Serve bacon along with the fries.

GRAIN-FREE, GLUTEN-FREE

EXTRA-CHEESY SWEET POTATOES AU GRATIN

PREP TIME: 30 MINUTES • COOK TIME: ABOUT 1 HOUR • SERVES 5–6 AS A SIDE DISH

2 pounds sweet potatoes

2 tablespoons butter, divided

1 tablespoon olive oil

1 yellow onion, chopped

½ tablespoon fresh thyme

1 teaspoon chopped fresh rosemary

1 teaspoon kosher salt

½ teaspoon freshly ground black pepper

1 cup heavy cream

1 cup (5 ounces) shredded Gruyère or fontina cheese

1 cup shredded Parmesan cheese, divided

1 Preheat oven to 400°F.

2 Peel and thinly slice sweet potatoes about ⅛-inch thick. To get even, thin slices, use a mandoline or slice with a sharp knife.

3 In a saucepan, add 1 tablespoon butter and olive oil. Once the butter is melted, add onion, thyme, rosemary, salt, and pepper. Sauté until the onion is soft, about 3–5 minutes. Set aside.

4 In another saucepan, add heavy cream and remaining 1 tablespoon butter. Bring to a simmer on medium-high heat. Once bubbling, remove from the burner and set aside.

5 In a 9×13 baking dish, add a layer of the sweet potatoes (it's okay if the potatoes slightly overlap each other). Then add a layer of the onion mixture. Then add some of the Gruyère and Parmesan cheese (only use ½ cup of the Parmesan for the layering, reserve the other ½ cup for step 8). Repeat layers of sweet potatoes, onion mixture, and cheese until all ingredients are used. The last item should be the onion mixture (do not add a top layer of Parmesan cheese yet).

6 Slowly pour the heavy cream sauce over the whole dish of sweet potatoes.

7 Bake for 40 minutes.

8 After 40 minutes, remove the baking dish from the oven. Set the oven to broil. Sprinkle the remaining ½ cup Parmesan cheese on top of the sweet potatoes and return to the oven. Broil until the cheese is melty and bubbly, about 5–10 more minutes.

9 Allow to sit for 10–20 minutes so the juices will settle and thicken. Serve!

GRAIN-FREE

PART 8

the art OF SOUP

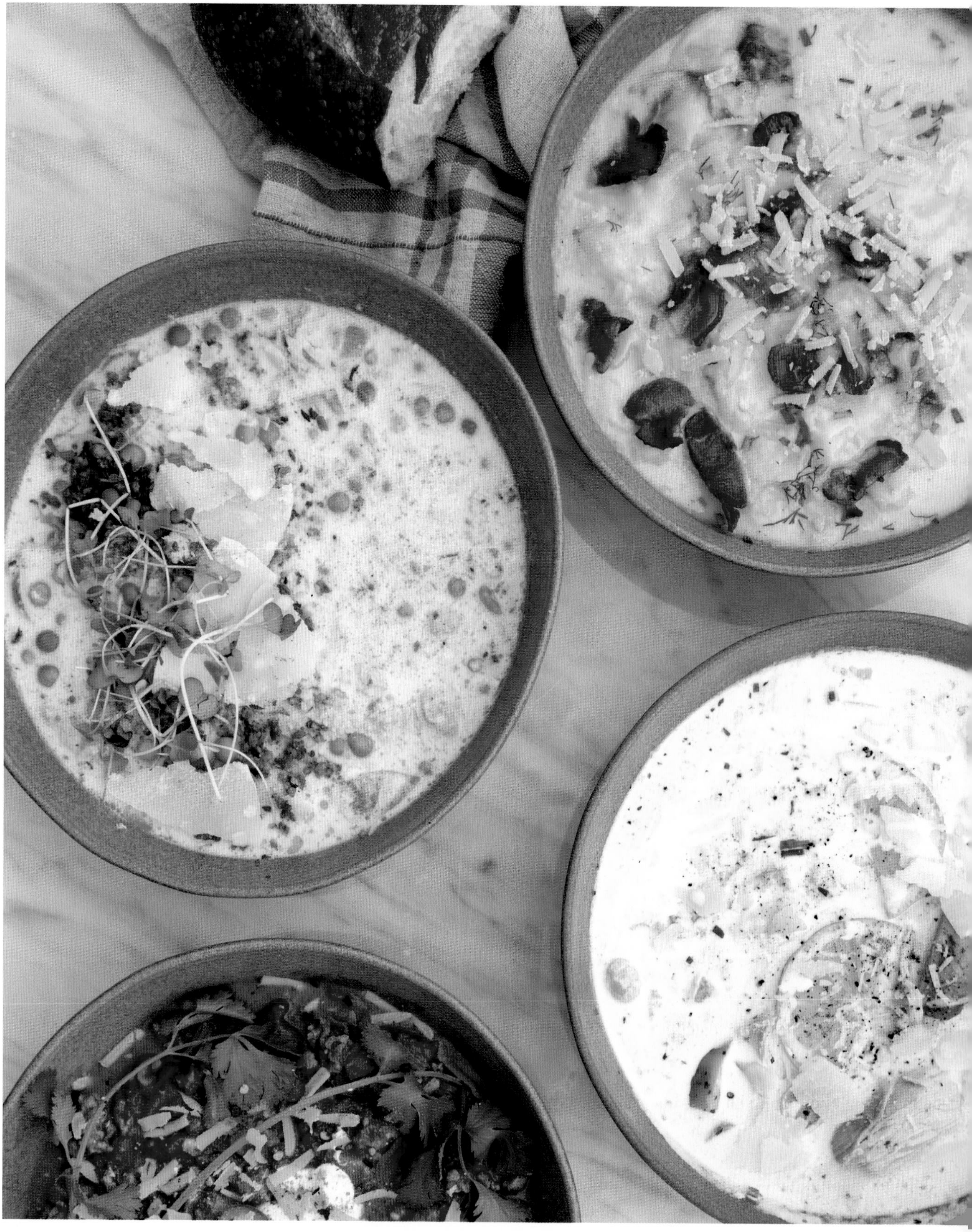

A CASE
for soup

Soup and I have a long, complicated relationship. Personally, I think soup always had a thing for me, but I didn't really start enjoying soup until my adult years. I used to have very lowkey-extra requirements for a meal:

- Must be presented with a fork and maybe even a knife
- Must come with sides
- Must require my concentration as I expertly construct the perfect bite with all that is on the plate

> **SOUP** *is a* *home cook's* **SECRET WEAPON.**

Then one day during a freak snowstorm in South Carolina, I wanted a bowl a really hearty bowl of soup. To celebrate this new craving and all that was to follow, I grabbed a bottle of champagne and shoved it into the snow that had accumulated on our deck. I then marched into the kitchen, grabbed my large dutch oven that had only known the likes of stews and roasts, and decided that was the day I would begin making soup.

I graduated from soup-resistant to soup-curious and am now the president of the soup fan club. In the fall and winter we do Soup Sundays, which is so perfect because it takes the guesswork out of what to have on Sundays and provides the most delicious leftovers for lunch the next day.

Soup is a home cook's secret weapon. In one pot you can pull together countless flavor profiles, from hearty and cozy to light and bright. Soup freezes well. It gets better over time. It travels well.

If you are already a card-carrying soup lover, welcome! If you're new to soup or you're not sure if you're a soup lover, I think you'll find a recipe in this book that will be your gateway to soups.

BEFORE WE SOUP! (A NOTE ON STOCK AND BROTH)

Stock and broth, while very often used interchangeably, do have some differences.

Stock. The main base of stock is bones. When you see a recipe that calls for bones (even bones without meat on them), you are making stock. Stock is typically thicker than broth because collagen is extracted from the bones during the cooking process, causing it to have that thick, gelatinous body to it. I almost always prefer using stock over broth because I like the thickness it brings, and it also tends to have an extra depth of flavor because it is typically made with veggies and additional seasonings.

Broth is made with the actual meat and rarely includes the bones or carcass. It is lighter in body since it does not have any collagen being extracted from the bones, and the main flavor truly is the meat (as opposed to stock, which can have a lot of other flavors from the vegetables and seasonings that are simmered with the bones).

For someone who loves soup as much as I do, it might come as a shock to you that I rarely make my own stock or broth. I have made it in the past, and I know it's delicious and has incredible health benefits. But there are so many delicious store-bought stocks and broths out there. I've made soup with homemade stock and I've made it with store-bought stock, and for me the taste is not so wildly different that it matters. And that is a personal preference.

BEST STORE-BOUGHT BROTH AND STOCK OPTIONS

There's a stock I love and have been using for years, but I decided to buy a bunch of different chicken broths and stocks from the most popular grocery stores to see if I've been missing out. Below are a few I want to highlight, along with my picks for gold, silver, and bronze medals.

1. *Kettle & Fire Organic Chicken Broth* ($$$). While this can be found in nearly every popular grocery chain, it is on the expensive side. It has great chicken flavor, but I probably won't use it to make soups

or stews since those need so much liquid. If, however, I wanted to drink a really healthy organic broth or make a delicious, rich sauce, I would go for this.

2. *365 by Whole Foods Market Organic Chicken Broth* ($). Simple, light flavor of chicken. Great price point.

3. *Bare Bones Organic Chicken Bone Broth* ($$$). Good chicken flavor and the spices are pronounced. Good for sipping, but I probably wouldn't buy it for soup because of the price point.

4. *Trader Joe's Organic Chicken Bone Broth* ($). Good chicken flavor and thickness. If you are looking for a stock that has that gelatinous consistency, this is it! Also note that though it's got the word *broth* in its name, "bone broth" is actually a stock.

5. *Better Than Bouillon Organic Roasted Chicken Broth* ($$). Very strong, rich chicken flavor. I know some people are very loyal to this, and I say use what you love. This does need to be prepared (1 teaspoon chicken base mixed with 8 ounces water). It also is very flavorful, so you might want to limit the amount of salt or seasonings a recipe calls for.

The Winners

1. *Kitchen Basics Original Chicken Stock* ($). Great flavor of chicken and seasonings but not so overpowering that it might mess with the other ingredients in my soup. This is the one I always reach for!

2. *Imagine Organic Free Range Chicken Broth* ($). Really great flavor of chicken and a hint of seasonings. This is a great backup to my Kitchen Basics.

3. *Pacific Foods Organic Free Range Chicken Stock* ($$). Light seasoning, hint of chicken. I grab this if I can't find Kitchen Basics or Imagine.

Whatever your stock or broth options are, the great thing about soup is that you get to control the flavors and make it as rich or as light as you like.

freezing SOUPS

Most soups do really well in the freezer and can last up to three months. Here are some golden rules to consider when deciding whether to freeze your soup:

- Avoid freezing soups with grains or noodles. These can get mushy and fall apart easily after being frozen and thawed. You can always make the base of the soup and freeze it and then add the noodles or grains when you reheat.
- If a soup recipe calls for dairy (such as cream, milk, or mascarpone), leave this ingredient out prior to freezing and add it only when you're ready to reheat and serve the soup. Sometimes dairy separates in frozen soups and can be a bit of a challenge when reheating.
- Make sure to label your soup so you know when you need to use it! I like to write the date that is three months from when I put it in the freezer.

There are lots of containers out there for freezing soup, but I prefer to just go with a gallon-size, freezer-safe baggie. This allows the soup to freeze in a nice thin block so it doesn't take up too much space. If I want to freeze individual portions, I place them in smaller freezer-safe baggies.

To thaw the soup, I move it to the refrigerator overnight and reheat on the stove or in the microwave the next day. To reheat the soup straight from the freezer, place the bag or container of frozen soup in hot water. Allow it to sit until it is liquid enough to be transferred to a bowl or pot to be fully reheated.

FAVORITE TOOLS
for making soup

The beautiful thing about soup is that generally it all comes together in one pot. You rarely need a lot of kitchen tools to bring together a delicious, rich, satisfying bowl of soup. That being said, I do have a few tools I always reach for when it's time to cook soup.

Garlic roller or frozen crushed cubes of garlic. You're no longer new here, so you know most of my recipes call for garlic. A garlic roller gets us a delightful naked clove of garlic in 10 seconds or less. I almost always use fresh garlic because nothing else compares, but the frozen and crushed cubes of garlic found in the freezer section are the next best option.

Trash bowl. There can be a lot of scraps and peels and whatnot when bringing a soup together. Having a bowl on the counter to collect all that trash makes everything easier.

Soup pot. You don't need a fancy or expensive pot to make soup, but if you're looking for a truly versatile and long-lasting pot, I highly recommend the 7¼-quart dutch oven from Le Creuset. It is so beautiful, conducts heat evenly, and can go from stovetop to oven to tabletop.

Soup ladle. For years I just used a regular stirring spoon to ladle out my soups, which is fine. But then I got a soup ladle, and it just makes getting the soup from the pot to the bowl a lot simpler—and for some reason more satisfying.

Soup bowls. We have a set of soup bowls we love. They hold a good amount of soup, are a little on the wide side so each bite of soup has a perfect amount of toppings, and are oven-safe, which I love for soups that I sprinkle with cheese and place under the broiler.

SOUP RECIPES

EASY HOMEMADE CHICKEN STOCK

If you make this on the stovetop, be sure you have a day you can hang at home to monitor the stock. Grab a good book or settle in to binge your favorite shows. Make a day of it!

PREP TIME: 10 MINUTES • COOK TIME: 7 HOURS

1 chicken carcass plus 4–5 raw chicken drumsticks with the meat (I like to add the drumsticks to infuse a little more chicken flavor into my stock)

4–5 carrots, unpeeled

4 stalks celery

1 small onion, peeled and cut in half

1 bunch thyme (about 10–15 sprigs)

1 bunch parsley

1 bunch dill

1 bulb garlic, unpeeled and cut in half lengthwise

2 teaspoons whole black peppercorns

½ cup apple cider vinegar

2 tablespoons kosher salt

2 bay leaves

6 quarts water (24 cups)

1 Put all ingredients into a large stock pot. Bring to a boil and then turn down to a simmer. Keep simmering on the stove, uncovered, for 7 hours.

2 Cool the stock slightly. Place a colander over a large bowl and pour the stock through, reserving the liquid. Some people then like to strain their stock through a cheesecloth, but this is optional. Let cool. Skim off any fat on the surface of the stock.

Makes 15 cups of stock

STORING THE STOCK

Refrigerate in an airtight container and use within 7 days. You can also freeze the stock. Add 2 cups cooled stock to small freezer-safe baggies (I like this method so I can easily stack the frozen broth). You can also pour stock into a soup cube tray, freeze, and put the cubes in a freezer bag to store in the freezer until use. Lasts up to 3 months in the freezer.

To use frozen stock, remove the amount needed from the freezer and thaw overnight in the refrigerator. If you need it thawed faster, put the baggie of stock in a bowl of hot water until it can be dumped into a pot, then heat on low until fully thawed.

DAIRY-FREE, GLUTEN-FREE, GRAIN-FREE

HOMEMADE CREAM OF MUSHROOM SOUP

This soup truly is delicious, but it's especially perfect for substituting in recipes that call for canned cream of mushroom soup. Try using it in my Welcome Home Pot Roast (page 122)!

PREP TIME: 5 MINUTES • COOK TIME: 30 MINUTES • SERVES 2–3

2 tablespoons butter

8 ounces shiitake or baby bella mushrooms, chopped

2 shallots, chopped

3 cloves garlic, minced

2 teaspoons kosher salt

1 teaspoon ground black pepper

2 cups vegetable broth

1 cup heavy cream

1 tablespoon cornstarch or arrowroot powder

1 tablespoon water

1 Melt the butter in a large soup pot over medium-high heat.

2 Add the mushrooms and sauté until golden brown, about 5–8 minutes.

3 Add the chopped shallots and cook until soft, about 3 minutes. Add the minced garlic and sauté until fragrant, about 1 minute.

4 Sprinkle salt and pepper over the mushroom mixture and stir to combine.

5 Add the broth slowly, using a wooden spoon to deglaze the pan as you add the liquid. Bring to a boil.

6 Stir in the heavy cream. Taste and add any additional salt or pepper to your liking. Reduce heat to medium-low and allow to simmer on the stove for 10 minutes or until thickened.

7 While simmering, in a small bowl make a slurry by adding 1 tablespoon cornstarch or arrowroot powder and 1 tablespoon water. Mix to combine.

8 After the soup has simmered for 10 minutes, slowly add the slurry to the soup and stir. Allow to simmer for an additional 3 minutes.

9 For a creamier soup, add 1 cup of the soup to a blender and blend until smooth. Add back to the soup pot. (Or place an immersion blender into the soup pot and blend until desired consistency.)

VEGETARIAN, GLUTEN-FREE

OPTIONAL: *Garnish as desired with fresh parsley, chopped fresh chives, or a swirl of balsamic vinegar for a deeper flavor. For a crunch, serve with Parmesan cheese crisps.*

191

GO-TO
weeknight soups

CHICKEN POT PIE SOUP

When my friend had her baby, I showed up at her door with two containers of this soup—one that they could freeze and the other that they could eat that evening. She later told me it was one of their favorite meals because it was a break from the many casseroles they had received. Now this is the meal I take anytime I sign up for a Meal Train.

 There is a lot of chopping for this dish! Prep ahead of time by chopping everything earlier in the day and placing in the refrigerator until you are ready to bring this soup together.

PREP TIME: 10 MINUTES • COOK TIME: 40 MINUTES • SERVES 5–6

4 tablespoons butter

½ yellow onion, diced

4 carrots, peeled and diced

4 stalks celery, thinly sliced

2 cups cooked, shredded chicken or turkey

½ teaspoon dried Italian herb blend

2 teaspoons kosher salt

½ teaspoon ground black pepper

½ teaspoon dried sage

2½ cups chicken broth

2 tablespoons cornstarch or arrowroot powder

2 tablespoons water

¼ cup heavy whipping cream or half-and-half (makes soup creamier but can be omitted)

½ cup frozen peas (optional)

1 Melt the butter in a large soup pot over medium-high heat.

2 Add the onion, carrots, and celery. Cook, stirring, until the onions start to turn translucent, about 5 minutes.

3 Stir in the chicken or turkey, then add the Italian herbs, salt, pepper, and sage. Stir to coat the veggies and meat with the seasonings. Pour in the chicken broth and bring to a boil. Reduce the heat to low and let simmer for 20 minutes.

4 Meanwhile, mix together equal parts cornstarch or arrowroot powder and water. Add the mixture to the soup and stir. Allow to simmer for 5 minutes.

5 When it starts to thicken, stir in the cream if using. Let the sauce bubble up and thicken for about 3 more minutes. If it seems overly thick, splash in a little more broth. Mix in frozen peas if using, and let cook for an additional 2 minutes. Taste and adjust seasoning to your liking. Serve warm.

> **TIP:** *I love making this soup with leftover turkey a few days after Thanksgiving.*

CRISPY SAUSAGE CHOWDER

PREP TIME: 10 MINUTES • COOK TIME: 35 MINUTES • SERVES 5–6

1 tablespoon olive oil

1 pound ground Italian sausage

½ cup white wine, divided

2 shallots, chopped

3 stalks celery, chopped

1 pound red potatoes, cut into chunks

3 teaspoons kosher salt

1 teaspoon ground black pepper

2 cloves garlic, minced

4 cups chicken broth or stock

1 cup frozen peas

1 cup heavy whipping cream

Parmesan cheese and freshly cracked black pepper for serving

1 In a large soup pot over medium-high heat, add 1 tablespoon olive oil. Add the ground sausage and sauté until browned and a little crispy, about 6–8 minutes. Remove the sausage to a paper towel–lined plate or bowl (this will help remove excess fat and oil). Set aside.

2 If your soup pot has more than 1 tablespoon oil and fat from the sausage, remove extra with a spoon or by wadding up some paper towel and dipping it into the soup pot to soak it up.

3 To the soup pot, add ¼ cup white wine or chicken stock to deglaze. Add the shallots, celery, potatoes, salt, and pepper. Allow to sauté until shallots are tender, about 3–4 minutes. Deglaze again with the remaining ¼ cup white wine. (A double deglaze adds even more flavor!)

4 Add the garlic and mix to combine. Add the broth. Bring to a boil and then turn the heat to medium-low and allow to simmer until the potatoes are fork-tender, about 15 minutes.

5 Add the sausage back to the soup pot. Add the peas and the heavy whipping cream. Allow to heat through gently, about 5 minutes.

Ladle into bowls and add a sprinkle of freshly ground black pepper and salt and some freshly grated Parmesan cheese. Serve!

CHICKEN TACO SOUP

1 tablespoon olive oil

1 yellow onion, chopped

3 cloves garlic, minced

2 cups cooked, shredded chicken

2 teaspoons chili powder

½ tablespoon kosher salt

1 teaspoon ground black pepper

2 teaspoons cumin

juice of 1 lime

1 (4-ounce) can diced green chiles

1 (28-ounce) can crushed tomatoes

2½ cups chicken broth

1 cup whole corn kernels, frozen

1 (15-ounce) can black beans, drained and
  rinsed

TOPPINGS

sliced avocado

shredded cheese

sour cream

lime

tortilla chips

cilantro

hot sauce

1 In a soup pot, heat olive oil over medium heat. Sauté onion until soft, about 4–5 minutes. Add garlic and stir until fragrant, about 1 minute. Add shredded chicken and stir in chili powder, salt, pepper, cumin, lime juice, and green chiles. Sauté for a few minutes, allowing the aromatics to coat the chicken.

2 Add tomatoes and broth. Bring to a boil, then turn the heat to low and simmer, covered, for 10 minutes.

3 Stir in corn and beans. Simmer for 10 more minutes.

4 Taste and add salt and pepper as needed.

Scoop into bowls and top with avocado slices, cheese, sour cream, lime wedges, tortilla chips, cilantro, and hot sauce.

GLUTEN-FREE , DAIRY-FREE OPTIONAL

RESTORATIVE CHICKEN SOUP

Whenever I am feeling under the weather, I want a big bowl of this chicken noodle soup. It's so comforting, and I feel restoration coming back to my body.

PREP TIME: 15 MINUTES • COOK TIME: 30 MINUTES • SERVES 5–6

1 tablespoon olive oil

3 carrots, peeled and chopped

3 stalks celery, thinly sliced

1 small onion, chopped

2 cloves garlic, minced

2–3 cups cooked, shredded chicken

1 teaspoon dried oregano

2 teaspoons kosher salt

½ teaspoon ground black pepper

8 cups chicken broth or stock

3 sprigs fresh thyme

1 bay leaf

1 (16-ounce) package egg noodles
(or 2 zucchini for zoodles)

WITH EGG NOODLES

1 Heat a soup pot on medium-high heat with the olive oil. Add the carrots, celery, and onion and sauté for 5 minutes or until the onions start to become translucent but not browned. Add the minced garlic and sauté until fragrant, about 1 minute.

2 Add the shredded chicken, oregano, salt, and pepper. Stir to coat the chicken and veggies with the seasonings. Add the chicken broth, top with the sprigs of thyme and bay leaf, and bring to a simmer.

3 Add egg noodles, bring to a boil, and then turn the heat to medium-low to simmer for 15 minutes.

4 Remove thyme sprigs and bay leaf.

WITH ZUCCHINI NOODLES

1 Follow steps 1–2 above.

2 Allow the soup to simmer over medium-low heat for 5 minutes and prepare your zoodles. Make them with a spiral vegetable slicer or with a julienne peeler. Add the zoodles to the soup and simmer for another 10 minutes.

3 Remove thyme sprigs and bay leaf.

Ladle into bowls and enjoy!

GRAIN-FREE OPTIONAL, DAIRY-FREE

LEMONY CHICKEN AND POTATO SOUP

I created this soup when I desperately needed summer weather to arrive. I wanted something bright, like the sunshine. This soup did just that and then gained a small cult following. This was the first soup I made in the Instant Pot. I was determined to use my IP for more than just potatoes and roasts. It is a perfect dish to make in the IP if you are just learning to use this appliance.

PREP TIME: 15 MINUTES • COOK TIME: 45 MINUTES TO 5 HOURS • SERVES 5–6

1 tablespoon olive oil

2 carrots, peeled and sliced

1 small yellow onion, chopped

1 pound Yukon Gold potatoes, quartered

3 cloves garlic, minced

1 teaspoon dried oregano

1 teaspoon Italian seasoning

1 tablespoon kosher salt

1 teaspoon ground black pepper

1½–2 pounds boneless, skinless chicken breasts or chicken thighs

4 cups chicken stock

¼ cup mascarpone cheese (or ½ cup heavy whipping cream)

¼ cup freshly squeezed lemon juice

Be sure to add the lemon at the end. It will surprise you!

INSTANT POT METHOD

1 Set the IP function to "Sauté." Add 1 tablespoon oil and allow to heat up.

2 Add carrots, onion, and potatoes. Sauté for 3 minutes.

3 Add garlic, oregano, Italian seasoning, salt, and pepper. Sauté for 1 more minute.

4 Add chicken and chicken stock. Place the lid on the IP and set the valve to "Sealing."

5 Cook on high pressure for 10 minutes.

6 Allow the pressure to release naturally for about 5–10 minutes. After 5–10 minutes, move the valve to "Venting" and remove the lid, then set to "Sauté" to keep the soup cooking as we prepare for the next step.

7 Move chicken to a bowl or cutting board and shred with two forks (or you can shred with a stand mixer or hand mixer). Place chicken back in the IP.

8 Add the mascarpone cheese (or heavy cream) and mix until melted and combined. Then add lemon juice. Stir until incorporated. Turn off IP (or put on "Keep Warm" setting).

SLOW COOKER METHOD

1 If your slow cooker has a sauté function, set to sauté and follow steps 1–4 of IP method. If not, just add all ingredients except mascarpone and jemon juice into the slow cooker and cover.

2 Cook for 3 hours on high or 5 hours on low. The chicken is done when it hits 165°F. It should easily shred with a fork.

3 Follow steps 7–8 of IP method.

Ladle into bowls and serve with freshly cracked black pepper and freshly grated Parmesan cheese.

GLUTEN-FREE

"IT'S DONE ALREADY?" CHICKEN SALSA SOUP

PREP TIME: 10 MINUTES • COOK TIME: 25 MINUTES • SERVES 5–6

1 tablespoon olive oil

½ medium white onion, diced

2 cloves garlic, minced

2 teaspoons kosher salt

6 cups chicken broth or stock

juice of 2 limes

2 cups cooked, shredded chicken

1 (16-ounce) jar salsa verde

1 (15-ounce) can cannellini beans (optional)

1 cup frozen corn (optional)

TOPPINGS

hot sauce

sour cream

shredded cheddar cheese

fresh cilantro

sliced avocado

lime wedges

1 Heat a soup pot over medium-high heat. Add the olive oil, and once oil is hot, add the diced onion. Cook, stirring, for about 3 minutes, until onion has softened. Add minced garlic and sauté until fragrant, about 1 minute.

2 Add all remaining ingredients and bring to a boil.

3 Lower heat to medium-low and allow the soup to simmer for 10–15 minutes, stirring occasionally.

Ladle into soup bowls and serve with your favorite toppings!

GLUTEN-FREE, DAIRY-FREE OPTIONAL

LOADED BAKED POTATO SOUP

PREP TIME: 15 MINUTES • COOK TIME: 45 MINUTES • SERVES 4–5

6 slices bacon, divided

1 tablespoon butter

2 stalks celery, chopped

½ sweet onion, chopped

3 cloves garlic, minced

3 large russet potatoes (about 3 pounds), peeled and cubed

3½ cups chicken or vegetable stock

½ cup mascarpone cheese or cream cheese

1 tablespoon kosher salt

1 teaspoon ground black pepper

½ cup shredded sharp cheddar cheese

1 teaspoon chopped fresh chives

1 teaspoon chopped fresh dill

sour cream and additional cheddar cheese for serving

FOR BACON

1 Line a large rimmed baking sheet with parchment paper or foil. Lay 5 bacon slices (reserving 1 slice) in a single layer.

2 Place baking sheet in the cold oven and set oven to 400°F. After 10 minutes, flip the bacon and bake for an additional 10 minutes. Place bacon on a paper towel–lined plate and set aside.

FOR SOUP

1 In a large soup pot over medium-high heat, add reserved slice of bacon. (We want some bacon fat for our soup, but frying all the bacon can create quite a mess, and we only need about 1 teaspoon of bacon fat!) If you prefer not to use bacon fat, substitute 1 tablespoon oil. Cook bacon fully, flipping every 45 seconds to cook both sides. Remove bacon to plate with the rest of the slices.

2 In the soup pot with bacon fat, add butter. Once butter is melted, add celery and onion. Sauté for 3 minutes, until the onion is translucent. Add garlic and stir until fragrant, about 1 minute.

3 Add the cubed potatoes. Sauté for about 3 minutes. Pour in chicken stock (the stock should cover the potatoes). Bring to a boil and cook for 15–20 minutes, until potatoes are easily pierced through with a fork.

4 Add mascarpone cheese, salt, and pepper. Mix until combined.

5 Turn off the heat. With a potato masher or immersion blender, lightly mash potatoes.

6 In a high-capacity blender, blend 1 cup of the soup for about 30 seconds. Please remember not to put the lid fully on the blender with hot liquid in it! Use a loose dish towel to cover the top of the blender. (You could also just continue to use the immersion blender to your preferred creaminess.)

7 Stir in the sharp cheddar cheese and fresh chives and dill.

Serve with crumbled bacon, sour cream, and additional cheddar cheese.

GLUTEN-FREE

CHILI

There's no debate here—chili absolutely deserves a seat at the soup table!
I love a good, hearty chili, especially in colder months. It's like a big, cozy
hug. So if you need a hug, these chilis have got you.

COLD WEATHER CHILI

PREP TIME: 15 MINUTES • COOK TIME: 30 MINUTES • SERVES 5-6

4–5 slices of bacon (optional)

1 red bell pepper, seeded and chopped

1 poblano pepper, seeded and chopped

1 jalapeño, seeded and chopped
 (omit if you do not want spicy chili)

1 red onion, chopped

3 cloves garlic, chopped

1½ pounds 90/10 ground sirloin (or 80/20
 ground beef)

2 tablespoons tomato paste

2 teaspoons kosher salt

1 tablespoon chili powder

1 teaspoon cumin

¼ teaspoon cayenne pepper

½ cup red wine, beef stock, or dark beer
 (choose your liquid!)

1 (28-ounce) can crushed tomatoes

1 (15-ounce) can black beans, drained and
rinsed (optional)

TOPPINGS

hot sauce

sour cream

shredded cheddar cheese

crumbled bacon

additional jalapeños

fresh cilantro

TIP: *To give this chili more depth of flavor,
use red wine or dark beer rather than beef
stock.*

1 In a soup pot, fry 4–5 slices of bacon, if using. Remove bacon to paper towel–lined plate and reserve 1 tablespoon bacon fat in the pan. Crumble bacon for topping the chili with later. (If you choose not to fry bacon, just add 1 tablespoon oil to soup pot.)

2 Add all peppers, onion, and garlic to pot and sauté on medium-high heat until veggies are tender, about 3–4 minutes.

3 Add beef and crumble, sautéing until browned, about 5 minutes.

4 Add tomato paste, salt, chili powder, cumin, and cayenne. Mix to combine for about 2 minutes.

5 Add your liquid of choice to deglaze the pan.

6 Add tomatoes and black beans (if desired).

7 Bring to a boil and simmer for at least 10 minutes. Taste and adjust seasonings as needed.

Ladle into bowls and add your favorite toppings like hot sauce, sour cream, cheddar cheese, crumbled bacon, jalapeños, and cilantro.

DAIRY-FREE OPTIONAL, GLUTEN-FREE

HARVEST CHILI

This is the official soup of fall! I created this recipe several years ago when I wanted to join in the pumpkin craze but preferred something savory instead of sweet. This chili is not sweet or overly pumpkiny. It is the perfect combination of fall flair and savory flavor.

There is a lot of chopping for this chili, so plan for this or chop everything the morning of. Also, this is delicious when made with pumpkin ale, but if you can't find that, any ale will work!

PREP TIME: 10 MINUTES • COOK TIME: 40 MINUTES • SERVES 6

1 tablespoon olive oil

1 pound ground turkey (or ground chicken)

1 pound ground hot or regular Italian sausage (chicken or pork)

1 onion, diced

1 bell pepper, chopped

3 carrots, peeled and diced

4 cloves garlic, chopped

1 tablespoon chili powder

1 tablespoon ground cumin

1 tablespoon dried oregano

2 teaspoons kosher salt

6 ounces pumpkin ale (half a beer; use gluten-free if desired)

1 (15-ounce) can pumpkin puree (NOT pumpkin pie filling)

1 cup chicken stock

TOPPINGS

shredded cheese

plain Greek yogurt or sour cream

green onions

cilantro

red pepper flakes (for those who like a little more heat)

1 In a dutch oven or large soup pot, heat the oil over medium-high heat. Add the ground turkey and sausage. Cook, crumbling, until the meat begins to brown and caramelize, about 7–8 minutes.

2 Add onion, bell pepper, and carrots. Cook until veggies are softened, about 5 minutes. Add garlic and cook for 1 minute.

3 Add chili powder, cumin, oregano, and salt and cook until very fragrant, 2–3 minutes.

4 Deglaze with the pumpkin ale, scraping up the browned bits from the bottom of the pot. Allow to cook for 2 minutes.

5 Add the canned pumpkin and chicken stock. Stir to incorporate all the ingredients. Bring to a boil, reduce to medium-low heat, and simmer for 20 minutes. If chili gets too thick, add a little bit more chicken stock.

6 Taste and add additional salt or red pepper flakes (for more heat) if needed.

Dish out chili and add your choice of toppings, like shredded cheese, plain Greek yogurt or sour cream, green onions, fresh cilantro, or red pepper flakes.

DAIRY-FREE OPTIONAL, GLUTEN-FREE OPTIONAL

WHITE CHICKEN CHILI

PREP TIME: 10 MINUTES • COOK TIME: 35 MINUTES • SERVES 5-6

1 tablespoon olive oil

1 medium onion, chopped

2 cloves garlic, minced

2–3 cups cooked, shredded chicken

¼ cup white wine (or chicken broth)

1 (15-ounce) can great northern or navy beans, drained and rinsed

1 cup frozen corn

2 cups chicken broth

1 (4-ounce) can diced green chiles

2 teaspoons kosher salt

1 teaspoon ground cumin

1 teaspoon dried oregano

½ teaspoon ground black pepper

¾ cup plain Greek yogurt (optional)

½ cup heavy whipping cream (optional)

TOPPINGS

avocado

cherry tomatoes, halved

hot sauce

1 In a large soup pot over medium-high heat, add the oil. Sauté onion in oil until translucent, about 3 minutes. Add garlic and stir until fragrant, about 1 minute.

2 Add shredded chicken. Stir to combine and then slowly pour in the white wine (or chicken broth), using a wooden spoon to deglaze the pan. Let sauté for another 2 minutes.

3 Add beans, corn, chicken broth, green chiles, and seasonings. Bring to a boil. Reduce heat and simmer, uncovered, for 20 minutes.

4 At this point you can taste and add any additional salt or pepper if needed, then serve just like this. But for a super creamy chili, proceed to step 5!

5 Remove from heat. Stir in Greek yogurt and cream.

Ladle into bowls and top with fresh avocado, cherry tomatoes, and hot sauce!

GLUTEN-FREE, DAIRY-FREE OPTIONAL

PART 9

HOME *cookish*

summer
chicken cutlets,
page 217

These are recipes I keep in my back pocket for evenings when I want something home cooked but without the effort. Everyone who eats these meals will think you were in the kitchen bringing together an elaborate meal. But, just between you and me, we'll know it is home cookish.

WONTON SOUP

6 cups chicken stock

12 frozen potstickers (I like the ones from Trader Joe's)

2 tablespoons soy sauce

1 teaspoon fish sauce

1 tablespoon rice wine vinegar

½ teaspoon sesame oil

juice from 1 lime

1 teaspoon kosher salt

1 inch ginger, minced (or one cube frozen ginger from Trader Joe's)

2 cloves garlic, minced

TOPPINGS

red chili peppers

green onions, chopped

fresh cilantro

lime wedges

In a large soup pot, add all ingredients except the potstickers. Bring liquid to a boil over medium-high heat and then add the potstickers. Turn down heat to medium-low. Simmer for about 10 minutes until the potstickers are cooked through.

Ladle into bowls and garnish as desired with a few slices of chili pepper, green onions, fresh cilantro, and a squeeze of fresh lime juice!

VERY EXTRA AVOCADO TOAST

PREP TIME: 5 MINUTES • COOK TIME: 5 MINUTES • SERVES 2

2 slices sourdough or favorite bread, toasted

1 avocado, peeled, pitted, and mashed

2 tablespoons crumbled goat cheese

2 slices cooked bacon, crumbled

1 tablespoon maple syrup

finishing salt such as fleur de sel

1 Spread mashed avocado evenly over both slices of toast.

2 Sprinkle goat cheese and crumbled bacon over the avocado. Drizzle with maple syrup.

3 Sprinkle with salt. Enjoy!

VEGETARIAN, GRAIN-FREE, GLUTEN-FREE, DAIRY-FREE

I TAKE MY EGGS . . .

Mastering how to make perfect eggs exactly the way you like is not only achievable but also ensures you have a quick meal at the ready whenever the craving strikes.

PREP TIME: NONE • COOK TIME: 5–8 MINUTES

FRIED EGG

1 Crack egg into a small dish or ramekin, making sure not to break the yolk.

2 Place a small nonstick skillet over medium-high heat and add 1 tablespoon oil or butter. Once fat is heated, slowly pour the egg into the pan.

3 Allow the bottom of the egg to cook until it can easily slide around the pan. You can test this by gently shaking the pan after about 1 minute.

4 Continue to gently shake the pan every once in a while to keep the egg in contact with the oil. For a runny yolk, cook for 2–3 minutes. For over-medium or over-hard, flip the egg after 2–3 minutes and cook for an additional 2–3 minutes. Serve with a sprinkle of salt and freshly cracked pepper.

POACHED EGG

1 Crack an egg into a small dish or ramekin, making sure not to break the yolk. In a small saucepan, add 4 cups water and bring to a gentle boil. Add 1 teaspoon salt and 2 teaspoons vinegar. Reduce heat to medium.

2 Using a spoon, swirl the liquid in a circular motion to create a whirlpool effect in the water. While the water is still swirling, remove the spoon and gently pour the egg into the vortex.

3 For an over-easy poached egg, cook 2–3 minutes. For over-medium, cook 4–5 minutes. Remove the egg with a slotted spoon. Serve with a sprinkle of salt and freshly cracked black pepper.

soft-boiled egg

medium-boiled egg

hard-boiled egg

SOFT-, MEDIUM-, AND HARD-BOILED EGGS

1 Place eggs into a saucepan and cover with water until eggs are fully submerged.

2 Bring water to a boil over medium-high heat. Remove pan from heat and cover.

   a. For hard-boiled eggs, keep covered for 13 minutes.

   b. For medium-boiled eggs, keep covered for 8 minutes.

   c. For soft-boiled eggs, keep covered for 6 minutes.

3 Remove eggs and place in a bowl filled with enough ice water to cover eggs and stop them from cooking further. After 5 minutes, remove from ice bath, peel, and eat!

JAMMY EGG IN THE INSTANT POT

(This is by far my favorite way to make an egg!)

1 Add a steamer basket or circular wire rack to IP. Place eggs in basket. Pour 1 cup water into the IP. Cook on low pressure for 5 minutes.*

2 Instantly release the pressure and transfer the eggs to a bowl filled with enough ice water to cover the eggs and stop them from cooking further. After 5 minutes, remove from ice bath, peel, and eat!

If your Instant Pot does not have a low pressure setting, place on high pressure and cook for 3–4 minutes.

fried egg

poached egg

jammy egg

RAMEN NOODLES

This is maybe my favorite go-to meal when I'm craving takeout! It comes together in about 10 minutes and is wildly delicious.

PREP TIME: NONE • COOK TIME: 10 MINUTES • SERVES 1

1 package instant ramen noodles (discard flavor packet if your ramen came with it)

1 tablespoon butter

1 tablespoon coconut sugar or brown sugar

1 tablespoon soy sauce

1 teaspoon fish sauce

1 teaspoon sriracha

frozen peas or any leftover veggies such as sugar snap peas (optional)

juice from half a lime

OPTIONAL TOPPINGS

nori seasoning

sliced avocado

toasted sesame seeds

1 Prepare ramen according to package instructions (omitting flavor packet), then drain water and return saucepan with noodles to the burner over medium-high heat.

2 Add butter, coconut sugar, soy sauce, fish sauce, sriracha, and any veggies. Stir to combine until butter is melted and all ingredients are incorporated. Turn off heat and add lime juice.

Dish noodles into a bowl and serve with favorite toppings like nori, sliced avocado, and toasted sesame seeds.

FANCY NOT FUSSY SHEET PAN NACHOS

PREP TIME: 10 MINUTES • COOK TIME: 10 MINUTES • SERVES 3–4

1 (15.4-ounce) can refried beans

1 bag (10–12 ounces) tortilla chips

1 bell pepper, chopped

½ red onion, chopped

1 cup cooked chorizo (optional)

8 ounces sharp cheddar cheese, shredded

4 ounces goat cheese, crumbled

OPTIONAL TOPPINGS

Pickled Red Onions (page 83)

sliced avocado

jalapeños

sour cream

fresh cilantro

hot sauce

fresh lime

1 Preheat oven to 400°F.

2 Place parchment paper or foil on a large sheet pan.

3 Scatter tortilla chips across the pan. Spoon dollops of refried beans evenly over the chips (I do this directly from the can). Use the back of the spoon to spread the beans over each chip.

4 Evenly scatter bell pepper and red onion over chips. (Add chorizo at this time if using.) Sprinkle with sharp cheddar cheese.

5 Place pan in the oven and cook until cheese is melted and bubbly, about 5–8 minutes.

6 Remove the pan from the oven, sprinkle with crumbled goat cheese, and serve.

Load nachos with toppings of choice such as pickled red onions, sliced avocado, jalapeños, sour cream, fresh cilantro, and hot sauce. Add lime wedges throughout the sheet pan for people to grab and squeeze over their nachos. Serve straight from the sheet pan! Sharing optional.

VEGETARIAN OPTIONAL

"GET ME OUT OF TAKEOUT MODE" ROAST

This is THE dish I make when I have been in an eating-out rut and I need something to get me back in the kitchen and enjoying a home-cooked meal. This roast does take time to cook, but bringing it together can take less than 5 minutes! It is perfect for making tacos, burrito bowls, and sandwiches, or just serving next to your favorite veggies.

PREP TIME: 5 MINUTES • COOK TIME: 2–6 HOURS • SERVES 5–6

1 (3-pound) chuck roast

3 teaspoons kosher salt

1 teaspoon ground black pepper

1 tablespoon olive oil

1 (16-ounce) jar pepperoncini with juice

5 cloves garlic, smashed

SLOW COOKER

1 Pat your roast dry and season with salt and pepper.

2 Optional: If your slower cooker has a sauté function, set it to sauté. Add 1 tablespoon olive oil. When oil is shimmering, add the roast and brown 2–3 minutes on each side.

3 Add roast to the slow cooker along with jar of pepperoncini and garlic cloves.

4 Cook on low for 6 hours or high for 4 hours. The meat is done when it easily shreds with a fork.

INSTANT POT

1 Pat your roast dry and season with salt and pepper.

2 Optional: Set IP function to "Sauté." Add 1 tablespoon oil. When oil is shimmering, add roast and brown on each side (about 2–3 minutes per side).

GRAIN-FREE, GLUTEN-FREE, DAIRY-FREE

3 Add garlic cloves and pour in jar of pepperoncini as well as ¾ cup water or beef broth.

4 Close and lock the lid. Turn valve to "Seal."

5 Set IP to high pressure for 1 hour 15 minutes.

6 Allow the IP to naturally release for about 15 minutes. Move the valve to "Venting" and open the lid.

DUTCH OVEN

1 Preheat oven to 325°F.

2 Pat your roast dry and season with salt and pepper.

3 Optional: Add 1 tablespoon olive oil to the dutch oven and place on medium-high heat. Once oil is shimmering, add roast and brown on each side (about 2–3 minutes per side).

4 Add jar of pepperoncini and garlic cloves.

5 Cover with lid and bake for 3 hours.

Shred meat and serve with the pepperoncini. Use to make tacos, burrito bowls, nachos, or sliders!

EAT, PRAY, LOVE PASTA

 The sauce comes together fast, so be sure to have everything prepped and ready to go before you get to the stove!

PREP TIME: 10 MINUTES • COOK TIME: 30 MINUTES • SERVES 4–5

1 pound rigatoni or other pasta of choice

1 tablespoon olive oil

½ sweet onion, thinly sliced

1 (7-ounce) jar sun-dried tomatoes in oil, drained and cut into strips

3 cloves garlic, minced

2 teaspoons kosher salt

½ teaspoon ground black pepper

¼ cup dry white wine or vegetable stock

1 cup heavy whipping cream

¼ cup freshly grated Parmesan cheese

1 Prepare pasta according to package instructions.

2 In a sauté pan over medium-high heat, add the oil. Once oil is heated, add onions and sauté until soft, about 3–5 minutes.

3 Add sun-dried tomatoes and sauté for another 2 minutes. Add garlic, salt, and pepper and stir until fragrant, about 1 minute.

4 Deglaze the pan by slowly pouring in the white wine or vegetable stock and scraping up any browned bits with a wooden spoon.

5 Reduce heat to medium and add cream. Bring to a boil, stirring occasionally.

6 Add Parmesan cheese and mix to combine. Allow sauce to simmer until cheese melts. If the sauce is too thick, add ¼ cup vegetable stock.

Serve sauce over pasta. Sprinkle with additional Parmesan cheese and freshly cracked black pepper. Enjoy!

VEGETARIAN

CLEAN-OUT-THE-FRIDGE FRIED RICE

This is the perfect meal if you have leftover rice and lots of veggies you need to use up.

PREP TIME: 5 MINUTES • COOK TIME: 15 MINUTES • SERVES 1–2

1 tablespoon olive oil

1 onion, thinly sliced

2 cups cooked (or leftover!) basmati or jasmine rice

1 cup diced assorted veggies

3 tablespoons sesame oil

¼ cup soy sauce

2 cloves garlic, minced

2 eggs, beaten

4 green onions, roughly chopped

1 Heat a large sauté pan or braiser over medium-high heat and add 1 tablespoon oil.

2 Once oil is heated, add onion and sauté until softened, about 2 minutes.

3 Add rice and any other veggies you have on hand (bell pepper, carrots, zucchini, etc.) along with 3 tablespoons sesame oil. Sauté 2–3 minutes, then add soy sauce and garlic. Sauté 2–3 more minutes.

4 Add eggs. Stir constantly as egg cooks, about 2 minutes. Remove pan from the heat and add chopped scallions.

VEGETARIAN

SUMMER CHICKEN CUTLETS

PREP TIME: 15 MINUTES • COOK TIME: 25 MINUTES • SERVES 6–8

3–4 boneless skinless chicken breasts (to make 6–8 chicken cutlets)

2 eggs, beaten

juice from half a lemon

½ cup all-purpose flour (or tapioca starch for gluten-free)

1½ teaspoons kosher salt

1 teaspoon ground black pepper

2 cups panko (gluten-free panko works too)

½ cup grated Parmesan cheese

2 tablespoons olive oil, divided

jar of favorite marinara sauce

Using your favorite store-bought marinara sauce makes this dish come together so fast!

1 Using a sharp knife, cut the chicken breasts into cutlets by filleting them. To do this, simply place your hand on top of the breast and run your knife horizontally through the chicken. Once you get about halfway through, lift the top half and hold it up while continuing to cut through the chicken.

2 Your cutlets should be ¼ to ½ inch thick. If chicken is still too thick after filleting, you can place each cutlet in a plastic bag and use a meat tenderizer or small, heavy skillet to pound out the fillet until it is thinner. (This is rarely necessary.)

3 Place eggs in a shallow bowl. Add lemon juice and whisk to combine. Combine flour, salt, and pepper into a second shallow bowl (be sure to mix thoroughly). In a third shallow bowl, combine panko and Parmesan.

4 Working with one cutlet at a time, dip chicken into flour mixture, then eggs, and then panko mixture, pressing well to coat. Set aside and repeat with remaining cutlets.

5 In a large sauté pan over medium-high heat, add 1 tablespoon olive oil. Once heated, add

GLUTEN-FREE OPTIONAL

217

half the chicken cutlets. Cook for 5–6 minutes, then flip and cook for 5 more minutes or until golden. Place the cooked cutlets on a baking rack resting on a baking sheet. (A baking rack helps to keep the breading from getting soggy, but if you don't have one, you can just place the cutlets on your baking sheet.) Add remaining 1 tablespoon olive oil to the pan. Wait for the oil to heat up (the pan is already hot, so this takes only about 30 seconds), then add the rest of the cutlets and cook.

6 Set oven to broil. Place all cutlets in a single layer in an oven-safe baking dish. Add a good spoonful of marinara sauce to each cutlet and then some extra shredded Parmesan cheese. Broil until cheese is melted and bubbly (about 4–5 minutes).

Serve chicken cutlets with salad greens, fresh steamed broccoli, or your favorite pasta.

SPICED CHICKPEAS WITH TZATZIKI

PREP TIME: 10 MINUTES • COOK TIME: 15 MINUTES • SERVES 5

1 tablespoon olive oil

1 (15.5-ounce) can chickpeas, drained and rinsed

½ red onion, diced

1 red bell pepper, chopped

2 cloves garlic, minced

½ teaspoon paprika

1 teaspoon cumin

1 teaspoon kosher salt

juice from half a lemon

FOR SERVING

pitas

hummus

Tzatziki (page 165)

lettuce greens

crumbled feta cheese

1 In a large sauté pan over medium heat, add olive oil. Once oil is heated, add chickpeas, onion, and bell pepper. Sauté for 5–8 minutes until soft.

2 Add garlic, paprika, cumin, and salt. Mix to combine and sauté for an additional 3 minutes.

3 Add lemon juice. Stir and remove from heat.

4 Spread hummus inside your pitas. Then spread tzatziki all around. Add spiced chickpeas, lettuce greens, and feta cheese. Enjoy!

VEGETARIAN

SWEET & SPICY CHICKEN STUFFED SWEET POTATOES

If you have leftover chicken and leftover Sweet Heat Wing Sauce, this dish comes together so fast! This is also perfect if you already have leftover baked sweet potatoes.

PREP TIME: 10 MINUTES • COOK TIME: ABOUT 1 HOUR • SERVES 4–5

4 sweet potatoes (slightly less than ½ pound each)

2 cups shredded cooked chicken (you can use a store-bought rotisserie chicken or cook your own chicken breasts and shred the meat)

½ cup Sweet Heat Wing Sauce (page 164), plus extra for drizzling

Cilantro Lime Yogurt Sauce (page 162)

fresh cilantro for garnish

OVEN METHOD

1 Preheat oven to 400°F.

2 Scrub sweet potatoes and cut in half lengthwise (this will give you 8 halves).

3 Line a baking sheet with aluminum foil. Oil flesh side of the sweet potato halves and place flesh side down on baking sheet. Bake for 45–55 minutes, until the flesh of the sweet potato is tender. (While the potatoes are baking, prepare the chicken mixture and the Cilantro Lime Yogurt Sauce.)

4 Remove the sheet pan from the oven and set the sweet potatoes aside on a platter. Turn on broiler.

5 In a bowl or directly on the foil-lined baking sheet, toss shredded chicken with ½ cup Sweet Heat Wing Sauce. Spread evenly over the sheet pan. Place under broiler for 5 minutes or until chicken gets a little crispy.

6 To serve, top each sweet potato half with about ¼ cup chicken. Drizzle with additional

Sweet Heat Wing Sauce and Cilantro Lime Yogurt Sauce. Garnish with fresh cilantro!

INSTANT POT METHOD

1 Place steamer basket in IP and add 1 cup water.

2 Scrub sweet potatoes and place on top of the steamer basket.

3 Secure and lock the lid and move the valve to "Sealing."

4 Cook at high pressure for 25 minutes.

5 Allow to release naturally and move the valve to "Venting."

6 Remove sweet potatoes and set aside on a platter. Turn on broiler.

7 Follow steps 5 and 6 of the oven method.

EVERYDAY
food and wine
PAIRINGS

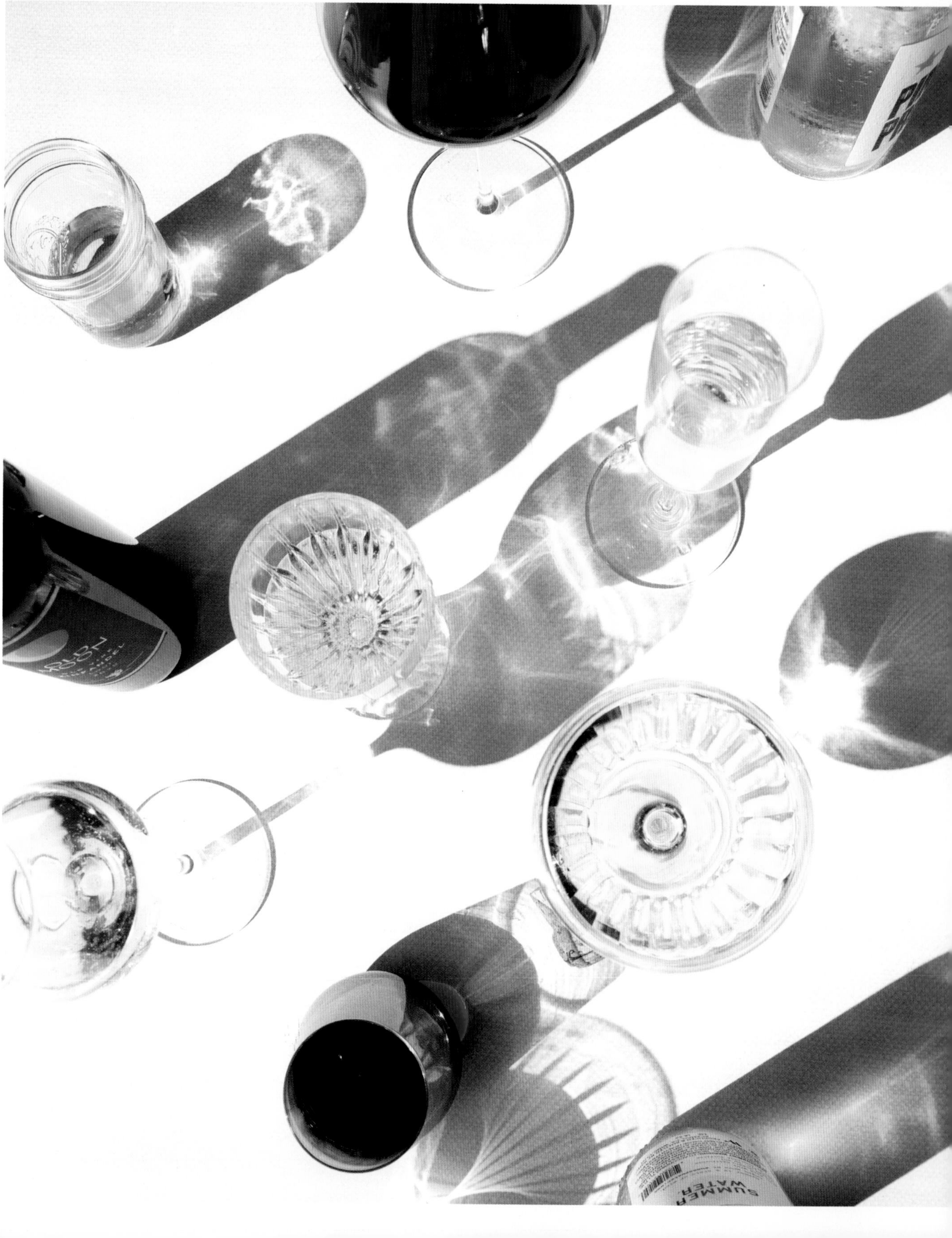
SUMMER WATER

In the summer of 2021, Jeremy tricked me into taking a Level 2 wine-tasting course from the internationally recognized Wine and Spirit Education Trust. It was a five-week intensive course that required fifteen hours of class time and over twenty hours of independent study time. We both passed the exam with merit. I say Jeremy tricked me because I thought this was going to be like a fun Napa getaway except remote. Drink wine all the time. But when I tell you I didn't even study this hard to get my undergraduate degree . . . well, it was a wild ride.

Maybe you're like, "But it's only Level 2?" To that I would say, you weren't there. You didn't see the maps. Maps on every page. Maps for every variety of grape. Maps to explain the maps. More maps than wine.

I blindly walked into this course thinking it was going to be all wine tasting and calling out notes: "Blackberry!" "Wet soil!" "Oak!" "My vacation to Barcelona in 1999!" And it turns out it was an *intensive* maps class complete with in-depth discussions on soil and weather and altitude. Because this is all-important to winemaking.

I don't think the everyday home cook needs to have such an in-depth knowledge of food and wine pairing, so I'm taking the knowledge I have and whittling it down to the most approachable and important lessons. Then you too can become an everyday expert at food and wine pairing.

In the following sections, you will see choices for each type of wine. I tried to select wines that are widely distributed and listed them as follows:

1. First choice—my favorite option based on tasting notes and how the wine is made.

2. Second choice—the next best option, which has similar notes to my first choice.

$. Budget choice—has similar notes but won't break the bank. You cannot go wrong with this less expensive option!

A GUIDE FOR
how to pair wine
WITH FOOD

If you fall too far down the wine-tasting rabbit hole, you'll run into some very pretentious tasters and rules. But this guide is for the everyday home cook, and while there are some helpful guidelines, the number one rule is to drink what you enjoy! We each have different preferences and palates because we are altogether different humans. You will really begin to hone your wine preferences as you take note of what you like and don't like in wines.

GUIDELINES FOR FOOD AND WINE PAIRING

The first step to successful food and wine pairing is to understand the components of wine and how to identify them on your palate. It will be helpful if you pour yourself your favorite glass of wine as you move through this section. To write this section, I poured a glass of one of my favorite and most approachable cabernets: Freakshow from Michael David.

Swirling and Smelling Wine

Yes, we do swirl our wine! Swirling can seem pretentious, but allowing the wine to interact with oxygen allows it to open up so you can smell all the aromas of the wine.

Smelling wine comes after swirling. This is so important because it prepares your palate for what you're going to taste—kind of like walking into your house after a long day and smelling a pot roast that's been slow cooking while you were gone. Smelling the pot roast makes your mouth water, and that's because taste and smell are connected.

To keep it simple, here is a high-level chart of the most common aromas that can be detected in wine.

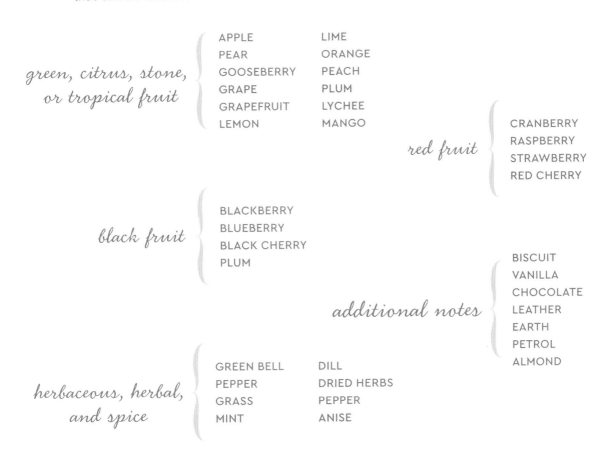

green, citrus, stone, or tropical fruit

APPLE
PEAR
GOOSEBERRY
GRAPE
GRAPEFRUIT
LEMON

LIME
ORANGE
PEACH
PLUM
LYCHEE
MANGO

red fruit

CRANBERRY
RASPBERRY
STRAWBERRY
RED CHERRY

black fruit

BLACKBERRY
BLUEBERRY
BLACK CHERRY
PLUM

additional notes

BISCUIT
VANILLA
CHOCOLATE
LEATHER
EARTH
PETROL
ALMOND

herbaceous, herbal, and spice

GREEN BELL
PEPPER
GRASS
MINT

DILL
DRIED HERBS
PEPPER
ANISE

As you taste more wine and get more comfortable with naming what you are smelling, this becomes more intuitive.

In my cabernet I smell a lot of dark fruit like blackberry and plum. I also smell some vanilla.

If you are really at a loss, it can be helpful to download the Vivino app and look up your wine there, as it will list the aromas and tasting notes you should get from a particular wine. As you hone this skill you can smell the wine, name what you smell, and then check Vivino to see if you are correct!

FOOD & WINE BESTIES

food

FATTY: ribeye, pork butt, cheese, fried chicken, avocado

SALTY: popcorn, french fries, oysters, cured meats, olives

SPICY: pad thai, curries, spicy shrimp pasta, Nashville hot chicken

GRILLED: burgers, BBQ, steaks, kabobs

ACIDIC: red pasta sauces, tomatoes, citrus

wine

TANNIC: cabernet sauvignon, syrah, Nebbiolo, malbec

ACIDIC: champagne, dry sparkling wine, pinot noir, riesling

SWEET: sweet riesling, gewürztraminer, Moscato

BARREL-AGED: chardonnay, zinfandel, bordeaux, syrah

MEDIUM-BODY, ACIDIC: Beaujolais, Chianti, Rhône blends

Tasting Wine

Tasting comes after smelling, which is essential because our palate is perfectly prepared. Cabernet sauvignons are known for having big personalities. They are big in almost every way.

When we taste a wine, we are looking for the following:

Sweetness: dry, off-dry, medium, or sweet

Acidity: low, medium, or high

Tannin: low, medium, or high

Alcohol: low, medium, or high

Sweetness: This one is the easiest to identify. Is the wine sweet or dry? My cabernet is dry.

Acidity: The pulp of the grape is what gives wine its water, sugars, acids, and flavors. As you learn more about wine and grape varieties, you will be able to know if your wine will be high or low in acid even before tasting it. Another great way to know about the acidity in your wine is how your palate reacts when you take a sip. If you feel the sensation like your mouth is watering, it is acidic. The deeper you feel this sensation, the more acidic it is, and vice versa. My cabernet has medium acidity.

Tannin: The seeds, skins, and stems of the grapes are what give wine its tannin. As a general rule, white wines have no tannin because the skins and stems are removed from the grapes. A great way to explain the sensation of tannin is to think of something bitter, like black tea that has steeped way too long. If you take a sip of wine and your mouth immediately goes dry, you have a wine with high tannin. My cab is high in tannin.

Alcohol: All bottles of wine need to list their ABV (alcohol by volume) content. In some cases, this can help identify whether or not a wine is of good quality. Red wines and dessert wines should have high ABV. You want to see 13.5% to 15% ABV for a red wine. White wines tend to have a lower ABV, anywhere between 12% and 13.5% (except for dry rieslings, which we will cover later). My cabernet has an ABV of 14.5%, which is excellent, so I know this wine is high in alcohol—but I can also know this by taste. When you taste a wine and there is a slight burning sensation in your throat after you swallow, this indicates the wine is high in alcohol.

After tasting and moving through the different categories, I've found my cabernet is dry, medium to high in acidity, high in tannin, and high in alcohol.

HOW TO ADVENTURE THROUGH THIS GUIDE

I created this guide so you can actually go through it as if you are at a wine tasting. To that end, I recommend wines you will want to try as a way of reinforcing the lesson. I also pair the wines with a dish for you to make so you can see how food and wine can come together to make each other shine. Typically, it's important to start with food first and then choose a wine to pair with it. It's easier to narrow down a wine that pairs with a dish once you understand the flavors of your dish. But to really dive into the lessons on the different varieties of grapes, I will first teach on the wine and then provide the recipe that pairs with the wine.

A note on the selections: I tried to choose wines that are widely available, but I also offer guidance on how to ask about certain varieties at your local wine shops and vineyards.

Pair sweet wines with foods that have heat.

SWEET WITH HEAT!

Pair smoky foods with wines that have oak notes.

SMOKE WITH OAK!

LET'S GET
bubbly

The first thing you need to know about bubbles is that they pair with virtually everything! Like popcorn. Or fried chicken. Or french fries. Or a New York strip steak.

VARIETIES OF BUBBLES

Champagne: Champagne can only come from Champagne, France. If you ask for champagne and someone opens a bottle of bubbles from California, this is not champagne but sparkling wine. Champagne is made in the traditional method in Champagne, France, and can be very labor intensive, which is why it can have more complex notes like brioche and almonds and also why it is generally more expensive than sparkling wine. Champagne is also typically high in acid.

When you see "Méthode Traditionnelle" on a bottle of bubbles, you know it has been through a more extensive process to produce the sparkling wine or champagne, and it will have extra depth of flavor. Méthode Traditionnelle starts with a base wine. Usually it is a mix of different grape varieties, which you can find listed on the back of the bottle (most commonly chardonnay and pinot noir). The wine goes through two fermentation processes, and it's during the second fermentation that the bubbles are formed.

This second fermentation also forms a sediment in the wine called *lees*. We will learn more about lees as these are present in other types of wines, but what is important to know is that lees imparts flavors of biscuit and bread. So if you ever taste a bottle of sparkling wine or white wine and get notes of bread or biscuit, you will know the wine has been aged on lees. This process can take a year or longer.

After several more steps (which are fascinating but also mind-boggling) the bubbles are almost ready to be sealed. It just needs to be topped off with a mixture of wine and sugar. The winemaker gets to determine the percentage of wine to sugar, and this is where the labeling for wine comes from. The following are the labels for the most dry bubbles (very little sugar has been added) to sweeter bubbles (a good amount of sugar has been added):

Brut nature: Bone dry. It can be tart and needs to age in the bottle for several years.

Extra brut/dry: Dry, but not as much as brut nature. Can be citrusy.

Brut: A hint of sweetness. Most sparkling wines are in this category. The sugar gives a little richness to the wine.

Sec or dry: Moderately sweet.

Demi-sec: Detectable sweetness.

Doux: This is the sweetest of sparkling wines.

Cava: This is the Spanish term for a traditional method of sparkling wine produced in Spain. Cava typically has medium acid and is not as bold as champagne. It can be fruity and acidic.

Prosecco: This is sparkling wine made in northeastern Italy. Unlike champagne, which is made from chardonnay and pinot noir grapes, prosecco is only made using prosecco (also called glera) grapes. Prosecco is most famous for being made using the tank method, which means the wine is fermented in a large tank instead of individual bottles. Prosecco is fresh, fruity, and simple with notes of green apple and melon. It is much less complex than champagne.

Sparkling wine: This can come from anywhere and can also be made in any form. For example, you will see that a bottle of Schramsberg (a sparkling wine from California) is made using the Méthode Traditionnelle. If a bottle of sparkling wine has the word *Crémant* on the label, that means it was made outside of Champagne, France, but is just as high-quality as champagne.

The most helpful thing to note about bubbles is that the label Méthode Traditionnelle means these bubbles will have more complex flavors and notes of bread and biscuit that come from lees. It took longer to make and went through a more intense process.

I love using prosecco or other inexpensive bottles of bubbles when I am adding something like orange juice for a mimosa or for making a French 75. If I want to celebrate something with a nice bottle of bubbles that will be enjoyed on its own, I like to find a bottle of bubbles with the label Méthode Traditionnelle!

THE BUBBLY GUIDE

champagne $$$
From: Champagne, France
Flavor: Complex, with toast and biscuit notes
Drink: By itself
For: Special occasions and nice dinners

prosecco $
From: Italy
Flavor: Fruity (white peach, melon), acidic, mildly sweet
Drink: With orange juice to make mimosas
For: Everyday gatherings or casual Sundays

cava $-$$
From: Spain
Flavor: Fruity, acidic (lemon, grapefruit), clean
Drink: In cocktails that call for bubbles!
For: Everyday gatherings or casual Sundays

sparkling wine $-$$$
From: Anywhere!
Flavor: Simple and fruity to complex and nutty
Drink: Alone or add fruit juice, depending on price
For: Any occasion

THE BUBBLY GUIDE: GATHERING

Special occasion or gifting: Spring for something nicer, like a brut champagne or sparkling wine.

> *Top picks:* Dom Perignon Brut Champagne, Perrier Jouet Belle Epoque Brut Champagne, Veuve Clicquot Vintage Brut Champagne, or Schramsberg "J Schram" Sparkling Wine
>
> *Local wine shop or vineyard:* Ask for a special-occasion bottle of bubbles with brioche notes that is made in the Méthode Traditionelle.

Picnic or casual outing: Go for something bright, acidic, and easy on the wallet like Cava.

> *Top picks:* Borrasca Cava or Rondel Brut Cava
>
> *Local wine shop or vineyard:* Ask for bubbles that are bright with notes of lemongrass and grapefruit—something less complex and less expensive than champagne.

Boozy brunch: Pick up a bottle of bubbles that is inexpensive and a little sweeter, such as prosecco.

> *Top picks:* PoLa Marca Prosecco or Borrasca Prosecco DOCG
>
> *Local wine shop or vineyard:* Ask for dry bubbles with a hint of sweetness like honeysuckle or white peach, which plays well with mixers (such as orange juice for mimosas).

TASTING BUBBLES

1 **Veuve Clicquot** (this one retails for about $50, but many stores carry a smaller version so you don't have to buy a whole bottle. I'm putting it on the list because it truly conveys the power of bubbles!)

2 **Schramsberg Blanc de Noirs**

3 **J Vineyards Sparkling Cuvee California**

Make sure your bubbles have been in your refrigerator for at least several hours (or all day) before opening! For this tasting, I will be pouring the Veuve Clicquot, which is champagne since it comes from Champagne, France.

Tip your glass slightly and slowly pour the bubbles in. Continue to pour as the bubbles subside.

serving temperature: well chilled or ice cold (38–45°F)

on the nose: notes of ripe fruit, also poached pear and baked apple, a bit of citrus like lemon, and maybe even some grated ginger

sweetness: dry

acidity: medium to high acidity

tannin: none

alcohol: medium to low

on the palate: notes of brioche and biscuit as well as poached pear, baked apple, and grated ginger

This bottle of champagne is well balanced with cream and citrus notes, which pairs perfectly with cheese.

I love a cheese board with sparkling wine. It's one of the most perfect pairings that pleases almost everyone. The platter in this section is different from the traditional cheese and charcuterie board. It's a little more festive and reminiscent of the holiday season—I call it The Cozy Platter.

This platter brings together creamy, citrusy, and savory notes. The star of the show is the baked brie with bright cranberry sauce. The best rule of thumb with any cheese platter is to start with the star of the show and build around that—keeping all flavor profiles (including salty, sweet, and savory) in balance.

Here are some of my favorite tips for building a charcuterie board:

- Keep it tight! A sparse cheese board can look sad and uninviting. Make sure to use an appropriately sized board relative to the size of your gathering.

- Prep some of the pairings together on the board so guests know what goes together. Go ahead—put some turkey and cranberry sauce on a mini croissant, or a piece of sharp cheddar on the appropriate cracker.

- Add the large items first and then use small items like fruits and nuts to fill in any gaps in the platter.

- Make sure to have plates and utensils around the platter so people won't be shy about grabbing the food.

- Color is fun! Use any leftover herbs you might have (like rosemary, thyme, or sage) to make the platter come alive.

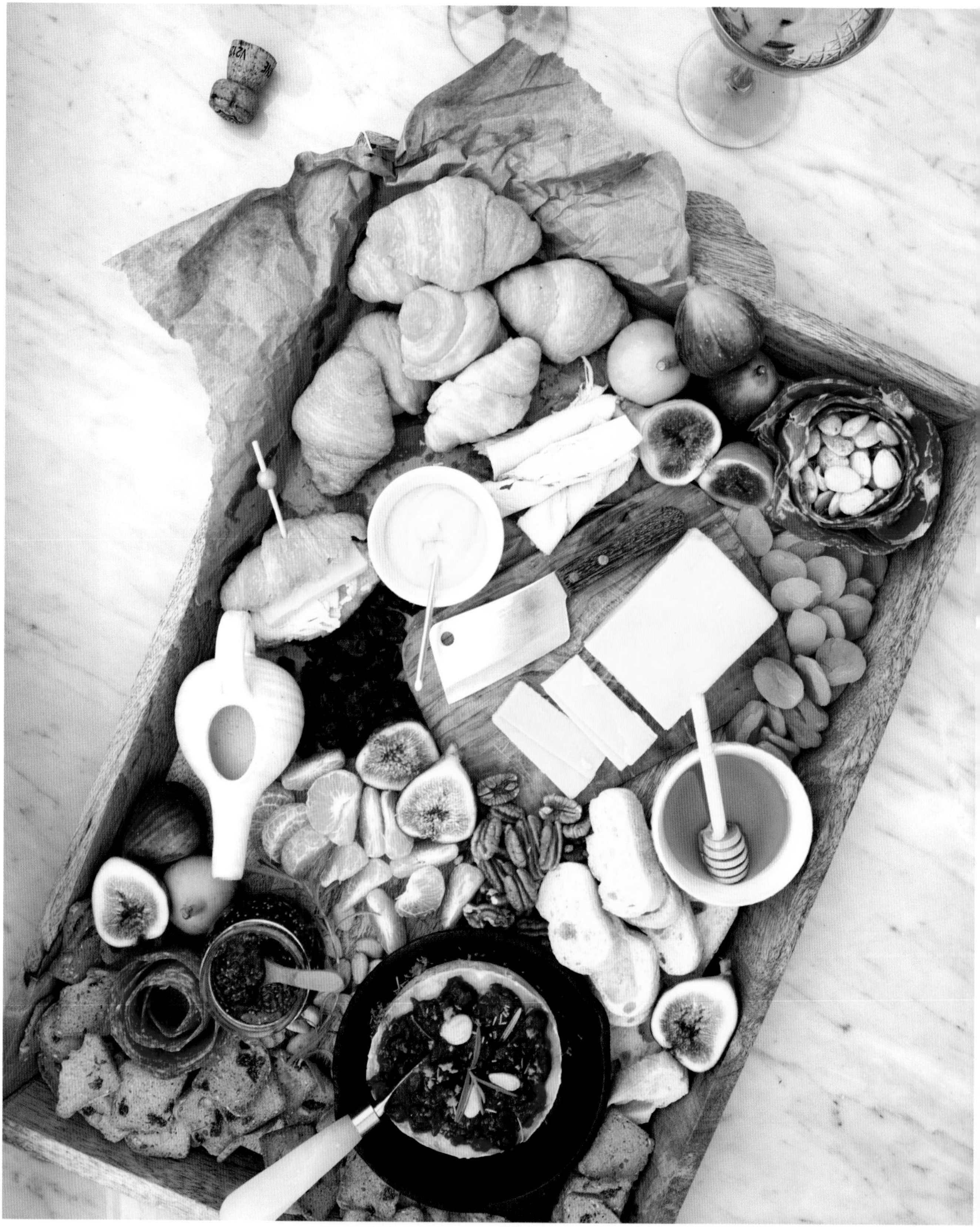

THE COZY PLATTER

This is the absolute perfect platter to prepare for winter holidays or after Thanksgiving. Use leftovers from your feast for this spread. You can even add a little mason jar of leftover gravy.

wine pairing options

1 Veuve Clicquot
2 Schramsberg Blanc de Noirs
3 J Vineyards Sparkling Cuvee California

CHEESE

Sharp white cheddar
Wheel of brie

MEAT

Coppa or salami
Turkey (I like to use deli slices of smoked turkey or leftover Thanksgiving turkey)

FRUIT

Fresh figs
Dried apricots
Dried cranberries
Fresh oranges or clementines

DIPS

Fig jam
Dijon mustard
Cranberry sauce (I use canned whole berry)

FOR SERVING

Crispy baguette or mini baked croissants/ crescent rolls

Favorite crackers (I like the cranberry hazelnut crackers from Raincoast and cornbread crisps from Trader Joe's)

Hazelnuts, walnuts, or pecans

ADDITIONAL INGREDIENTS FOR BAKED BRIE

½ cup cranberry sauce
1 tablespoon coconut sugar or brown sugar
zest of one small orange or clementine
1 teaspoon vanilla extract

BAKED BRIE WITH CRANBERRY SAUCE

1 Preheat oven to 425°F. Slice the top rind off the round of brie. With a spoon, smoosh down some of the cheese in the middle to create a small well. Wrap the brie in foil, leaving the top exposed, so it will not melt all over the place while baking. (If you have a small oven-safe bowl or ramekin, you can place the brie into this dish instead of wrapping in foil.)

2 Place a second piece of foil or parchment paper on a sheet pan (this will help in transferring the brie to the platter). Place the foil-wrapped brie (or the dish with the brie) on the sheet pan. Bake for 8 minutes or until it is oozing.

3 In a small saucepan over medium-high heat, add ½ cup cranberry sauce, 1 tablespoon brown sugar or coconut sugar (if you want your sauce to be more on the sweet side, add a second tablespoon), orange zest, and vanilla.

4 Stir together until the ingredients have incorporated and come to a simmer. You can also mash some of the berries in the pan if you would like a smoother sauce.

5 Remove brie from the oven. Using the parchment paper or foil "handles," transfer to your platter (or carefully transport your hot baking dish). Pour cranberry sauce over the brie and garnish with chopped nuts.

ASSEMBLING THE PLATTER

1 With the brie in the middle of the platter, build around it!

2 Add the additional cheese and meats to the outer edges of the platter.

3 In little mason jars (or any kind of jars) add the fig jam, Dijon mustard, and leftover cranberry sauce. I place the fig jam and the Dijon mustard next to the sharp cheddar, as they pair together. Place the cranberry sauce in the opposite section.

4 Add the items to be used for eating the cheese and spreads. I group the mini croissants with the meats and crackers near the brie.

5 Fill in any gaps with fruits and nuts.

And that's The Cozy Platter! It's festive and puts leftovers to the most glamorous use.

ROSÉ
all day

There's a reason "Rosé all day" is a popular phrase! Rosé is known for being easy to drink and appropriate during most hours of the day. Besides the easy-drinking character of rosé, its color is what it's known for.

A common misconception is that rosés are just a mixture of red and white wines, but that's usually not the case. Red, white, and rosé wines all begin with crushing the grapes. The difference is when the skins are removed. With rosé, after a few hours the wine is drained from the skins before any fermentation begins, which is what gives them their pink hue. Another difference with rosés is they are typically ready to be enjoyed the year that they are bottled instead of undergoing a long aging process.

A lot of wines are titled by their grape variety. For example, chardonnay is made from the chardonnay grape. However, rosés are a blend made from a variety of grapes such as pinot noir, grenache, and syrah red grapes. Their flavor profile is fresh and fruity with a little citrus. Generally you will pick up notes of red fruit like strawberries, cherries, and raspberries.

Rosés can be either dry or sweet. Sweet rosés like white zinfandel are not as popular as dry rosés, so in this lesson we will be tasting a dry rosé.

1 Chateau Miraval Côtes de Provence Rosé

2 Chateau d'Esclans Whispering Angel Rosé

$ Chateau d'Esclans The Palm Whispering Angel

I will be opening the Chateau Miraval.

serving temperature: chilled or cold (about 45–50°F).
on the nose: notes of red fruit, like strawberry and raspberry.
You also might get some notes of melon or grapefruit.
sweetness: dry
acidity: high
tannin: none
alcohol: medium
on the palate: strawberry, melon, and some citrus. It's bright and juicy!

This bottle of rosé will pair with a variety of dishes because of its high acidity and bright flavors. Pairing it with something as earthy and savory as mushrooms really allows its red fruit notes to shine, and its acidity cuts through rich foods like the cheesy sausage mixture in our next recipe: Mascarpone Stuffed Mushrooms.

MASCARPONE STUFFED MUSHROOMS

This is the appetizer you want to be known for! Take it to every holiday party and gathering and watch as the mushrooms disappear within seconds! I almost called these magic mushrooms because they are so delicious you'll have an out of body experience, but then I realized people might think the secret ingredient is marijuana, and I assure you it is not. So Mascarpone Stuffed Mushrooms it is!

The stuffing is a decadent mix of shallots, fresh sage, garlic, Parmesan cheese, and sweet Italian sausage. It is the ultimate savory flavor. What binds the mixture together and makes these stuffed mushrooms extra creamy is the mascarpone cheese. Mascarpone has just two ingredients: whole cream and citric acid, which makes the cream thick and tangy. I can eat it by the spoonful.

PREP TIME: 10 MINUTES • COOK TIME: 50 MINUTES • SERVES 6–8 AS AN APPETIZER

wine pairing options

1 Chateau Miraval Cotes de Provence Rosé

2 Chateau d'Esclans Whispering Angel Rosé

3 Chateau d'Esclans The Palm Whispering Angel

1 pound whole baby bella or white mushrooms

2 tablespoons olive oil

¾ pound (or 3 links) sweet Italian sausage, casings removed

1 tablespoon chopped fresh sage

1 shallot, chopped

2 cloves garlic, minced

2 teaspoons kosher salt

1 teaspoon ground black pepper

¼ cup dry white wine or chicken stock

5 ounces mascarpone cheese

⅓ cup freshly grated Parmesan cheese

chopped fresh parsley (optional, for garnish)

I make the stuffing the day before my gathering and store it in the refrigerator. The next day, about 30 minutes before guests arrive, I fill my mushrooms with the mixture and pop them in the oven. I serve them right from the cast-iron skillet. (Also, your house will smell amazing!)

1 Preheat oven to 350°F.

2 Remove and finely chop the stems from the mushrooms. Set aside. Place mushroom caps hollow side up in a baking dish or cast-iron skillet large enough to hold them in a single layer. Set aside.

3 Heat 2 tablespoons olive oil in a sauté pan over medium heat. Add sausage, crumbling it with a spatula or wooden spoon. Cook sausage for 8–10 minutes, stirring frequently, until completely browned.

4 Add chopped mushroom stems and cook for 3 more minutes. Stir in sage, shallot, garlic, salt, and pepper and cook for another 2 minutes, stirring occasionally.

5 Slowly pour in white wine or chicken stock while scraping up the browned bits to deglaze the pan.

TIP: *If you prefer to make this a meal instead of an appetizer, try my Creamy Italian Sausage Pasta (page 95), which has the same flavor profile as the mushrooms and pairs perfectly with the selected wines.*

6 Add mascarpone and Parmesan cheese. Continue cooking until the sausage mixture is creamy and the cheese has completely melted.

7 Fill the inside of each mushroom cap with the sausage mixture (about 1 tablespoon per cap). Bake for 30 minutes, until the stuffing is crusty and the mushrooms have cooked through. Serve warm.

This recipe calls for a dry white wine for deglazing (which is also a good pairing for these mushrooms), but a rosé really shines too. You can open a bottle of white (I like using pinot gris or sauvignon blanc) and then either enjoy a glass while you cook or offer it to your guests. Alternatively, you can deglaze with chicken stock.

THE MAKEUP
of white wine

Welcome to the wonderful world of white wine! Here's a fun fact to really mess with your head: not all white wine is made from white grapes. Of all the types of wine, whites have the least contact with the skin of the grape. As a reminder, the skin of the grape gives wine its color, tannin, and flavor. The pulp, which is where most of the flavor comes into play for white wine, gives wine its water, sugar, acids, and flavors.

The fermentation process for white wine begins right after the grapes are pressed and the liquid is extracted. During fermentation, yeast eats the natural sugars occurring in the juice and turns it into alcohol. The yeast can be naturally occurring or can be added by the winemaker. After fermentation, the yeast dies and falls to the bottom of the fermentation vessel. This yeast forms a layer of dead cells called lees, which you may remember reading about in the bubbles section. When the wine is ready to age, the winemaker can either remove the lees or stir up the lees throughout the aging process to keep the wine in contact with it.

Lees are what give white wines their biscuit and bread notes. Most aromatic white grape varieties, or wines that have floral and herbal notes, are not put in contact with the lees because the bread and biscuit notes can overwhelm those flavors. Aromatic white wines include riesling, viognier, and gewürztraminer.

A process called *malolactic conversion* also takes place after fermentation. This is carried out by the bacteria. Bacteria lowers the acidity in the wine and can give it buttery flavors. Malolactic conversion almost always happens in red wine making, but the winemaker can decide if they want their white wine to have buttery notes or not. If they are making wine from an aromatic grape like a riesling, they will stop the malolactic conversion from happening. But if they are making chardonnay and want those buttery notes, they will allow the malolactic conversion to happen.

Lees give white wines their bread and biscuit notes. Malolactic conversion gives wines their buttery notes.

Another important factor in creating white wine is the vessel in which it ages. The most common vessels are made of stainless steel or oak.

Stainless-steel vessels can be used for both fermentation and the aging process. The stainless steel does not affect the flavor of the wine. These vessels can also be sealed airtight to prevent oxygen from interacting with the wine, which would change its flavor. Stainless vessels keep the wine very crisp and clean on the palate.

Oak barrels add flavor and allow oxygen to interact with the wine, which can also add flavor and generally gives the wine fuller body. Oak barrels enable flavors such as dried fruit, hazelnut, almond, and even caramel to come through in the wine.

The way the oak is toasted while a barrel is being made gives the wine aromas of sweet spice and charred wood. A brand-new barrel is called "new oak," and it can give the wine a lot of higher intensity flavors such as vanilla, coconut, charred wood, and spice. The more a barrel is used, the duller these flavors become.

If you taste a chardonnay that is creamy and buttery, you can be sure that it was aged with the lees in an oak barrel.

IT DOESN'T HAVE TO BE BUTTERY
to be chardonnay

Let's go to France! Chardonnay is the main white grape variety of the Burgundy region in France. If you see a wine labeled "white burgundy," it is most likely made from the chardonnay grape in that region. Throughout the different regions you will come across very different chardonnays due to the changes in climate. These can range from some with high acidity all the way to others that are full-bodied and have complex layers of flavors.

Chablis is a village in the Burgundy region that produces wine from chardonnay grapes. If you are holding a bottle of wine that says Chablis (and not chardonnay), that's because France puts the name of the appellation on the bottle, not the grape variety. So all Chablis is chardonnay. Another common French chardonnay is Pouilly-Fuissé, which means it's a chardonnay from the Pouilly-Fuissé region of France.

I specifically picked a Chablis for this tasting because I want people who don't like buttery chardonnays to give this one a try. Chablis is dry with high acidity and flavors of apple and lemon. It is very approachable and refreshing. I also picked a Chablis for those who love a big, buttery, oaky chardonnay so you can explore the other varieties.

If you are not able to find a Chablis, look for a California or Washington chardonnay that was fermented and aged in a steel vessel. These bottles often have the label "unoaked" on them.

Here are the options for this pairing:

1 **Domaine Chatelain Petit Chablis**

2 **Domaine Trouillet Pouilly-Fuissé**

$ **River Road Chardonnay Unoaked**

serving temperature: chilled or cold (45–55°F)

on the nose: green apple, lemon, and some pear. Also a bit of minerality.

sweetness: dry

acidity: high

tannin: none

alcohol: medium

on the palate: green apples and pear! Also just a bit of stone.

This fruity, acidic wine is the perfect pairing for a decadent roasted chicken as it cuts through the richness of the sauce while still being able to hold its own.

My recipe for Come to the Table Chicken and Fries is so good it will bring everyone to the table! In the fall and winter I make this chicken about once a month. Even if I'm just making it for Jeremy and me, the leftover chicken is perfect for soups or BBQ chicken pizza. You can even shred the leftover chicken and freeze it to use later for soups.

COME TO THE TABLE
CHICKEN AND FRIES

COOK TIME: ABOUT 1 HOUR 45 MINUTES • PREP TIME: 20 MINUTES • SERVES 5–6

wine pairing options

1 Domaine Chatelain Petit Chablis

2 Domaine Trouillet Pouilly-Fuissé

$ River Road Chardonnay Unoaked (or your favorite unoaked chardonnay)

FOR THE CHICKEN

1 (4–5 pounds) whole chicken

1 tablespoon kosher salt

2 teaspoons ground black pepper

⅓ cup olive oil

1 lemon, halved

1 bulb fresh garlic, cut in half lengthwise (unpeeled)

1 small onion, skin removed and quartered

½ cup dry white wine such as Chablis or pinot gris

FOR BASTING

¼ cup butter, melted

2 cloves garlic, minced

¼ cup dry white wine (optional)

¼ cup olive oil (optional)

FOR THE FRIES

2 medium russet potatoes

1 tablespoon olive oil

1 tablespoon kosher salt

1 teaspoon dried Italian herbs

FOR THE SAUCE (OPTIONAL)

¼ cup dry white wine

1 tablespoon cornstarch or arrowroot powder

½ cup heavy cream

1 tablespoon butter

½–1 teaspoon kosher salt

½ teaspoon ground black pepper

GRAIN-FREE, GLUTEN-FREE

FOR THE CHICKEN

1 Preheat oven to 425°F.

2 Remove and discard the chicken giblets. Pat the outside of the chicken dry with paper towels.

3 In a small dish, whisk together 1 tablespoon salt, 2 teaspoons black pepper, ⅓ cup olive oil, and the juice from half of the lemon.

4 In a small (11×14-inch) roasting pan or in your enameled cast-iron braiser, add the chicken, breast side up. (If you have a rack or an oven-safe trivet to raise the chicken, place that in the dish first.) Brush the olive oil mixture all over the outside and under the skin of the chicken.

5 Quarter the remaining half a lemon and place inside the chicken, along with the halved garlic bulb and quartered onion.

6 Pour white wine into the bottom of the pan. Place in oven uncovered and bake for 1 hour.

7 Meanwhile, combine melted butter with minced garlic. Set aside for basting chicken later.

8 After 1 hour, remove chicken from the oven. Baste with the mixture of melted butter and garlic. For the optional pan sauce, add ¼ cup dry white wine and ¼ cup olive oil to the pan at this time. Return to the oven and cook for another 30 minutes, or until the chicken reaches 165°F when a meat thermometer is placed in the thickest part of the chicken. For extra crispy skin, at the end of the cooking time, broil chicken for 3–5 minutes.

9 Remove chicken from the oven, place on a platter, and tent with foil to rest. (See next page for how to make the sauce.) Before carving, discard the garlic, lemon, and onion from the chicken.

Serve chicken with the warm pan sauce as soon as fries come out of the oven!

FOR THE FRIES

1 Preheat oven to 425°F (if you aren't making these while the chicken is already in the oven).

2 Scrub and rinse potatoes. To make wedges, cut each potato in half lengthwise, then cut each half into another half lengthwise. Then cut each quarter at a slight diagonal to make wedges.

3 Soak potato wedges in water for 10 minutes. Drain and gently pat dry with a cloth.

4 On a large rimmed sheet pan covered in foil or parchment paper, add potato wedges. Pour olive oil, salt, and Italian herbs over wedges and toss to evenly coat. Arrange on the pan so wedges are not touching.

5 Place in the oven for 25 minutes, then flip the wedges and bake for another 25 minutes or until crispy and golden!

If you are making the fries alongside the Come to the Table Chicken, add them to the oven during the last 20 minutes of the chicken baking time—this will allow them to finish cooking and stay hot while the chicken rests and you make the sauce.

FOR THE SAUCE (OPTIONAL)

1 Place the pan or braiser on top of the stove and turn the heat to medium-high. (If your pan cannot go on the stovetop, add all the pan juices to a sauté pan.) Add ¼ cup wine to deglaze, slowly pouring it in and stirring with a wooden spoon to scrape up the browned bits. To thicken, mix together equal parts cornstarch (or arrowroot powder) and water until fully combined. Very slowly pour the mixture into the pan while also vigorously stirring the sauce to incorporate.

2 Once the sauce thickens, add the cream and butter, stirring to incorporate. Allow to come back to a simmer. Cook for 3–4 minutes.

Taste. If it needs salt and pepper, start by adding ½ teaspoon salt and ¼ teaspoon pepper. If it needs a little citrus, add juice from a wedge of lemon! Stir until combined. Remove from heat and serve with chicken.

To determine whether you can make a pan sauce, first taste the drippings in the pan. If you get some good flavor, then let's pull together a sauce. If the sauce is mostly evaporated or has a lot of burnt bits in it, or if it just tastes unpleasant, skip the sauce.

SAUVIGNON BLANC:
brightness in a glass

Is there anything better than a chilled glass of sauvignon blanc on a hot day?! Sauvignon blanc is known for its big flavor, high acidity, and herbaceous notes. For some people, sauvignon blanc might be a bit much, which is why pairing it with food that has a lot of spices can complement this wine.

Sauvignon blanc is typically unoaked, so you will not get those notes of oak or vanilla. It also rarely has contact with lees, so there will be no bread or biscuit notes. The most popular regions for sauvignon blanc are New Zealand, France, and Austria.

New Zealand sauvignon blanc is the boldest! You will really get notes of grass and strong minerality. If you want a sauvignon blanc that is *slightly less bold*, one from Austria will be your perfect pick. It still has those minerality notes but is a little less herbal.

If you want a sauvignon blanc that is *smooth with a little bit of zest*, one from France will be the perfect selection. You will want to look for a bottle of wine that says "Sancerre" or "Pouilly-Fumé" on the label. Both these regions in France produce sauvignon blanc.

For our tasting, I have a bottle of the Cloudy Bay sauvignon blanc from New Zealand. I love New Zealand sauvs! My next favorite, and one I always have on hand, is the Decoy sauvignon blanc from California. Both of these are incredibly bright, crisp, and bold.

Let's taste our sauvignon blanc!

1 Cloudy Bay Sauvignon Blanc
2 Decoy by Duckhorn Sauvignon Blanc
3 Kim Crawford Sauvignon Blanc

serving temperature: chilled or cold (45–55°F)

on the nose: grapefruit, also some lemon. Maybe a little bit of pineapple. And the grass. (Most sauvignon blancs are known for their grassy notes.)

sweetness: dry

acidity: high

tannin: none

alcohol: high

on the palate: grapefruit right up front! And then you'll get hit with other citrus and finally grass.

Greek food is one of my favorite meal pairings with sauvignon blanc. There can be so many bold flavors happening in Greek food, from oregano to cinnamon to garlic to fresh dill and lemon. It needs a wine that can stand up to those flavors without competing with them. In the following recipe, the sauvignon blanc cuts through the richness of the Greek meatballs while allowing some of the more subtle flavors to shine through.

GREEK PLATTER WITH LEMON GARLIC SAUCE

Making these meatballs is simple, and they come together fast! If you don't like ground lamb, you can use ground beef instead.

PREP TIME: 15–20 MINUTES • COOK TIME: 15–20 MINUTES • SERVES 5–6

wine pairing

1. Cloudy Bay Sauvignon Blanc
2. Decoy by Duckhorn Sauvignon Blanc
3. Kim Crawford Sauvignon Blanc

MEATBALLS

1 pound ground chicken

1 pound ground lamb (or ground beef)

½ cup panko or breadcrumbs (or gluten-free panko)

2 teaspoons paprika

2 teaspoons dried oregano

1 teaspoon cumin

¼ teaspoon cinnamon

juice from 1 large lemon

1 teaspoon kosher salt

3 cloves garlic, minced

LEMON GARLIC SAUCE

¼ cup plain Greek yogurt

juice from 1 lemon

2 cloves garlic, minced

1 teaspoon kosher salt

TOMATO SALAD

1 cup halved cherry tomatoes

1 cucumber, sliced

¼ red onion, sliced

1 teaspoon kosher salt

¼ cup crumbled feta

1 tablespoon olive oil

1 tablespoon red wine vinegar

FOR SERVING

Basmati rice, lettuce greens, or pitas

Hummus

Crumbled feta

GLUTEN-FREE OPTIONAL

 You can serve this however you like—in a pita, over rice or a bed of greens, or with pita chips. I love including a small tomato salad with feta for some freshness, and you cannot go wrong with Trader Joe's Mediterranean Hummus!

1 Preheat oven to 400°F.

2 Place all the ingredients for the meatballs in a large bowl and mix using your hands or a fork. Make sure all the ingredients are well-incorporated. Using a spoon or small ice cream scoop, form golf-ball-size meatballs. I usually get about 20 meatballs.

3 On a large rimmed baking sheet covered with foil or parchment paper and coated with oil, add the meatballs. Bake for 15 minutes or until a meat thermometer reads 165°F. If you would like them a little browned on top, place under the broiler for 3–5 minutes.

4 While the meatballs bake, make the lemon garlic sauce. Mix all ingredients together and place in the refrigerator to chill.

5 To make the tomato salad, add all ingredients to a bowl and stir to combine. Place in the refrigerator to chill until the meatballs are done.

To serve, I like to set out all the sides and dressings along with the meatballs and allow everyone to create their own plate. Drizzling the meatballs with the lemon garlic sauce is divine!

For a dairy-free option, try this with Greek Vinaigrette (page 167) instead of Lemon Garlic Sauce.

These meatballs freeze well. So if you need to freeze some of them, form the meatballs and place them into a freezer-safe container or bag. When you are ready to enjoy them, thaw overnight in the refrigerator and then bake the next day following the method above.

RIESLINGS:
the gateway into wine

For many people, their love for wine began with a riesling, most likely a sweet or off-dry one. These wines are extremely approachable thanks to their delicate sweetness and drinkability.

Rieslings grow best in cool or moderate climates and are most famously produced in Germany and in the Alsace region of France (which used to be part of Germany). The most famous regions in Germany for rieslings are Mosel, Rheingau, and Pflaz. If you have a bottle from one of these regions, you've got a winner.

German rieslings are known for their high acidity, minerality, and aromatic intensity. Typical notes are apricot, petroleum, and wet slate. And yes, you read that correctly—petroleum is a pronounced aroma for a German riesling and occurs through a compound that appears during the ripening of the grape. Common labels you will see on German rieslings are *Trocken*, which means dry, or *Halbtrocken*, which means the wine has some sweetness.

French rieslings are very dry, light-bodied, and have high minerality with notes such as green apple, lime, and smoke.

To sum it up, rieslings can range from dry to sweet, are unoaked, can be low to high in acidity, and can be light- to full-bodied.

What truly sets riesling grapes apart is their susceptibility to noble rot, which is caused by a fungus called botrytis. This fungus can grow on ripe grapes in climates with damp, misty mornings and dry afternoons. Noble rot essentially creates tiny holes in the grape skins, allowing water to evaporate. This leads to concentrated sugars and acids in the fruit.

Think of it like the difference between pure cranberry juice and cranberry juice with added sugar. A grape subjected to noble rot is like the juice with added sugar, which is why these grapes are almost always used to make sweet wines. To be clear, rieslings are not sweet because of added sugar; they are sweet because by decreasing the water content of the grape, noble rot caused the naturally occurring sugars to become more concentrated.

Even though rieslings are made with sweeter grapes, some of them can range from dry to off-dry (meaning some sweetness) to sweet. A great way to know if the riesling you are holding is dry or sweet is to look at the alcohol content. If it is 12% or above, it will be dry. If it is 8% to 11%, it will be sweeter.

Gewürztraminer is another sweet wine worth mentioning. This grape is most commonly grown in the Alsace region of France. It has notes of peach, apricot, and lychee. Like riesling, it is also known for being a sweeter wine. It can have a lower acidity than riesling but a slightly higher alcohol content. Gewürztraminer is said to be the grown-up version of Moscato. So if you are ready to graduate from Moscato (which is almost dessert-like in its sweetness) but not quite ready for the high acidity of riesling, gewürztraminer is your pick!

For this section, I am going to compare two rieslings. First up is the Domdechant Werner Estate Riesling Trocken. You can assess that this riesling will be more dry because it's labeled as *Trocken*, which means dry.

serving temperature: well chilled or ice cold (38–45°F)

on the nose: pear, grapefruit, honey, and petrol

sweetness: dry to off-dry

acidity: high

tannin: none

alcohol: high (for a sweet wine)

on the palate: notes of minerality, green apple, and pear

Now we'll compare this with the Dr. Loosen "Dr. L" Riesling to show you how versatile these wines can be. A lower alcohol content shows that the Dr. Loosen riesling will be on the sweeter side.

on the nose: apple, honey, and some citrus
sweetness: sweet
acidity: high
tannin: none
alcohol: low
on the palate: notes of almond, pineapple, and citrus

SWEETER WHITES AND UNEXPECTED PAIRINGS

Spicy foods are some of the hardest to pair with wine. This is because spice can elevate a wine's alcohol sensation (that warm feeling going down the back of your throat), making it very unpleasant.

Remember, when pairing food and wine, heat goes with sweet! You don't want to pair a dish with a lot of spices with a wine that has a high alcohol content because it will just result in an unpleasant burning sensation. If you are enjoying spicy foods, reach for a sweet or off-dry wine.

Remember, WHEN PAIRING FOOD AND WINE, **HEAT GOES WITH SWEET!**

Because most rieslings have lower alcohol content and are highly aromatic, they complement a dish like curry without competing with the flavors. Jeremy and I once went to a renowned Indian restaurant in DC and did their tasting menu along with their wine pairing. With almost every dish, they served some kind of riesling or sweeter white wine, and it was perfect!

Pairing wine with your favorite takeout foods, especially Thai, Indian, or Vietnamese cuisine, is such a treat. Curry is a great dish to pair with sweeter whites, so our featured recipe for this section is Make Me Smile Yellow Curry. Curry can be rich and packed with flavor, which is elevated by the spices used in this dish.

MAKE ME SMILE YELLOW CURRY

 There is a good amount of chopping for this recipe! Allow time for prep or prep ahead of time. If you cannot find fresh ginger, frozen crushed ginger works great. Use 3 cubes.

PREP TIME: 15 MINUTES • COOK TIME: 50 MINUTES • SERVES 4–5

wine pairing options

1 Domdechant Werner Estate Riesling Trocken

2 Dr. Loosen "Dr. L" Riesling

3 S Sohne Riesling-Blue

CURRY

¼ cup butter (half a stick)

2 small yellow onions, finely chopped

2 cloves garlic, minced

1 tablespoon grated fresh ginger

3 tablespoons medium yellow curry powder (for less spice, use mild yellow curry powder)

2 teaspoons kosher salt

1 teaspoon cumin

½ teaspoon cayenne pepper (use less for less heat)

2 pounds boneless, skinless chicken breasts or thighs, cut into 1-inch cubes

1 (14.5-ounce) can diced tomatoes

¾ cup canned coconut cream (the solidified cream that forms at the top of a can of full-fat coconut milk; make sure not to shake the can so the cream stays separate from the liquid)

¾ cup dry roasted cashews, finely chopped (by hand or in food processor)

Cilantro Lime Yogurt Sauce (page 162)

RICE

1¼ cups basmati or jasmine rice

½ cup golden raisins

¼ cup dry roasted cashews, roughly chopped

GRAIN-FREE, DAIRY-FREE

FOR THE CURRY

1 Heat butter in a large sauté pan over medium heat until melted and slightly bubbly.

2 Add onions, garlic, and ginger, stirring until softened, about 5 minutes.

3 Add curry powder, salt, cumin, and cayenne and stir to fully coat the onion mixture with the spices.

4 Add chicken, stirring to coat, and cook for 3 minutes. Add the can of tomatoes, including the juice, and bring to a simmer. Cover and simmer gently for 20 minutes, stirring occasionally.

5 Uncover and add the coconut cream. Stir and then cover for another 15 minutes, stirring occasionally.

6 Add cashews. Stir and cook for an additional 5 minutes.

FOR THE RICE

1 Follow the package instructions for making rice.

2 Once the rice is done, add golden raisins and cashews. Stir to incorporate and serve immediately!

Spoon rice into bowls and add curry. Drizzle with Cilantro Lime Yogurt Sauce. Enjoy!

PINOT GRIGIO
is always a good idea

Pinot grigio and pinot gris are names for the same grape but from different areas. Pinot grigio comes from Italy, and pinot gris comes from France! This grape is a mutation of pinot noir, which explains why pinot noir can be paired with so many dishes that usually call for white wines.

Pinot grigio/gris, like riesling, also grows in cool to moderate climates. There are two styles a winemaker can take with this grape, the first being a simple white wine with high acidity and flavors of lemon and apple. In Italy, pinot grigio is in such high demand that the grapes are picked earlier for this simple, clean, but still delicious white wine.

The second style occurs when the winemaker allows the grapes to stay on the vine longer, which is typically how pinot gris grapes are handled in France, letting them ripen further and create more complex flavors. These grapes are higher in sugar and lower in acidity. Like rieslings grown in Alsace, pinot gris can also be susceptible to botrytis, making it sweeter than Italian pinot grigio.

Unlike some chardonnays, pinot grigio/gris is not aged in oak barrels because the oak would interfere with the delicate fruit flavors.

Another great characteristic of pinot grigio/gris is its versatility in cooking. Whenever a recipe calls for a dry white wine I always know I can reach for a pinot grigio/gris, which is what we'll use in preparing Self-Care Creamy Risotto. These wines are typically inexpensive while still being delicious, so you can feel okay about sharing some of your wine with your food!

For the tasting, the following options are perfect, and I'll be doing a comparison tasting of the first two.

1 Poderi di Carlo Friuli Pinot Grigio

2 King Estate Domaine Pinot Gris

3 J Vineyards Pinot Gris California

Poderi di Carlo Friuli Pinot Grigio

serving temperature: well chilled or ice cold (38–45°F)

on the nose: notes of green apple, lemon, and some honey.
Clean with a crisp aroma.

sweetness: dry to off-dry

acidity: medium to high

tannin: none

alcohol: medium to high

on the palate: notes of apples and honey with an acidity that hits at the
end. Very simple and crisp wine, which is the style for Italian pinot grigios!

This next one is a French-forward pinot gris.

King Estate Domaine Pinot Gris, 2019

on the nose: notes of grapefruit and pear, some honeydew,
and some minerality

sweetness: dry

acidity: medium

tannin: none

alcohol: high

on the palate: notes of honeydew, lemon, and pear. It has more body
than the pinot grigio and is a little bit more complex in its flavor profile.

Both of these wines are delightfully approachable and enjoyable. Either one
would be a perfect pair for rich and creamy risotto. The crispness of the Italian
pinot grigio will cut through its richness, and the pronounced fruit notes in the
pinot gris will complement its rustic flavors.

SELF-CARE CREAMY RISOTTO

Let's first refute a myth: Risotto is not hard to make. It truly is not. It takes time, and sometimes the length of time can be confused with the level of difficulty. My risotto recipe is cozy and mouthwatering and approachable, but it does take time and attention.

This is a dish you hang out with while you make it. Pour yourself a glass of wine, turn on your favorite podcast or playlist, and enjoy the ride.

PREP TIME: 10 MINUTES • COOK TIME: 30 MINUTES • SERVES 4–5

wine pairing options

1. Poderi di Carlo Friuli Pinot Grigio
2. King Estate Domaine Pinot Gris
3. J Vineyards Pinot Gris California

6 cups vegetable broth or chicken stock
2 tablespoons olive oil, divided
5 tablespoons butter, divided
5 ounces shiitake mushrooms, sliced
2 shallots, diced
3 cloves garlic, minced
1½ cups Arborio rice
½ cup dry white wine, such as pinot grigio
1 tablespoon kosher salt
1 teaspoon freshly ground black pepper
½ cup frozen peas
⅓ cup freshly grated Parmesan cheese

1. In a small saucepan, bring the broth to a simmer. Turn heat to low to keep it warm while you make the risotto.

2. Add 1 tablespoon olive oil and 1 tablespoon butter to a large sauté pan or dutch oven over medium-high heat. Once melted, add mushrooms.

3. Sauté mushrooms for about 2 minutes on each side. Remove mushrooms and set aside.

4. Add remaining 1 tablespoon olive oil to the sauté pan, and add shallots. Sauté for 1 minute. Add garlic and sauté for an additional minute.

5. Add rice, stirring to coat with oil, and cook for about 2 minutes. When the rice has taken on a pale, golden color, pour in wine, stirring until the wine is fully absorbed. Add salt and pepper.

VEGETARIAN

6 Using a ladle, add ½ cup of the simmering broth to the rice and stir until the broth is absorbed. Continue adding broth ½ cup at a time, stirring until the liquid is absorbed and the rice is cooked, about 15 to 20 minutes. Once the broth is used up, don't forget to turn off the heat under the small saucepan.

7 Once rice is cooked and liquid is absorbed, add frozen peas and stir to incorporate. Turn heat to low and stir in mushrooms. Add remaining butter and Parmesan. Stir until butter is melted and cheese is melty.

Dish up the risotto and sprinkle with finishing salt, freshly cracked black pepper, and extra Parmesan cheese. A great side dish is my "Do I Have to Share?" Balsamic Glazed Carrots (page 177).

Risotto is best eaten while it's still hot! To reheat the next day, add a little broth so it isn't as thick. Reheat on the stove over medium heat or in the microwave.

the white wine
GUILD

		made in	acidity	body	flavors	try it with
EXTRA DRY	PINOT GRIGIO	Italy	High	Light	Lemon, melon, almond	Sushi or fried calamari
	CHABLIS	France	High	Light	Green apple, lime, pear	Roasted chicken or crab legs
	ALBARIÑO	Spain	High	Medium	Lemon, grapefruit, apple	Ceviche or risotto
VERY DRY	SANCERRE (French sauvignon blanc)	France	Medium to high	Medium	Grass, grapefruit, lime	Trout or salad with goat cheese
	GRÜNER VELTLINER	Austria	Medium	Light	Lime, lemon, nectarine	Oysters, California rolls, or pecan-crusted chicken
	CHENIN BLANC	France, South Africa	High	Medium	Apple, pear, spice	Pad thai, Nashville hot chicken, or wonton soup
DRY	CHARDONNAY	California	Low to medium	Medium	Pineapple, vanilla, caramel	Grilled veggies or lobster
	WHITE BURGUNDY	France	Medium	Light	Lemon, pear, hazelnut	Pasta with white sauce or chicken
	SAUVIGNON BLANC	New Zealand	High	Light	Grass, grapefruit, melon	Greek kabobs or lobster rolls
OFF-DRY	PINOT GRIS	France, United States	Medium	Light	White peach, lemon zest, almond	Grilled fish, ramen, or ceviche
	DRY RIESLING	France, Austria	High	Light	Lime, jasmine, petrol	Curry, jalapeño poppers, or jambalaya
	VIOGNIER	France, California	Medium	Medium	Tangerine, peach, mango	Orange chicken or tikka masala
SWEET	MOSCATO D'ASTI	Italy	Medium	Light	Peach, orange blossom	Baked brie or a breakfast-for-dinner spread
	GEWÜRZTRAMINER	Germany	Low	Medium	Lychee, grapefruit, rose	Sharp cheddar cheese or quiche
	SWEET RIESLING	Germany	High	Lights	Peach, apricot, floral	Blue cheese or drink alone as dessert

a love letter
TO RED WINE

When I first started drinking red wine, I stayed with the most popular and approachable reds. Pinot noir. Cabernet sauvignon. Merlot. I had no idea what a vast world was out there for red wine. No idea that I could chill my red. No idea, in fact, that most reds should be served at around 60°F. No idea that I could enjoy a glass of smoky, bold red but then also enter the land of juicy, jammy red. A winemaker can have so much fun when creating a bottle of red because there are so many ways to add flavor or make the flavor of the grape shine.

Red wine is made from red grapes, but the wine's color actually comes from the grape skins, not the juice. After the grapes are picked, they are then crushed and allowed to macerate with the skins, seeds, and in some cases the stems. The skins give the wine not only its red color but also its tannin. Tannin is apparent in most red wines, unlike white wines. Tannin is also important for allowing a wine to age. Red wines made with high tannin can age in the bottle anywhere from several months to years.

Once the grapes are crushed, they go into their first fermentation. During this process yeast consumes the sugar from the grapes and converts it into alcohol. For most reds, this process can take anywhere from one to three weeks. After the first fermentation, the liquid is drained from the tank and then the skins are pressed to extract even more liquid. The liquid is then put into a vessel to undergo its second fermentation through malolactic conversion. Unlike white wine, almost all red wine goes through malolactic conversion as it transforms very sharp flavors into creamier, more pleasant notes. (But remember, chardonnay is one white grape that can go through malolactic conversion, and this is where its buttery notes come from.)

The next step for red wines is aging. There are so many different vessels a red wine can be aged in, but the most common are oak barrels or stainless-steel tanks. Because so many red wines can stand up to aging in oak barrels, these are frequently used. Newer oak barrels will give red wine flavors of spice while older oak barrels can give flavors such as vanilla or coconut. After aging the wine in oak barrels, a winemaker may choose to blend it with other red wines. In a later chapter we'll learn more about the power of red blends, but for now just know that this is done often.

Most red wines that can be purchased at your local wine store are ready to open and enjoy right away. But there are more complex red wines such as Brunello di Montalcino that require aging in a bottle.

When someone is serving a glass of red wine, you'll often see them place an aerator on the bottle before pouring, or they will pour the wine into a decanter to sit for anywhere from several minutes to an hour or so. The primary reason for decanting is that it allows the wine to interact with oxygen, which causes aromas and flavors to open up so the wine is its most delicious! A fun experiment is to pour a glass of red and take a sip. Then give the wine a nice swirl and let it sit for 15 minutes before coming back to it. You might notice the wine is a little softer or that some of the notes are a little more pronounced.

For everyday red wines that are ready to drink upon purchase, I like to use an aerator. It's simple, and it allows the wine to interact with oxygen as it is being poured from the bottle. After that, it's swirl and sip time!

No matter what your preferred tastes are, I believe there is a red wine out there for you! Whether it's a juicy and fresh grenache, an earthy but light pinot noir, or a big, bold, smoky syrah, there is a bottle of red just waiting for you to obsess over. I hope this introduction to red wine opens you up to some unlikely reds!

IF YOU LIKE BORDEAUX,
you don't hate merlot

I would like to specifically speak to the people who proclaim they do not like merlot.

Merlot was widely loved in America before the movie *Sideways* hit theaters. In this movie the main character passionately declares his hatred of merlot and refuses to drink it. After the movie came out, merlot sales allegedly plummeted and pinot noir came on the scene as the new go-to red wine. People started to associate merlot with cheap red wine.

What is truly comical is that at the end of this movie, this main character declares that his favorite red wine is a Right Bank bordeaux. And if you're holding a bottle of bordeaux from the Right Bank of France, it's either a merlot or a red blend made from mostly merlot grapes.

So let's travel to Bordeaux, which is a region on the west coast of France that is itself split into two regions—the Right Bank and the Left Bank. Both are famous for their red wine grapes.

Bordeaux's Right Bank produces mostly merlot grapes and merlot-blended red wines. The Left Bank produces mostly cabernet sauvignon grapes. As mentioned earlier, French wines are not labeled according to the type of grape used but according to the region where the wine was produced. So if you are holding a bottle of wine with the title bordeaux, you are either holding a bottle of cabernet sauvignon or a merlot blend, depending on whether it is from the Right or Left Bank.

Let's say a bottle is made with 70% merlot, 15% Cabernet Franc, and 15% cabernet sauvignon. Seeing that it is dominated by merlot grapes, we know this is a bordeaux from the Right Bank. If the dominant grape variety were cabernet sauvignon, then it would be a Left Bank bordeaux.

Now let's dive into the differences between cabernet sauvignon and merlot, and why they make an excellent red blend.

Cabernet sauvignon, as we've learned, is high in everything. High acidity, high tannin, high alcohol, and a big flavor profile. We will generally get black fruit notes such as black currant and black cherry. It is often matured in oak barrels, which causes the wine to have notes of charred wood, vanilla, and baking spices. Aging cabernet sauvignon in oak barrels is also very important because oxygen can interact with the wine, which is what softens the tannin.

Unlike cabernet, merlot is a middle-of-the-road red wine, which is why it can make for such easy drinking. Go-with-the-flow merlot. Merlot has medium tannin and medium acidity. Its most common notes are more in the red fruit category, such as ripened strawberry and red cherry. Because it isn't high in tannin, merlot does not have to be aged as long in oak barrels and therefore can go to market sooner. It is also incredibly approachable and perfect for anyone wanting to dip their toes into the world of red wine or for people who need a break from big, bold reds.

So why are most bordeaux wines, whether from the Right Bank or the Left, turned into red wine blends? Because they are delicious, that's why! But there's also a science behind it. Merlot softens the tannin of cabernet and lowers its acidity, which allows for it to be enjoyed earlier and makes the wine a bit more approachable. It also lends some brightness to cabernet by adding some of the red fruit notes.

Whether you are trying a Right Bank or Left Bank bordeaux, you have a delicious, complex red blend that is the perfect pairing for rich dishes with red meat. Here are some options for this pairing:

1　Château Bel-Air Lussac Saint Émilion
2　Old Merelo Merlot Single Vineyard
3　Decoy by Duckhorn Merlot

> **TIP:** Fruity, light-bodied red wines such as Beaujolais and grenache like to be served at room temperature or slightly chilled (55°F). Full-bodied red wines like cabernet sauvignon should be served at 60°F.

For this section I am drinking the Chateau Bel-Air Lussac Saint-Émilion. Pouring red wine through an aerator spout allows the red wine to interact with oxygen, which softens the tannin.

serving temperature: room temperature or slightly cool (60°F)

decant/aerator: yes

on the nose: notes of plum, blackberry, also some oak, vanilla, and some smoke

sweetness: dry

acidity: medium

tannin: medium to high

alcohol: medium to high

on the palate: notes of plum, black cherry, blackberries, and earth

This delicious, complex, but still approachable bordeaux complements Beef Bourguignon (French beef stew) so well. The complex notes of the Cab Franc and cab sauv in this red blend will not be outshined by the richness of the stew. But the fruity notes of the merlot are also able to cut through the decadence of Beef Bourguignon in a way that makes you go back for more!

If anyone asks me how rich I want to be, I will say, "As rich as French beef stew!" Introducing the most extra meal of all time: Beef Bourguignon.

Julia Child was famous for her Beef Bourguignon recipe. It is involved, takes time, and is extremely decadent. Many people have tried to make a shortcut recipe for it. I've tried some of them and am not a fan. However, I did try Ina Garten's spin on this classic recipe and loved it. But then I made my own changes. So this is what I envision would come out of a kitchen (or a bar or what have you) if Julia, Ina, and I walked in.

A couple things to note before we get started. First, I cook my bacon in the oven to avoid a lot of grease splatter, but you can cube it and add it to a dutch oven and cook it that way.

Second, this recipe calls for one full bottle of red wine (which is why we love Julia!). So opt for a delicious but inexpensive option such as merlot or Côtes du Rhône.

"JULIA, INA, AND BRI WALK INTO A BAR" STEW

PREP TIME: 20 MINUTES • COOK TIME: ABOUT 3 HOURS • SERVES 6–8

wine pairing

1 Château Bel-Air Lussac Saint-Émilion

2 Old Merelo Merlot Single Vineyard

$ Decoy by Duckhorn Merlot

6–8 slices bacon

3 pounds chuck roast, cut into 1-inch cubes

1 tablespoon + 2 teaspoons kosher salt, divided

3 teaspoons ground black pepper, divided

2 tablespoons olive oil

1 pound carrots, sliced diagonally into 1-inch chunks

5–6 ounces shiitake mushrooms, sliced

2 small yellow onions, sliced

4 cloves garlic, minced

1 (750 ml) bottle dry red wine such as Côtes du Rhône or merlot

½ cup beef stock or broth

2 tablespoons tomato paste

8–10 sprigs fresh thyme

2 tablespoons butter

1 cup frozen peas (optional)

1 tablespoon cornstarch or arrowroot powder (optional)

1 Add the slices of bacon to a sheet pan lined with foil or parchment paper. Place pan in the cold oven and turn oven to 400°F. After 10 minutes, flip bacon and cook for an additional 10 minutes. Once the bacon is crispy, remove pan from the oven and place bacon on a paper towel–lined plate. Reserve the sheet pan with the bacon fat.

2 While bacon is cooking, start prepping the chuck roast by cutting it into 1-inch cubes. Pat the beef cubes dry with a paper towel and sprinkle with 2 teaspoons salt and 1 teaspoon pepper. Set aside.

3 Reset oven temperature to 325°F.

4 In a large dutch oven over medium-high heat, add 2 tablespoons olive oil. Once the oil is heated, add beef cubes in a single layer. You might have to do this in batches if there is not enough room in your pan. We want each cube to be browned. Sear on all sides for 2–3 minutes.

5 Remove beef to a large plate or bowl. Tent with foil and set aside.

6 Into the dutch oven, add carrots, mushrooms, and onions along with 1 tablespoon reserved bacon fat from the sheet pan,

1 tablespoon salt, and 2 teaspoons pepper. Stir to coat the veggies in the bacon fat and seasonings and continue cooking for 6–8 minutes, stirring occasionally, until onions are lightly browned. While veggies are cooking, chop the bacon.

7 Once onions are lightly browned, add garlic and cook for 1 more minute.

8 Put beef and bacon into the pot with the juices from the meat. Add the whole bottle of red wine. If meat is still not covered, add ½ to 1 cup beef broth. Add tomato paste and stir. Bring to a simmer, add the bunch of thyme, cover pot with a tight-fitting lid, and place it in the oven for about 2½ hours, or until the meat and vegetables are fork-tender.

9 Remove the dutch oven to the stovetop. Check to make sure the meat is fork-tender. Turn the burner to medium-high heat and add butter and frozen peas. Bring to a boil, then lower the heat and simmer for 15 minutes.

10 If you like thicker stew, combine equal parts cornstarch (or arrowroot powder) and water. Slowly pour into the stew over low heat, mixing vigorously. Allow to simmer until thickened.

Spoon the beef stew over Savory Mashed Sweet Potatoes (page 173) and sprinkle with freshly cracked black pepper and finishing salt.

IS IT SYRAH
or shiraz?!

Besides a lemon drop martini, I do not think anything is as delicious to pair with steak as a bold, delicious red wine! And when it comes to a rich cut like the ribeye in the recipe that follows this chapter, everyone will tell you the right pairing is syrah or shiraz.

Syrah and shiraz both refer to the same grape variety. Syrah is its French name, but in Australia it is called shiraz.

The syrah grapes grown in France are small and have very thick skins. The result is a wine with medium to high levels of acidity and tannin. Syrah is medium-bodied and usually portrays notes of black fruit like blackberry and black cherry. It is also set apart for its peppery and herbal notes like green bell pepper.

The shiraz grapes from Australia are grown in a warmer climate, which allows for a more ripe grape. This leads to cooked or stewed black fruit aromas and licorice notes.

Syrah/shiraz is almost always aged in oak barrels to soften the tannin. Because of this, it will have notes of smoke and spice. Because of its high tannin, this wine can also stand up to aging in the bottle. Excellent bottles of syrah/shiraz can age for up to a decade or more. Over time, bottle aging adds notes of dried fruit as well as meat and earth.

Syrah/shiraz grapes produce many delicious wines on their own, but they also have become very important in making red wine blends like merlot. Syrah/shiraz grapes add color, black fruit notes, and tannin to other wines. They are generally blended with grenache and mourvèdre grapes to produce what is known as a Rhône blend or a GSM (which stands for grenache, syrah, mourvèdre blend).

Using an aerator when pouring is a good idea because these wines have medium to high tannin. Here are my picks:

1 **Two Hands Shiraz Angel Share**

2 **Mousset Tendance Syrah**

3 **Radius Syrah**

serving temperature: this is a medium-bodied red wine and is best served at 54°F, just under room temperature.

decant/aerator: yes

on the nose: blackberry, plum, oak, pepper, potential hint of vanilla

sweetness: dry

acidity: medium

tannin: medium

alcohol: medium

on the palate: blackberry and oak right up front. A little bit of pepper or maybe baking spice.

You are going to be amazed at how the flavor profile of a shiraz/syrah changes with ribeye. The buttery, garlicky richness and peppery notes of the meat really allows the red fruit notes of the wine to shine! That's because the pepper and smoke of the steak balance out the pepper and the oak in the wine, allowing a delightful brightness to present itself.

YOU'RE WORTH IT RIBEYE

You are worth a delicious, decadent meal—even on a Tuesday. Even if you're the only one eating it. (Side note: Do we make this ribeye while listening to Fifth Harmony sing "Worth It"? I don't think they're talking about pan-seared ribeye in that song, but still . . .)

This meal is best enjoyed by just two people. The ribeye is very large (24 ounces, or nearly 2 pounds). It is not recommended to cook another 24-ounce ribeye in the same pan after the first one is finished, because the browned butter will quickly burn and your second steak will be blackened and not browned. If you really want to make two large ribeyes, you will either need to use a second skillet or let the first pan cool off and then wipe out the existing oil and butter. But really, I like to think of this meal as a special treat for just me or to share with another person.

PREP TIME: 5 MINUTES • COOK TIME: 45 MINUTES • SERVES 1–2

wine pairing

1 Two Hands Shiraz Angel Share

2 Mousset Tendance Syrah

3 Radius Syrah

FOR THE STEAK

1 (24-ounce) bone-in ribeye, 2 inches thick

2 teaspoons kosher salt

½ teaspoon freshly cracked black pepper

1 tablespoon avocado or vegetable oil (it helps to have an oil with a high smoke point)

2 tablespoons butter

3 cloves garlic, peeled and smashed

1 rosemary sprig

1 bunch thyme (about 3–5 sprigs)

finishing salt, such as fleur de sel

FOR THE GARLIC BUTTER SAUCE

3 tablespoons butter

2 cloves garlic, minced

FOR THE BAKED POTATOES

2 russet potatoes

1 tablespoon olive oil

1 teaspoon kosher salt

TOPPINGS

sour cream

crumbled bacon

shredded cheddar cheese

chives

butter

GRAIN-FREE, GLUTEN-FREE

FOR THE RIBEYE

1 Remove steak from the refrigerator. Pat dry with paper towels and season each side with salt and pepper. Set aside for 20 minutes to come to room temperature.

2 Place a large cast-iron skillet on the stovetop and heat on medium-high heat for 3 minutes. After 3 minutes, add 1 tablespoon oil.

3 Add the ribeye to the pan and let it sear for 5 minutes without touching it. Then flip and sear the other side for 4 minutes.

4 Reduce heat to medium-low. Flip the ribeye again and add the butter, garlic, rosemary, and thyme to the skillet. Using a spoon, baste the ribeye with the melted butter for 3 minutes, then flip the steak and baste the other side for another 3 minutes.

5 Remove the steak to a plate and tent with foil to rest for 5 minutes. Your steak should be medium-rare (120–130°F). If you prefer it rare, only baste your steak for 2 minutes on the first side and 1 minute on the second side. For medium-well, keep your steak in the pan for an additional 3 minutes while basting, and for well-done, keep your steak in the pan for an additional 6 minutes while basting.

FOR THE GARLIC BUTTER SAUCE

1 While the steak rests, make the Garlic Butter Sauce: simply add the garlic to melted butter and stir!

FOR THE BAKED POTATOES

1 Preheat oven to 450°F. Scrub potatoes and pierce all over (at least 10–12 times) with a fork. Dry potatoes and rub all over with olive oil and salt. Place potatoes on a foil-lined baking sheet and into the oven for 45 minutes or until easily pierced with a knife.

2 Serve warm with favorite toppings such as sour cream, crumbled bacon, shredded cheddar cheese, chives, butter, and salt!

Slice the ribeye and discard the bone and any fat. Fan out the steak slices and drizzle with the Garlic Butter Sauce. Sprinkle with finishing salt. Serve alongside loaded baked potatoes.

GRENACHE:
the magic of a red blend

Grenache is the best kept secret from the everyday home cook. We generally hear of the more popular wines like cab sauv, pinot noir, zinfandel . . . but grenache is one of my favorite wines, and I didn't realize this until recently. The grenache grape is high in natural sugars and low in acidity. It has medium tannin, which makes it approachable. It also has red fruit flavors like strawberry and red cherry. Because of this, grenache grapes are commonly used to make rosé. I really like drinking a chilled bottle of grenache on a summer day when I prefer a red over a white.

Grenache not only shines as a grape in rosé; it is the perfect grape for blending with shiraz/syrah. The grenache softens the tannin and acidity in the shiraz/syrah and complements the red fruit notes. Mourvèdre grapes have a nice smokiness to them that also complement the shiraz/syrah grapes. When these three grapes are blended together you get a nicely balanced red blend known as GSM. My favorite GSM blends (and even my favorite grenache wines) come from Paso Robles. They have notes of black raspberry, fig, ginger, and bacon fat. GSM blends from France (also called the Rhône blend) will have notes of dried cranberry, dried herbs, cinnamon, and leather. These lighter reds are a perfect pairing for dishes you might only consider pairing with white wines, such as my decadent pasta dish Send Noods, which is made with butter, garlic, and Parmesan cheese. Read on for the recipe!

SEND NOODS

These noodles are so decadent and creamy, and whenever I have an intense food craving, I want someone to send me a big bowl of these noodles immediately! They pair perfectly with a slightly chilled grenache or red blend.

PREP TIME: 5 MINUTES • COOK TIME: 35 MINUTES • SERVES 5–6

wine pairing

1 Pallas Old Vine Garnacha Special Selection

$ Chronic Cellars Purple Paradise

1 pound bucatini pasta

1 tablespoon olive oil

4 tablespoons butter

5 cloves garlic, minced

2 cups chicken (or vegetable) broth

1 cup heavy cream

2 teaspoons kosher salt

1 teaspoon ground black pepper

½ cup grated Parmesan cheese

juice from 1 lemon

1 Bring a large pot of water to a boil. Add a generous amount of salt and the pasta. Cook for 6 minutes (or half the time the instructions on the box call for) and drain (the noodles will continue cooking in the sauce).

2 In a large braiser or dutch oven over medium-high heat, add oil and butter. Once butter melts, add garlic and sauté until fragrant, about 1 minute.

3 Pour in broth, heavy cream, salt, and pepper. Bring to a boil and then lower heat to medium. Add noodles. Simmer, stirring occasionally, for about 10–12 minutes, until pasta is al dente.

4 Turn heat off and sprinkle in the grated Parmesan cheese and the juice from half a lemon. Mix to combine. Serve right out of the pan!

VEGETARIAN (OPTIONAL)

the red wine GUIDE

	made in	tannin	body	flavors	try it with
NEBBIOLO	Italy	High	Full	Cherry, rose, anise	Gnocchi, mushroom risotto, or braised pork
MALBEC	Italy	High	Full	Red plum, blackberry, cocoa	Blue cheese, grilled lamb chops, or baked salmon
CHIANTI	Italy	High	Medium	Cherry, plum, tomato leaves	Bolognese, pizza, or Italian sandwiches
CABERNET SAUVIGNON	Australia, California	High	Full	Black cherry, black currant, cedar	Cheeseburgers, steak with peppercorns, or dark chocolate
SANGIOVESE	Italy	Medium to high	Full	Cherry, balsamic, oregano	Red-sauce lasagna, prosciutto, or grilled eggplant
SYRAH/SHIRAZ	France, Australia	Medium to high	Full	Blueberry, oak, peppercorn	Ribeye, shawarma, or hard cheeses (e.g., gouda)
PINOT NOIR	France, Oregon	Low to medium	Medium	Cherry, raspberry, mushroom	Beef stroganoff, grilled salmon, or chocolate-covered strawberries
MERLOT	France, California	Medium	Medium	Cherry, plum, vanilla	Beef bourguignon, roasted pork, or grilled lamb
BEAUJOLAIS	France	Low	Light	Pomegranate, herbs, banana	BBQ pulled pork, cedar plank salmon, or ham sandwiches
ZINFANDEL	Italy, California (Paso Robles)	Medium	Medium	Blackberry, strawberry, vanilla	Pizza, Asian BBQ, or roasted turkey
GRENACHE	France, Italy	Medium	Medium	Stewed strawberry, blood orange, dried herbs	Roasted veggies, chili, or cassoulet
GSM BLEND	France	Medium	Medium	Raspberry, blackberry, baking spices	Beef stew, mushroom risotto, or quiche lorraine

BOLD

DRY

LIGHT

FRUITY

PART 11

THE *beginner's* BAR CART

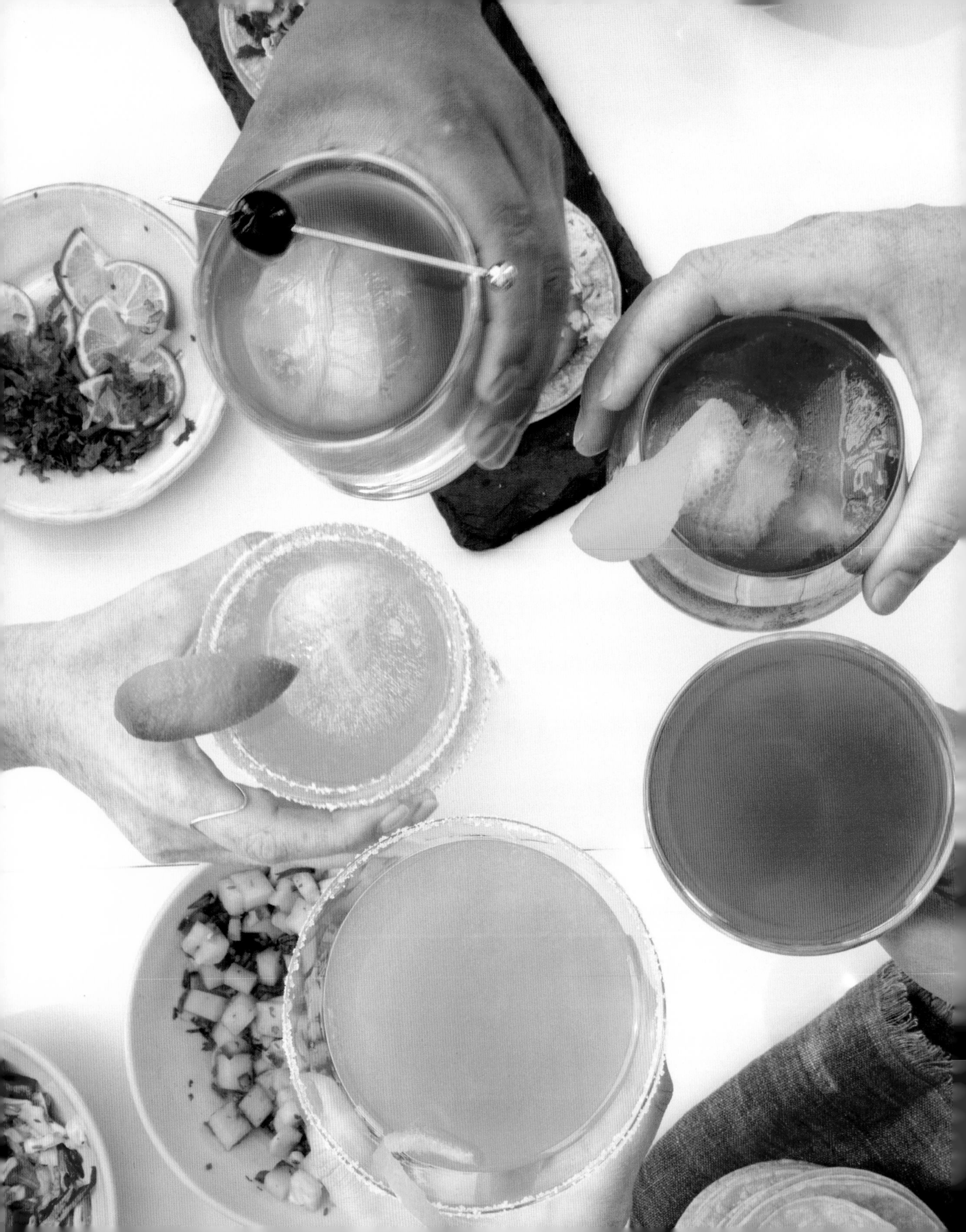

BAR
basics

One of my favorite parts of being a home cook is feeding people, which is closely followed by making sure everyone has a beverage they are obsessed with. I am a beverage queen. I move throughout my day via beverage. Coffee in the morning, crisp ice water perfectly filled in my tumbler throughout the day, sparkling water at lunch, an iced shaken espresso for mid-afternoon, and a cocktail, mocktail, or glass of wine to look forward to in the evening.

I was delighted to learn that, with a few tools and staples, I can make cocktails worthy of being served at high-end restaurants. And that is what we are all going to learn in this section.

BUILDING YOUR CART

I like to think of building a bar cart the same way I think of building a home: it takes some time. You don't need to get everything all at once (unless you want to!). And some ingredients and tools are worth the investment.

Here are some guiding principles as you build your bar cart:

1. *High-quality alcohol is worth it.* I promise you can tell the difference in your drink. A margarita made with low-quality tequila can taste like burning as it goes down. A margarita made with high-quality tequila is smooth and has beautiful notes of agave.

2. *This is an investment—but one that lasts.* A $40 bottle of rye might seem extreme, but remember, you're just using ounces at a time. And alcohol has a very long shelf life.

3. *Build over time.* You don't have to go out and get all the bar tools and alcohol today. Start with what piques your interest. The best way to find out what you like without buying a whole bottle of alcohol is to try drinks at restaurants known for their cocktails. Sit at the bar when the restaurant is slow and make friends with your bartender. Tell them what you like and don't like. It's the best education.

4. *Remember that cocktails are luxury items.* This is not an everyday indulgence! Making your own cocktails at home is fun and a huge money saver, but they are an occasional treat. This mindset helps your alcohol to last and can make cocktails something fun to look forward to after a long week—or, say, on Taco Tuesday!

Now that we have our mindset, let's talk about tools.

ESSENTIAL BAR TOOLS

The first thing you might want to consider is an actual bar cart, cabinet, or special shelf where you can place all your tools and alcohol. This is especially helpful when making cocktails because it means everything you need is in one spot. (If you need to place the alcohol out of reach of children, please do so! And still use the bar cart for the tools and fun glasses!)

Now let's talk about what we place on the bar cart. These first few items are essential.

Shaker. Shaking a drink in a stainless-steel container filled with ice makes it extra cold, which is why I will always opt for a stainless-steel shaker over a glass one. Sometimes this means it will take a little toying with the lid after shaking, because metal contracts once it is cold, but I've never had so much trouble with this that it bothered me. Shakers also generally come with strainers, which helps keep the ice or muddled ingredients from going into the glass when pouring.

Ounce Measurer. Recipes often call for alcohol to be measured in ounces, so it helps to have a smaller measurer. Lots of people like cocktail jiggers, but I do not prefer them since they can be messy to pour from. I like my little OXO Good Grips ounce measurers. I also like that they are angled, so I can easily see what I'm pouring. Hot tip: one shot usually equals 1–1½ ounces. Half a shot is ½–¾ ounce. Measuring in ounces is much easier.

Muddler. This is great for muddling fresh herbs, citrus, or other fruit to extract their flavors into your drink.

Large Sphere Ice Mold. These are amazing! This is an easy-to-use ice tray that makes beautiful ice spheres. The larger size of the ice sphere melts very slowly, so it will keep your drink cold without watering it down.

These next items are not essential but are useful.

Cocktail Mixing Glass with Long Spoon and Strainer. These are perfect for a cocktail that is stirred, not shaken, such as a martini, Manhattan, or negroni. And now seems like a good time to inform you that Bond, James Bond, has led us astray. He likes his martinis shaken, not stirred—which is ironic because martinis are supposed to be stirred. Why? A good rule of thumb for knowing whether you need to shake a drink or stir a drink is to take stock of your ingredients. If the drink consists mostly of alcohol (a martini, for example, is generally vodka or gin and dry vermouth) or thin liquids (think cranberry juice), then stirring them is perfect. But if the ingredients are of varying densities (think thick simple syrup and tequila), you want to shake those ingredients to really incorporate everything into one delicious drink.

Cocktail Picks. I love these picks for drinks that call for a garnish such as cherries or olives.

Bottle Opener. If you don't already have one, spring for one that is magnetic so it lives on your refrigerator and is easy to locate.

GLASSWARE

Have you ever been served a cocktail at a restaurant and enjoyed it more because of the actual glass it was served in? Or vice versa—have you ordered a fancy drink and felt disappointed that it was served in a plain water glass? Part of the fun of cocktails is what we serve the drink in! The following glasses are fun and classic glassware useful for serving your favorite cocktails.

Fortessa Old-Fashioned Glasses. Several years ago we were eating at a Mexican restaurant in DC, and they served their margaritas in these. I immediately went on the hunt and found them. We like to serve margaritas and any kind of bourbon drink in these beauties!

Coupe Glasses. These are so adorable, I cannot get over them. We like to serve martinis in these, as well as champagne.

Moscow Mule Copper Mugs. These serve a purpose besides being fun to look at. They keep your drink super cold thanks to the copper. Perfect for any kind of mule!

Martini Glasses. These can hold a bit more liquid than some of the smaller coupe glasses. They are, obviously, perfect for martinis—especially ones that include olives or cocktail onions.

ALCOHOL
basics

Below are the top mixing alcohols to have for making your favorite cocktails at home. I list two options for each, depending on your price range and store availability!

   The first one listed is my favorite and in most cases is higher-end.

VODKA

Vodka basically takes on the flavor of whatever you mix it with. People commonly like using vodka with juice, such as orange or cranberry juice. It's really versatile.

   Gold Star: Belvedere (maybe the smoothest vodka I've ever tried)

   Runner-Up: Tito's (it has a cult following)

WHISKEY

Bad whiskey is very bad. It basically tastes like burning. I could write a whole ebook on whiskey, but I won't. For the beginner, here is what you need to know: there is *bourbon* and there is *rye*. Rye tends to be a little more savory and has subtle spice notes. Bourbon can be a touch more on the sweet side. I prefer rye and always go for that when making or ordering a whiskey drink (unless it is an old-fashioned, and then I like bourbon).

   If you're using it for mixed drinks, don't buy the most expensive whiskey. Expensive whiskey is only for sipping. But the following options are still great quality and perfect for mixing drinks.

   Gold Star: FEW (rye or bourbon)

   Runner-Up: Bulleit (rye or bourbon)

GIN

Some people love gin and other people hate it. Gin is traditionally made with juniper berries, so it definitely has a piney taste to it. My second-favorite cocktail is made with gin. If you are unsure about gin, wait until you can try it at a restaurant or a friend's house.

Gold Star: Monkey 47

Runner-Up: Gray Whale

Honorable Mention: Hendrick's (also has a cult following)

TEQUILA

It took me a long time to like tequila, and I think that's because when I had my first margarita, in a restaurant, it was filled with store-bought sweet-and-sour mix and low-quality tequila. Since discovering amazing tequila, I am forever changed. Now I almost never order margaritas from a restaurant unless they are known for them.

Gold Star: Don Julio (Blanco or Añejo—right now I love Añejo)

Runner-Up: Casamigos

Honorable Mention: Patron Silver

RUM

Rum is generally for sweeter and fruitier cocktails. You can get dark, light, or spiced rum. Dark rum is aged longer, which means its flavor is deeper and more pronounced. Light rum has a much more subtle flavor, and spiced rum has notes of vanilla, brown sugar, and warming spices.

I generally have light rum on hand for mojitos.

Gold Star: Zaya dark rum

Runner-Up: Cruzan Aged Light Rum

HOUSEHOLD LIQUEURS

Liqueurs are technically liquor, but they stand out because they have sugars or fruits added to them. I like to have a few on hand.

Orange Liqueur. This is the perfect float for a margarita. People also use this to top other drinks or even in champagne.

Gold Star: Grand Marnier

Runner-Up: Cointreau

Elderflower Liqueur. This liqueur is known for its floral notes. It also has a hint of grapefruit.

Gold Star: St-Germain (the elderflower blossoms are hand-picked in the foothills of the Alps)

Raspberry Liqueur. This liqueur has an intense raspberry taste that is delightful and really delicious in desserts.

Gold Star: Chambord (you only need the small bottle, because a little goes a long way)

Vermouth. This is usually mistaken as a liqueur but is actually a fortified wine. It can be sipped by itself but is usually used in cocktails.

There are two types of vermouth. Sweet vermouth is used in Manhattans and negronis (I like Manhattans, so we always have this on hand). Dry vermouth is very versatile, but I generally use it in vodka or gin martinis.

Dry Vermouth

Gold Star: Dolin Vermouth de Chambery Dry

Runner-Up: Noilly Prat Extra Dry

Sweet Vermouth

Gold Star: Carpano Antica Formula

Amaro. If you like negronis or any kind of cocktail with a pleasant bitterness and hints of citrus, this is a must-have liqueur. It is also a fun red color, which can make your cocktails look summer-ready!

Gold Star: Aperol (much preferred because it is not as intense with the bitter notes)

Runner-Up: Campari (aged longer and has a deeper color, which also means the bitterness really comes out swinging)

TO BE CONSIDERED

Cocktail Cherries. The absolute best cocktail cherries are soaked in bourbon. These are what you get when you go to a fancy cocktail bar. A bit pricey, but worth every penny.

Bitters. It's always a good idea to have different bitters on hand, such as aromatic, cherry, and orange bitters. Just a few drops greatly enhance a drink. I like cherry bitters in a Manhattan and orange or aromatic bitters in an old-fashioned. Bitters are to your drink as finishing salt is to your dish. It just brings everything together.

Honey Simple Syrup. I rarely use white sugar or white sugar simple syrup in my drinks because I just never have it on hand. I like using honey simple syrup instead, which is just equal parts honey and water. I generally combine 1 cup of each in a small saucepan, then let the mixture come to a simmer on the stovetop over medium heat. Once simmering, just turn to low and continue cooking until the honey and water are incorporated. Allow to cool and pour into a container with a lid. Will last in the refrigerator for up to 3 weeks. (You can even infuse your simple syrup with mint or rosemary or orange and clove . . . the options are endless!)

CRAFTING YOUR FAVORITE COCKTAILS

Most cocktails have a combination of something sweet, something with citrus or spice, and something fresh, like an herb or sparkling water. There really is no end to the combinations of ingredients you can put together to make a delicious cocktail, so it can be very helpful to know and be able to express what you like.

For example, a few years ago I was at a brunch with friends. All my friends ordered champagne, but champagne can sometimes give me a headache. The server asked what I liked in a cocktail and told me the bartender could make me something.

I like bourbon (not a big vodka or rum fan). I do not like overly sweet or fruity drinks. I like drinks that have some citrus. And I like my drinks strong (I don't want a piña colada where I can't even taste the alcohol).

Do you know what you like?

What is (are) your favorite alcohol(s)?

Do you like your drink to be sweet, tart, dry, fruity, smoky?

Do you want to be able to taste the alcohol?

This can change over time—it's not set in stone. You can also have different preferences based on when you are drinking the cocktail—before, during, or after dinner. But a general understanding will be a helpful guide for you whether you're making your own cocktails or ordering them. Bonus: no more spending way too much on a cocktail you don't enjoy the taste of.

The following thirteen cocktails each feature a different alcohol, and each showcases an important aspect of cocktail making.

Fresh Is Next Level: It's always a good idea to use fresh ingredients when making cocktails. Fresh citrus, fresh herbs, fresh fruit. It's a game changer!

THE ABSOLUTE BEST MARGARITA

We learn two things about cocktails in making this margarita. First, we can make our own simple syrup, which really elevates the drink (no more buying store-bought mixers or syrups). Simple syrup is always a 1-to-1 ratio: 1 cup sweetener to 1 cup water. I like to use honey, especially for margaritas. The great thing about making your own simple syrup is that you can add flavor by using ingredients such as mint, lavender, cranberries, or orange and clove. The options are limitless!

Second, quality alcohol matters. Crafting a margarita is a great lesson in the importance of using top-shelf or high-quality alcohol. A top-shelf tequila is smooth and has beautiful notes of sweet agave.

2 ounces tequila

1 ounce freshly squeezed lime juice (half a large lime or one small lime)

1 ounce honey simple syrup

1 ounce Grand Marnier

kosher salt

1 (Optional) Salt rim of glass by taking a lime wedge and rubbing it around the rim of the glass, then turning the glass upside down onto a plate of salt. Move around to salt rim of glass. Next, add a large ice sphere to the glass.

2 In a shaker filled with ice, add tequila, lime juice, and honey simple syrup. Shake.

3 Pour mixture through a strainer into your glass.

4 Pour Grand Marnier over the top of the ice sphere to finish the margarita with a fun float!

OLD-FASHIONED

First is the enjoyment of a cocktail. An old-fashioned is just a few ounces of liquid. It is meant to be sipped and enjoyed, not just knocked back like a shot or gulped like a tall glass of water. When you are crafting a cocktail, because you are using high-quality, pure ingredients, it's important to take the time to savor it.

Second is the magic of opening up the senses with different techniques. An old-fashioned generally contains about 1 teaspoon of cold water. A few drops of water added to whiskey allows the whiskey to open up, or bloom, therefore allowing some of the notes of the whiskey (such as cedar and smoke) to come through. A little water can change the whole experience, from smell to taste.

Another way to enhance the senses in any cocktail—and especially in an old-fashioned —is by using the oil from a citrus peel. The peel is not just a pretty garnish. It also engages your sense of smell. Most bartenders will take an orange peel, twist it to release the oils, and rub it around the rim and inside of the glass before adding the liquid ingredients. That way when you tip the glass up to take a sip, your sense of smell is immediately engaged with the scent of orange.

Finally, an old-fashioned shows us that simplicity is beautiful. You do not need ten ingredients to make a delicious and vibrant cocktail. Just a few quality ingredients can bring a drink together!

2 ounces bourbon or rye whiskey

2 teaspoons simple syrup (honey or white sugar)

1 teaspoon cold water

2 dashes orange bitters

2 dashes aromatic bitters

orange peel

bourbon-soaked cherries (for garnish)

1. In a mixing glass filled with ice, add all ingredients except orange peel and cherries.

2. Stir with a long spoon for several seconds.

3. Twist the orange peel to release the oils. Rub the peel along the rim and inside of the glass you will pour your drink into.

4. Next, add a large ice sphere. Using a strainer, pour from the mixing glass into the old-fashioned glass.

5. To garnish, add orange peel and cherries (I use 2).

CRANBERRY MOSCOW MULE

A Moscow mule teaches us that we are in charge of how we create our drink. Want it a little sweeter? Add more simple syrup. A little more tart? Add more cranberry juice! A little more fizzy? Add more ginger beer. A little stronger? Add more vodka. Once you have the guide for a cocktail, you can make it your own based on your preferences.

A Moscow mule also teaches us about effervescence in a cocktail. Effervescence is the fizz or bubbles that come from sodas, sparkling water, and champagne or sparkling wine. It's a great way to add a playful element to your cocktail.

FOR CRANBERRY HONEY SIMPLE SYRUP

½ cup honey

½ cup filtered water

½ cup fresh cranberries

FOR CRANBERRY MOSCOW MULE

4 ounces 100% cranberry juice

2 ounces Cranberry Honey Simple Syrup

2 ounces vodka or gin (optional)

8 ounces ginger beer (Bundaberg is the tastiest, with clean ingredients)

FOR CRANBERRY HONEY SIMPLE SYRUP

1 In a small saucepan over medium heat, simmer the water and honey until the honey is fully dissolved.

2 Add the fresh cranberries and continue simmering for 8 minutes (until the cranberries split or pop).

3 Remove from heat and allow to cool. Place in a container with an airtight lid. Seal.

FOR CRANBERRY MOSCOW MULE

1 Fill a copper mug with ice.

2 Add cranberry juice, Cranberry Honey Simple Syrup, and vodka or gin (optional—omit for a virgin cocktail). Top off with the ginger beer. Enjoy!

There are no limits to the variations you can do with a Moscow mule. A typical mule has ginger beer, vodka, and lime juice. It is refreshing and bright. But you can also make a Kentucky mule, which uses whiskey instead of vodka. We're going to make a cranberry mule with vodka. Festive and bright!

WHISKEY SOUR

A whiskey sour is a masterclass in how to use herbs in cocktails. Adding herbs is a really fun way to add different layers to your classic cocktails and especially engages your sense of smell.

The best way to handle herbs in cocktails is to muddle them. Place the herb in the middle of your palm and with your other palm, simply clap over it a few times. A clap around the herb releases the oils just enough that it isn't overpowering or bitter.

2½ ounces rye or bourbon whiskey

1 ounce lemon juice

½ ounce maple syrup

sprig of rosemary (optional)

1 In a shaker filled with ice, add whiskey, lemon juice, and maple syrup. Shake vigorously for 10–15 seconds.

2 Strain into old-fashioned glass with a large sphere ice cube. Muddle a sprig of rosemary and place in the glass with the drink.

CLASSIC NEGRONI

1½ ounces gin (a barrel-aged gin makes this drink so special)

1 ounce amaro (Campari is preferred)

1 ounce sweet vermouth (level up this negroni by using Carpano Antica Formula sweet vermouth)

orange peel (optional)

1 In a mixing glass filled with ice, add gin, amaro, and vermouth. Stir for several seconds.

2 Take the orange peel and twist to release its oil. Rub the peel around the rim of your glass (I like to use a coupe glass). Add a large ice sphere to the glass.

3 Using a strainer, pour negroni from the mixing glass into the coupe glass.

MANHATTAN

2 ounces rye whiskey

1 ounce sweet vermouth

3 dashes cherry bitters

3 dashes aromatic bitters

bourbon-soaked cherries

In a mixing glass filled with ice, add whiskey, vermouth, and bitters. Stir. Strain into a coupe glass. Place 1–2 cherries onto a cocktail stick and add to glass as a garnish.

PAPER PLANE

1 ounce amaro (preferably Amaro Nonino)

1 ounce Aperol

1 ounce bourbon

1 ounce freshly squeezed lemon juice

Add all ingredients to a shaker filled with ice. Shake vigorously for 15 seconds. Strain into a coupe glass.

SUNSHINE MARTINI

white granulated sugar for rim (optional)

2 ounces vodka or gin

1 ounce Cointreau or Grand Marnier

1 ounce freshly squeezed lemon juice

¾ ounce honey simple syrup

1 (Optional) Sugar the rim of glass by taking a lemon wedge and rubbing it around the rim of the glass. Turn the glass upside down onto a plate of sugar. Move around to sugar rim of glass.

2 In a shaker filled with ice, add vodka or gin, Cointreau, lemon juice, and honey simple syrup. Shake vigorously for 10–15 seconds.

3 Strain into martini glass.

SUMMER IN A CUP

I also call this a "quarantini" because I started making it during the pandemic.

2 ounces vodka, gin, or tequila

1 ounce freshly squeezed grapefruit juice

1 ounce St-Germain

In a shaker filled with ice, add all ingredients and shake vigorously for 10–15 seconds. Pour into a glass and enjoy! (I like using the coupe glass for this.)

CRANBERRY BOURBON SMASH

2 ounces bourbon

1½ ounces Cranberry Honey Simple Syrup (page 290)

1 ounce cranberry juice

juice from one clementine

Add all ingredients to a shaker filled with ice. Shake vigorously for 10–15 seconds. Strain into a glass with a large ice sphere.

NOTHING TO RYE ABOUT

2 ounces rye whiskey

2 ounces fresh squeezed grapefruit juice

1 ounce honey simple syrup

6 ounces IPA beer

In a shaker filled with ice, add whiskey, grapefruit juice, and honey simple syrup. Shake. Strain into a 12-ounce glass. Top off with IPA beer.

THE GATHERING COOK

When I first was learning to cook, I dreamed of the delicious food I would bring to the table to serve the many guests who would come into our home. My visions ranged from five-course meals complete with palate cleansers to elaborate feasts that would be talked about for weeks after.

But of course I first had to learn to cook. Good food. Really good food. In the beginning, the bar I set for myself was so low:

No one got food poisoning from the burnt chicken I served last night. Win! Win! Win!

The pork was so tough no one could cut through it. *But* those potatoes were a dream. WINNING!

Our table wasn't big enough to seat everyone, but we still had so much fun. Tiny mercies!

As I got better at cooking, and people started doing those things I dreamed about—talking about my food, complimenting my food, asking me for my recipes—the bar I set for myself got higher and higher. I inadvertently placed an impossible standard on myself. And this standard had me bringing fewer people to my table less often. Which is absolutely ridiculous, because I wanted to learn how to cook so I could bring *more* people to my table *more* often.

This shift in bringing people to my table was such a learning experience for me that I wrote a whole book about it called *Come & Eat: A Celebration of Love and Grace Around the Everyday Table*. Learning how to cook brought me more confidence, and I wanted this confidence to lead to joy, not scrutiny and judgment.

And I want this for you too. I want to give you the skills and recipes you need to bring more people to *your* table. I want you to know that being efficient and confident in the kitchen does not mean you don't get to mess up or burn another meal or drop a tray of biscuits on the floor. I'm not very good at math, but I'm fairly sure it is mathematically impossible to not have another, or many more, cooking mishaps.

There are 365 days in the year, and three meals a day. That's 1,095 meals! Let's say you cook 900 meals in that year (that might be low for some, high for others). NINE HUNDRED MEALS. They will not all be perfect. They will not all be the best thing you ever ate. They will not all follow you into your dreams. And that does not mean you're not a good cook or you're not doing a good job feeding your people. It just means you're human.

Most likely it also means you're showing up. Even with an oversalted casserole. Even with slightly burned bread. Which leads us back to the first point of the Home Cook's Manifesto:

YOU ARE THE MOST IMPORTANT ITEM IN THE KITCHEN.

And that holds true at the table too. Your *presence* is more important than your perfectly roasted chicken. A confident and joyful cook knows this and believes it.

Your effort is worth it. Your food is enough. Your presence is valued.

COOK'S CLUB
SOUS CHEFS

Thank you to everyone who recipe-tested for this book! This book is yours as much as it is mine.

Alaina Falk
Alice Harvey Jones
Alicia Casady
Alison Markley
Amy
Amy Chalk
Amy King
Amy L.
Ann Combs
Annah Mary Summy
AnnDee Reiff
Annette White
Becky Fowler
Beth Richardson
Bri Ballschmidt
Brittany Littleton
Brittany McDonald
Cally Gagnon
Caroline Worf Long
Carrie Beth Davis
Casey Jeffers
Catherine & Sean Burke
Charissa Garside
Cheri Pieters
Chrissy Deming
Chrissy Joy Anderson
Christina Benard
Claire

Claire Johnson
Crystal Gorwitz
Dawn Bradley
Debbie Day
Debra Sim
Diana Alexander
Diane Egelston
Doris J Morris
Elizabeth Hubler
Emily Cradick
Emily Monahan
Emily Okerson
Emily Thompson
Erica Galindo
Faith Powers
Gina Murawski
Gwen Beattie
Hallie L. Kaiser
Holly Bryant
Jenn Topete
Jennifer Fiedel
Jennifer James
JeriLynne Clifford
Jess Sawyer
Jessica Gallagher
Josh Pratt
Julie & Ella Salay
Julie Cox
Julie Grubb

Kandice Kipp
Kara Keene
Karen Quilty
Karen Stenstrom
Kari Klinedinst
Katherine Albin Koch
Katie & Ed Altman
Kayla & David Craddock
Kayla Craddock & Josh Duval
Kelcey Petersen
Kellie Keddy
Kelly Warning
Kelsey Brandon
Kimberly W. LaBorde
Kimbers Gormley
Kimmie Simunds
Kirstjen Pratt
Kristen Kasmire
Kyra Joy Craig
Laura Oberkrom
Lauren Burns
Lauren Clark
Lauren Coyle
Lauren Mey
Leanne Johnston
Leslie Young
Letoya Monteith

Libba McCluskey
Lisa Neuweg
Liz Wine
Lolo McClure
Louisa Denomme
Malia
Marija Crosson
Martie Buzby
Mary Kate Cragg
Meg Garner
Megan J. Acito
Melanie Morris
Melissa Caudill
Melissa Freeman
Melissa Paugh
Melissa Scott
Meredith Plaud
Michele DeMichieli
Michelle Clark
Michelle Tuller
Nika Bevis
Rachael Smith
Rebecca Core
Ronda Jones
Samantha Mays
Sara Boudrie
Sara Laverty
Sara Plomp
Sara Voigt

Sarah Bakun
Sarah Blaeser
Sarah Cox
Sarah Craft
Sarah A Denning
Sarah Griffin
Sarah Masterson
Sarah Thacker
Sarah Towner
Shawn Slade
Shelby Watwood
Stacey Adams
Steph Jones
Stephanie Horlocker
Suzanne Winn
Tammy Robinson
Taylor Laman
Teri Barr
Terri Abblett
Theresa Diulus
Traci Hoffe
Tracy Hall
Valerie Morris Rodriguez
Veronica Hummel
Wendy Muller
Willow's Mom
The Wood Family

ACKNOWLEDGMENTS

To everyone who has tried my recipes, joined my Cook's Club, and taken my courses. This book would not be here without you all! It will always be a wonder to me that you trust my recipes to feed your people. The honor of it all. Thank you for being in my space with me.

To my family—my mom, dad, sister, and brother. Thank you for being the greatest encouragement to me and for being so enthusiastically excited for me during every step of this journey!

To my grandma, who passed away shortly after I signed this book contract. I am so sad she will not get to hold this book in her hands, but I am so grateful for all the ways she brought me to her table and showed me how to feed and welcome people.

To everyone who was part of the photoshoot for this book. What a fun, exhausting, creative, delicious few days those were! Special thanks to photographer Laura Klynstra and food stylist Mumtaz Mustafa. You are both brilliant. Thank you for coming alongside me in such a collaborative way to bring this book to life. I hope we get to do this again sometime soon. Also to Kelsey, Brianna, Jeremy, Kyle, Maureen, and Victor for jumping in and chopping, dicing, slicing, and cleaning. I thought I was going to feel so alone during this project; I had no idea how wrong I would be.

To Jamie B. Golden, Kendra Adachi, and Laura Tremaine. Thank you for catching every tear, holding space for every fear, and joining me in all my celebrations. My life would look very different if we didn't, all of us, sit down in front of that first zoom call over three years ago and say, "Should we start a mastermind?" I'm so glad we all said yes. I'm so glad we keep saying yes.

To my agent, Lisa Jackson. What a journey we have been on! I will never forget that first time you reached out to me, and I will never stop being amazed at how we came to work together. Thank you for believing in me before I even believed in myself.

To the team at Revell: Kelsey Bowen, thank you for taking a chance on me and for immediately understanding the vision for this book. Amy Nemecek, thank you for your incredible attention to detail and the energy you put into this book. Jane Klein, you are incredibly talented. Thank you for designing this book and making my vision come to life. Brianna DeWitt, you are a delight. Thank you for getting this book out into the world.

To Jeremy. I mean, I already dedicated this whole book to you, but here we are again. You are my favorite. Thank you for making sure I had every beverage desirable at my side as I was writing. Thank you for all the ways you showed up for me before I even had to ask. (And to Stout—you are the true MVP in all of this. How come you make me the most happy?!)

INDEX

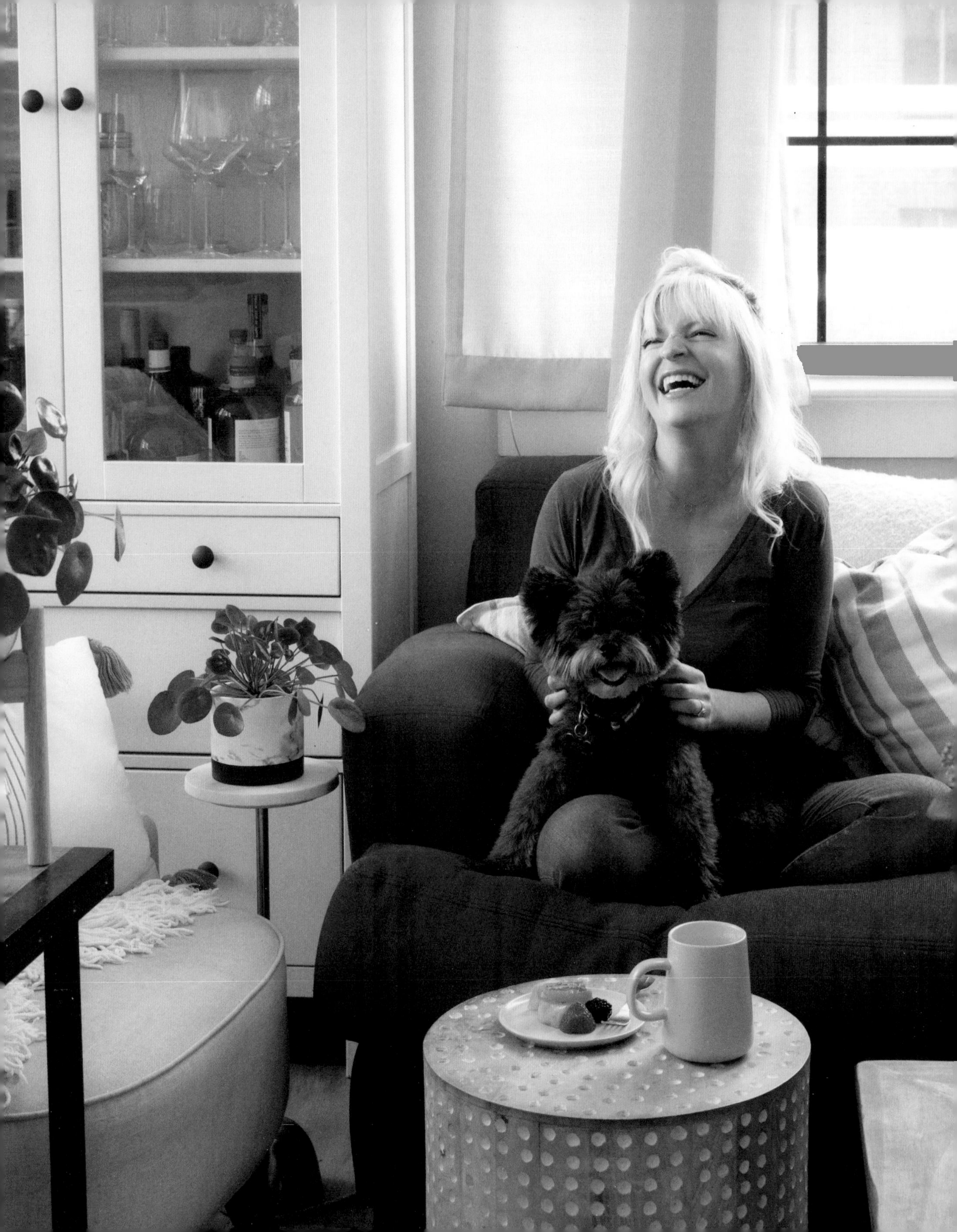